1,000,000 Books

are available to read at

Forgotten Books

---

www.ForgottenBooks.com

Read online
Download PDF
Purchase in print

ISBN 978-0-282-23729-5
PIBN 10845118

This book is a reproduction of an important historical work. Forgotten Books uses
state-of-the-art technology to digitally reconstruct the work, preserving the original format
whilst repairing imperfections present in the aged copy. In rare cases, an imperfection in
the original, such as a blemish or missing page, may be replicated in our edition. We do,
however, repair the vast majority of imperfections successfully; any imperfections that
remain are intentionally left to preserve the state of such historical works.

Forgotten Books is a registered trademark of FB &c Ltd.
Copyright © 2018 FB &c Ltd.
FB &c Ltd, Dalton House, 60 Windsor Avenue, London, SW19 2RR.
Company number 08720141. Registered in England and Wales.

For support please visit www.forgottenbooks.com

1 MONTH OF
FREE
READING

at

www.ForgottenBooks.com

By purchasing this book you are
eligible for one month membership to
ForgottenBooks.com, giving you
unlimited access to our entire
collection of over 1,000,000 titles via
our web site and mobile apps.

To claim your free month visit:
www.forgottenbooks.com/free845118

* Offer is valid for 45 days from date of purchase. Terms and conditions apply.

English
Français
Deutsche
Italiano
Español
Português

www.forgottenbooks.com

Mythology Photography **Fiction**
Fishing Christianity **Art** Cooking
Essays Buddhism Freemasonry
Medicine **Biology** Music **Ancient
Egypt** Evolution Carpentry Physics
Dance Geology **Mathematics** Fitness
Shakespeare **Folklore** Yoga Marketing
Confidence Immortality Biographies
Poetry **Psychology** Witchcraft
Electronics Chemistry History **Law**
Accounting **Philosophy** Anthropology
Alchemy Drama Quantum Mechanics
Atheism Sexual Health **Ancient History**
Entrepreneurship Languages Sport
Paleontology Needlework Islam
Metaphysics Investment Archaeology
Parenting Statistics Criminology
Motivational

ANALYTICAL INQUIRY

INTO THE

PRINCIPLES OF TASTE.

BY RICHARD PAYNE KNIGHT.

THE THIRD EDITION.

Quid placet aut odio est, quod non mutábile credas ?

Τοιος γαρ νοος εςτιν επιχθονιων ανθρωπων,

Οἱον επ᾽ ημαρ αγησι πατηρ ανδρων τε θεωντε.

London :

Printed by Luke Hansard, near Lincoln's-Inn Fields,

FOR T. PAYNE, MEWS-GATE; AND J. WHITE, FLEET-STREET.

1806.

[iii]

CONTENTS.

INTRODUCTION, p. 1.

Containing a Sceptical View of the Subject.

1. In its Principles.
2. In Building, Furniture, Gardening, and Dress.
3. In imitative Art.
4. In Style.
5. In the Productions of Nature.
6. Of the Word Beauty.
7. Applied to intellectual as well as sensible Qualities.
8. Variations in its Meaning.
9. As to the Sexes in Mankind.
10. Mr. Hume's Opinion considered.
11. Sexual Tastes of Brutes.
12. Double Meaning of the word Taste.

PART I. p. 19.

OF SENSATION.

CHAP. I. OF THE SENSE OF TASTE.

1. Its Organs.
2. Primary or simple Sensation.
3. Variation.
4. Irritation.
5. In different Individuals.
6. Mixed Flavours.
7. & 8. Vitiated and morbid Palates.
9. Their Pleasures and Habits.
10. Why fixed and indispensable.
11. Intoxicating Qualities.

CHAP. II. OF SMELL.

1. Its Organs, and their Modes of Action.
2. Connected with mental Sympathies in Brutes.
3. In Dogs.
4. In Oxen.
5. Mr. Burke's Opinion considered.
6. Sexual Sympathies of Brutes.

CHAP. III. OF TOUCH.

1. Its Modes and Limits—Smoothness.
2. Sexual Sympathies—Irritation.
3. Titillation.
4. Sir Joshua Reynolds's Position confirmed.
5. Internal Stimuli.
6. External Stimuli in Plants.
7. Sensation of Plants, organic Sensations in general.
8. Have no Resemblance to Objects or Ideas. Evidence of Sense.
9. Ideas—according to Plato.
10. Scepticism.
11. Its Origin.
12. Inverted Action of the Nerves. Cessation.
13. Various Pleasures of Cessation or inverted Action.

CHAP. IV. OF HEARING.

1. Organs and Modes of Action.
2. Sound—how conveyed.
3. Its Nature and Causes.
4. Its Effects, Modes, and Degrees of Irritation.
5. Simple and mixed Tones.

6. Connected with mental Sympathies in Animals.
7. In Mankind.
8. Expression in Music.
9. Articulate Sounds.
10. Verse.
11. Compared with Music.
12. Measure and Quantity.
13. How violated in the dead Languages.
14. How far addressed to organic Sense.
15. Musical and Poetical Melody.
16. Distance and Direction of Sounds.
17. Their Grandeur and Sublimity.

CHAP. V. OF SIGHT.

1. Its Causes.
2. Primary Effects.   Projection.
3. Distance.
4. Visible Magnitude.
5. Error of Mr. Burke.
6. Irritation—its Effects on the Organ.
7. Pleasures and Pains.   Colours.
8. Reflected and refracted Lights.   Effects of
    Colours, simple and mixed.
9. Sensual or visible Beauty.
10. Degrees of Sensibility in the Organs.
11 & 12. Smoothness, Sharpness, and Brilliancy in
    polished and transparent Objects.
13. In the Coats of Animals.
14. In Buildings, Gardens, Pieces of Water, &c.
15. Neatness.
16. General Principles of visible Beauty.
17. Illustrated by particular Instances.   Deceptions
    of Sight.

18. Mixed Qualities and Sensations—how separated.

19. Adverse Opinions of Mr. Price and Boileau.

20. Grottesques.

21. Mixed Qualities and Sensations further explained.

22. Consequence of Mr. Burke's Doctrine of Beauty.

23. Mr. Burke's System compared with that of Sir Joshua Reynolds.

24. Illustrated by Examples of the Temples of Vesta and Indian Domes.

25. The latter further examined. Mental Sympathies.

26. Beauties of Colour and Form in Animals. Appropriated Beauties of particular Kinds, depending on Habit. Irregularity.

27. Sexual Predilections—their Influence and Effects.

28. Force of Light—as reflected.

29. As acting directly upon the Eye. Mr. Burke's Error.

30. Darkness. Mr. Burke's Notion of it examined.

31. Other Privations compared with it.

32. Difficulty of considering Sensation alone.

33. Particularly in Vision.

34. Progress of Perception.

35. Its Effect in reducing the Pleasures of Sense.

PART II. p. 99.

OF THE ASSOCIATION OF IDEAS.

CHAP. I. OF KNOWLEDGE OR IMPROVED PERCEPTION.

1. Artificial Perception—how far independent of organic Sensation.

2. Imitative Art.

3. Imitation in general.

4. Its Pleasures of short Duration.

5. Science in Art—its Pleasures.

6. Whence derived.

7. Originals and Copies—their Difference.

8. Drawings and unfinished Sketches.

9. Juvenile and imperfect Works.

10. Mental Habits—their Effect on Sensation.

11. Exactitude of Imitation—where vicious.

12. Where just and necessary—in Painting.

13. In Sculpture.

14. Sculpture compared with Painting.

15. Poetry with Music.

16. Articulate Language and inarticulate Notes.

17. Idiom in Language, Rhythm, Prosody.

18. Melody in Language.

19. Modes of Articulation.

20. Verse considered in the Abstract.

21. As connected with Sense or Meaning.

22. With Passion, Sentiment, and Sympathy.

23. Irregularity and Variety comparatively considered—in Poetry and Music—in Sculpture and Painting.

24. Pope and Milton.

25. English Verse—its Nature and Character.

26. General distinct Characters of Verse and Prose.

27. Verse necessary to Poetry, and wherefore.

28. Paradise Lost.

29. English Blank Verse—its Defects in Milton.

30. In Thomson and Cowper.

31. Inversions and Transpositions.

32. Collocation of Words. Order of the Imagination. Order of the Understanding.

33. Their different Effects in Poetry.

A 4

34. Various Effects of Verse.
35. Vicious Modes of pronouncing Greek and Latin.
36, 37. Why they do not destroy the Character of
    Verse.

CHAP. II.   OF IMAGINATION.

1. Association of Ideas—when become habitual,
    involuntary.
2. Its Effects on Temper and Disposition. Lunacy.
3. Intoxication.
4. Dreams.
5. Anxiety, Grief, and Vexation.
6. Vivacity, Wit, Madness.
7. Idiocy.
8. Memory—how connected with Imagination.
9. Memory—artificial.
10. Natural, but unregulated.
11. Prosers and Prattlers.
12. Pleasures of Intellect—in natural Objects.
13. In social and moral.
14. In the fine Arts.
15. The Picturesque.
16. Origin and Use of this Word.
17. Its proper Meaning.
18. Style of Painting at its Revival.
19. Its Defects.
20. How changed and corrected.
21. Thence the Distinction of Picturesque.
22. Which could not have existed before.
23. In what Sense picturesque Objects may not be
    beautiful.
24. Objects purely picturesque.
25. Pleasures of Sense and Intellect improve each
    other.

26. Hence Objects of Sense receive their Character from the Mind.

27. Such are picturesque Objects, which are therefore indefinite in Number and Kind.

28. Neatness, Freshness, Lightness, Symmetry, Regularity, Uniformity and Propriety.

29. Dress and Culture. Consistency and Propriety.

30. In Houses and Gardens.

31. In Parks and Forests.

32. Sense of Propriety or Congruity, artificial and acquired. Mixed Architecture.

33, 34. Its Advantages.

35. Gothic Architecture, military and monastic.

36. Buildings of the Goths, Celts, Scandinavians, &c.

37. Military Architecture of the Greeks and Romans.

38. When employed in Houses and Villas.

39. Rise and Progress of Monastic or Cathedral Gothic.

40. Sacred Architecture of the Greeks and Romans.

41. Improperly copied and applied to Houses.

42. In Decorations of Grounds.

43. Ancient Coins, &c. why interesting.

44. Symmetry--in Animals.

45. In the Orders of Architecture.

46. Its Reasons.

47. Its Origin and Progress.

48. Refinement and Excess—opposed to the Gothic Principle of Contrast.

49. Scale by which the Eye measures.

50. Consequent Effects of Proportion in St. Peter's.

51. And of Contrast in Gothic Cathedrals.

52. Of Intricacy and Extent.

53. Lightness in Sculpture and Building.

54. Errors of Imitation in Principles.

55. Lightness in Painting. Flowing Lines. Rubens.
56. Corregio.
57. Sexual Beauty—its Principle.
58. Sudden Love.
59. Love, as existing among civilized and savage Men, and brute Animals, comparatively considered.
60. Power of Imagination.
61. Sensual and Social or Sentimental Love.
62. Metaphysical Love. Petrarch. Cowley, Waller.
63. Pastoral Love in Theocritus, &c.
64. In modern Dramas, &c.
65. Sculpture compared with Painting.
66. Forms appropriate to Sculpture.
67. Sculpturesque.
68. Grottesque.
69. Other distinct Characters, as
70. Classical.
71. Romantic.
72. Pastoral.
73. Commercial, Naval, Agricultural, &c.
74. The Pleasures, derived from all, belong to the Mind and not to the Objects.
75. Uniformity and Regularity.
76. Irregularity and Mutilation.
77. As affecting general Characteristics or Mental Sympathies.
78. As differently perceived by the Mind or the Eye.
79. Mr. Price's Illustration.
80. His general Mistake of Ideas for Things.
81. Deceptions of Sexual and Social Sympathies. Mistatement.
82. Regularity and Irregularity in Features and Attitudes.

83. Ease, Grace, Elegance, and Dignity of Gesture and Attitude.

84. Belong to Character and Expression, and not to particular Lines and Forms.

85. In inanimate as well as animal Bodies.

86. Dignity and Elegance, wherein different.

87. Dancing.

88. Grace of Savages.

89. Of the Greeks.

90. Lines of Grace.

91. Spiral Columns, scooped Pediments, &c.

92. Regularity in Architecture.

93. In Gardening.

94. Clumps and Canals. Terraces and Borders.

95. Composition in Houses, Offices, and Plantations.

96. Hanging Terraces.

97. Irregularity in Architecture.

98. Exemplified.

99. Trick and Affectation in Houses.

100. In Lodges, Cottages, Gateways, &c.

101. Mixed Architecture.

102. Situations.

103. Sir John Vanbrugh.

104. Mr. Brown.

105. Made Water.

106. Walks.

107. Smallness of Size.

108. In Women. In Animals or other Objects.

109. Gradual Diminution or Tapering.

110. General Rules.

111. In Morals.

112. Affections. Abstract Principles.

113. Their Effects.

114. Whether negative or affirmative.

115. In Taste and Manners.
116. Academies, their Effect on Art.
117. Accounted for.
118. Mechanical and liberal Arts, their Difference.
119. Feeling, Sentiment, and Science in Painting.
120. In Sculpture.
121. Public Schools of Rhetoric; their Effect on the Latin Language.
122. Freedom of Study; its Effect on the Greek.
123. On the English.
124. Instanced in Dr. Blair's Criticism on a Passage of Pope.
125. Criticism examined.
126. The Passage justified by others, from Euripides and Shakespeare.
127. Theoretical Criticism in general.

CHAP. III. OF JUDGMENT.

1. Judgment; in what it consists.
2. Reason, as applied to Taste.
3. Demonstration and Analogy.
4. Laws of Nature.
5. In Matters of Demonstration; in Matters of Belief.
6. Use of the Distinction.
7, 8. Illustrated by Instances.
9. Aristotle's Opinion examined.
10. Probability in Epic Fiction.
11. In Dramatic.
12, 13. Oratory.
14. Acting.
15. Epic and Dramatic License in Fiction; their Difference.

16. Poetical Probability.
17. Unities of Time and Place.
18. Of Action.
19. Action, and Subject or Cause of Action; their Difference.
20. Exemplified.
21. In the Tragedy of. Macbeth.
22. In the Iliad.
23. Both compared.
24. Unity of Subject.
25. Tragi-comedy.
26. Dramatic not to be judged by Epic Style.
27. Effect of Style on Probability of Fiction.
28. Of gradual Elevation and Exaggeration.
29. Of circumstantial Minuteness.
30. Mixture of Truth in the Iliad.
31. In the Productions of all unpolished Nations. Ossian.
32. Odyssey. Gulliver's Travels.
33. Novel of Clarissa Harlowe.
34. Politeness or good Breeding; in Language.
35. In Dress and Demeanor.
36. Its Principles.
37. Permanent Principles and fluctuating Modes
38. General and individual Nature.
39. Allegorical Personages ; Limits of Fiction.
40. In Epic and Dramatic Poetry.
41. In Painting.
42. Symbolical Figures.
43. Of Deities.
44. From Poetry, particularly the Iliad. Uniformity of Design among the Greeks.
45. Truth of Expression. The Laocoon.
46. Michael Angelo.

47. Extravagance in Invention.

48. Truth in Action and Gesture. Greek Artists. Michael Angelo.

49. Reasons for his Deviation from it. Abstract Form.

50. Character and Expression of Form.

51. Raphael's Vision of Ezekiel. Salvator Rosa's Witch of Endor.

52. Titian, Rubens, Rembrandt.

53. Difference of Character between Sculpture and Painting.

54. Similar to that between Epic and Dramatic Poetry.

55. Homeric Heroes, how far suited to the Stage.

56. Reasons for Horace's recommending them. His Character of Achilles examined.

57. Ulysses of Euripides, and Æneas of Virgil.

58. Judgment of Virgil.

59. His peculiar Excellence.

PART III. OF THE PASSIONS, p. 315.

CHAP. I. OF THE SUBLIME AND PATHETIC.

1. Sympathy.

2. Semblance of Truth.

3. Mr. Burke's Opinion.

4. Examined as to

5. Fiction and Reality.

6. Degrees of Sympathy. Romans. Asiatics.

7. Sympathies with Exertion, not with Suffering, please.

8. Roman Mime of Laureolus.

9. Fights of Gladiators.

10. Cruelties of the Americans to their Captives.

11. Attending Executions.
12. Stoic Opinion of the Deity.
13. Passive and Active Fortitude. Combats; Cock-fighting; Bull-baiting; and Boxing.
14. Tragedy and Comedy; their radical Difference.
15. Dramatic Distress always known to be fictitious.
16. Terror and Pity.
17. Longinus's Opinion. Ecstacy.
18. Selfish Sufferings not tragic.
19. Energetic Passions sublime.
20. Rapture. Enthusiasm. Love.
21. Hatred. Malignity.
22. Fortitude. The Laocoon.
23. Sculpture and Poetry; their comparative Influence on the Passions.
24. Acting and Reading.
25. Energies of Reason and Passion. Cato. Achilles.
26. Passion in Poetry may be too reasonable.
27. Madness. Folly. Perverted Energy. Weakness.
28. Morality of Tragedy.
29. *False Terrors* of Horace, what.
30. No Terror felt at Dramatic Exhibitions.
31. Pity melting the Mind to Love.
32. Only when Sympathy is with Energies of Mind.
33. Active and Passive Courage.
34. Weakness. False Delicacy.
35. Timidity. Modesty.
36. Pliability. Stubbornness. Themistocles.
37. Tenacity in Trifles.
38. Sublime and Pathetic, how connected; both energetic. Macbeth.
39. Otway's Venice Preserv'd. Shakespeare's Julius Cæsar.
40. Achilles.

41. Pathetic must be sublime.
42. Extreme Suffering. Horror.
43. Selfish Passions.
44. Distress remote from Self. Milton's Satan.
45. Remembrances of past Sufferings.
46. Power.
47. Infinity. Extent. Vastness.
48. Magnificence. Richness. Splendor.
49. Darkness. Vacuity. Silence.
50. Storms. Earthquakes. Volcanos, &c.
51. Power and Terror.
52. Passage of Virgil.
53. ———— of Lucretius.
54. Superstition and Enthusiasm.
55. Their Principles in common Observation.
56. Plague. Pestilence. Famine. Discord, &c.
57. Terror in the Character of Achilles.
58. Augmentatives and emphatical Expletives de‑
      rived from Terror.
59. Pain and Terror not Sources of the Sublime.
60. Mr. Burke's Philosophy on the Subject.
61. Not clearly understood by himself.
62. Leads to Materialism.
63. His progressive Scale of the Sublime.
64. Contrary in its Principles to the System of Lon‑
      ginus and all others known.
65. Considered in its different Graduations of Re‑
      spect, Awe.
66. Astonishment and Terror, as applicable to him‑
      self.
67. Deduction from it.
68. Treatise on Oriental Gardening; Experiments
      tried.
69. Others proposed.

70. Noxious and Innocent; Tame and Wild Animals. Game Cock.
71. Dog.
72. Ulysses's Dog.
73. Destroying and preserving Powers compared, as to Energy.
74. — as to the Effect of that Energy in the Sublime.
75. Description and Reality compared.
76. Illustrated by Virgil's Bees, and
77. By Homer's Moor Fowl.
78. Acquired Tastes.
79. Passage of Horace explained.
80. Mr. Burke's Opinion of Description examined.
81. Obscurity. Things distinct and Things determinate.
82. Energies. Images. Virgil's forging of the Thunderbolts. Homer's Girdle of Venus.
83. Consequences of Obscurity being thought sublime.
84. Impassioned Modes of Speech. Ideas. Ossian.
85. Sound Sense and Mental Energy in Character.
86. — in Description.
87. Enthusiastic Language. Heroic Style.
88. Lyric Style. Pindar. Sophocles. Gray.
89. Milton's Imagery sometimes obscure; not so in the Instance quoted by Mr. Burke.
90. Where really so, faulty. Instance.
91. Influence of Authority.
92. Images limited; Mental Energies not.
93. Instances and Illustrations.
94. Exceptions.
95. Comparative Influence of Music on the Passions.
96. Fabulous Stories concerning it.

b

97. Homeric Music.
98. Fanciful Theories.

CHAP. I. OF THE RIDICULOUS.

1. Laughter; its Nature and Causes.
2. Comedy as opposed to Tragedy, in Manners.
3. In the Passions.
4. In Attitude and Countenance. Raphael. Rembrandt.
5. Wit, as opposed to Judgment; as exciting Mirth.
6. Ludicrous, as opposed to sublime Imagery.
7. Humour.
8. Parodies.
9. Incongruities in Dress, Deportment, and Dialect.
10. Mimicry.
11. Good Nature and Good Humour, wherein different.
12. Sympathy in Joy. Contrast.
13. Selfish Passions ludicrous.
14. Morality of Comedy, in the prudential Concerns of Life.
15. In Love and Marriage.
16. In the domestic relations of Parent and Child, &c.
17. More immoral than Tragedy, but equally ineffective.

CHAP. III. OF NOVELTY.

1. All unvaried Continuity tires.
2. Change, therefore, necessary.
3. The Cause of corrupt Taste. In Literature.
4. In Art.
5. Abuse of Words.

6. Artists and Authors : how far the Corruptors of, or corrupted by the Public Taste.

7. Art and Dress connected, but not Literature.

8. Instances and Illustrations.

9. Perfection from the same Source as Corruption. Michael Angelo and Bernini. Ariosto and Marino.

10. Excess of Ornament and false Brilliancy.

11. From unfair Comparison, and

12. The natural Progress of Speech.

13. Novelty and Contrast the Principles of ornamental Gardening, as hitherto practised.

14. In China.

15. In England.

16. Intricacy and Variety.

17. Curiosity. The Marvellous.

18. Surprize. Progress of Fiction.

19. Horrible Stories and Events.

20. Avowed Fiction. Novels.

21. Their Effects on the Understanding.

22. On Temper and Disposition.

23. On Morals and Behaviour.

24. On Religion.

25. Their relation to Comedy.

26. Moral Effects of all Narrative and Dramatic Fiction weak.

27. Self-Importance of Poets, Painters, &c.

28. How far they are really useful to Society.

29. Erroneous Estimates of Life and Manners.

30. Causes of Disgust between the Sexes.

31. The most trivial most effective.

32. In other Objects. Mental Pleasure and Pain.

33. Knowledge and Ignorance.

34. Their moral Effects.

35. Love of Life and Fear of Death. Habitual At-
    tachments.
36. Love of Property.
37. Sensuality, Prodigality, or false Generosity.
38. Desire of perpetuating Property.
39. Perpetual Imprisonment.
40. Real Principle of Happiness.

PRINCIPLES OF TASTE.

INTRODUCTION.

—εστι δε τοις ευπορησαι βχλομενοις προυργχ το διαπορησαι καλως· η γαρ υστερον ευπορια λυσις των προτερων απορχμενων εστι. Aristot. Metaphys. Lib. III. C. i.

1.

TASTE is a subject upon which it might naturally be supposed that all mankind would agree; since all know instinctively what pleases, and what displeases them; and, as the organs of feeling and perception appear to be the same in the whole species, and only differing in degrees of sensibility, it should naturally follow that all would be pleased or displeased more or less, according to those different degrees of sensibility, with the same objects.

2. This is, however, so far from being the case, that there is scarcely any subject, upon which men differ more than concerning the objects of their pleasures and amusements: and this difference subsists, not only among individuals, but among ages and nations; almost every generation accusing that which immediately preceded it, of bad taste in building, furniture, and dress; and almost every nation having its

B

own peculiar modes and ideas of excellence in
these matters, to which it pertinaciously ad-
heres, until one particular people has acquired
such an ascendancy in power and reputation,
as to set what is called the *fashion*; when this
fashion is universally and indiscriminately
adopted upon the blind principle of imitation,
and without any consideration of the differences of climate, constitution, or habits of
life; and every one, who presumes to deviate from it, is thought an *odd mortal—a
humourist* void of all just feeling, taste, or
elegance. This fashion continues in the full
exercise of its tyranny for a few years or
months; when another, perhaps still more
whimsical and unmeaning, starts into being
and deposes it: all are then instantly astonished that they could ever have been pleased,
even for a moment, with any thing so tasteless, barbarous, and absurd. The revolutions
in dress only, not to mention those in building,
furnishing, gardening, &c. which have taken
place within the last two centuries, afford ample
illustration; and it is not the least extraordinary circumstance in these revolutions, that
they have been the most violent, sudden, and
extravagant in the personal decorations of that
part of the species; which, having most natural,
has least need of artificial charms; which is
always most decorated when least adorned;

and which, as it addresses its attractions to the
primordial sentiments and innate affections of
man, would, it might reasonably be supposed,
never have attempted to increase them by distortion and disguise. Yet art has been wearied, and nature ransacked; tortures have been
endured, and health sacrificed; and all to
enable this lovely part of the creation to appear in shapes as remote as possible from that
in which all its native loveliness consists.
Only a few years ago, a beauty equipped for
conquest was a heterogeneous combination of
incoherent forms, which nature could never
have united in one animal, nor art blended in
one composition: it consisted of a head, disguised so as to resemble that of no living
creature, placed upon an inverted cone, the
point of which rested upon the centre of the
curve of a semieliptic base, more than three
times the diametre of its own. Yet, if high-
dressed heads, tight-laced stays, and wide
hoops, had not been thought really ornamental,
how came they to be worn by all who could
afford them? Let no one imagine that he
solves the question by saying, that there have
been errors in taste, as there have been in religion and philosophy: for the cases are totally
different; religion and philosophy being matters of belief, reason, and opinion; but taste
being a matter of feeling, so that whatever was

really. and considerately *thought* to be ornamental must have been previously *felt* to be
so: and though opinions may, by argument or
demonstration, be proved to be wrong, how
shall an individual pretend to prove the feelings of a whole age or nation wrong, when the
only just criterion which he can apply to ascertain the rectitude of his own, is their congruity
with those of the generality of his species?

3. Is there then no real and permanent principle of beauty? No certain or definable combinations of forms, lines, or colours, that are in
themselves gratifying to the mind, or pleasing
to the organs of sensation? Or are we, in this
respect, merely creatures of habit and imitation; directed by every accidental impulse,
and swayed by every fluctuation of caprice or
fancy? It will be said perhaps, in reply, that
we must not found universal scepticism in occasional deviations, or temporary irregularities:
for, though absurd and extravagant fashions
have, at intervals, prevailed in all ages, and, in
later times, succeeded each other with little
interruption; yet there are certain standards
of excellence, which every generation of civilized man, subsequent to their first production, has uniformly recognized in theory, how
variously soever they have departed from them
in practice. Such are the precious remains of
Grecian sculpture; which afford standards of

real beauty, grace, and elegance in the human
form, and the modes of adorning it, the truth
and perfection of which have never been questioned, although divers other modes of producing and exhibiting those qualities have since
prevailed in different ages and countries. The
superiority, however, of these pure and faultless models has been invariably recognized by
all; so that the vicious extravagancies and corruptions, which temporary and local fashions
introduced and maintained, were tacitly and
indirectly condemned even by those who most
obstinately persevered in practising and encou-
raging them.

4. But is it certain that this condemnation
was sincere? and are not men's real feelings
and inclinations to be judged of more by their
practice than their professions? Established
authority, both in literature and art, is so imposing, that few men have courage openly to
revolt against it, and renounce all allegiance;
though they may tacitly secede from its controul, and let their own taste and inclination
govern them entirely in their practice: and
that, too, by the force of habit, in a manner,
and to a degree imperceptible to themselves.
When we find every florid and affected rhetorician, who has successively contributed to the
corruption of Greek, Latin, and English eloquence, applauding, in quaint phraseology and

epigrammatic point, the simple purity of Xenophon, Cæsar, and Swift; and condemning
in others the very style which he employs, we
can scarcely believe that he knew, at the time
of writing, how widely the taste, which he had
acquired by habit, differed from the judgment
which he exercised under the influence of authority. Both Michel Angelo and Bernini
were enthusiastic in their admiration, or at
least in their applauses, of the Grecian style
of sculpture; but nevertheless Michel Angelo
and Bernini were, in opposite ways, the great
corruptors of this pure style; the one having
expanded it into the monstrous and extravagant, and the other sunk it into effeminacy and
affectation. The late Sir Joshua Reynolds
expressed, throughout his life, the most un-
qualified admiration for the works of Michel
Angelo; while both in his writings and conversation he affected to undervalue those of
Rembrandt, though he never attempted to
imitate the former, but formed his own style
of colouring and execution entirely from the
latter; for whose merits he had the justest feeling, while he had none at all for those of the
other, as his own collection abundantly proved;
for the pictures which it contained of the Dutch
master were all genuine and good, while those
attributed to the Florentine were spurious and
below criticism. His feeling was just, though

his judgment was wrong; and so far he was the reverse of Michel Angelo and Bernini, whose judgment was true while their feelings were false. As the vices, however, of both these celebrated artists were more enthusiastically admired, in their respective ages, than ever the merits of either Rembrandt or Reynolds were, it may reasonably be doubted whether they dictated to, or complied with, the taste of their contemporaries: either supposition equally favours the sceptical side of the question concerning any real and permanent principles of taste.

5. In judging, however, of the works of Nature, it must be owned that there appears to have been less inconstancy; the beauties of particular kinds of trees, plants, flowers, and animals, having, I believe, been universally recognized in all ages and all countries: but, over these, it must be remembered that the power of man is more limited, nor *can* he indulge those partial and extravagant caprices of his taste, which he has so abundantly displayed in the productions of his own art and labour. As far, however, as he has been able, he has done it most profusely. At one time he crops the tail and ears of his dogs and horses; and, at another, forces them to grow in forms and directions, which nature never intended: his trees and shrubs are planted in fantastic lines,

or shorn into the shapes of animals or implements; and all for the sake of beauty. Happily for the poor animals, it has never appeared
possible to shear or twist them into the shapes
of plants, or it would, without doubt, have
been attempted; and we should have been as
much delighted at seeing a stag terminating in
a yew tree, as ever we were at seeing a yew
tree terminating in a stag. These metamor-
phoses of plants are not now, indeed, in
fashion: but it is merely fashion, that has exploded them; and as both fashions have had
their respective admirers, not only among the
vulgar, but among the most discerning and
enlightened of mankind*, it may reasonably be
doubted, whether either of them be at all consonant to the real principles of beauty, if any
such there be. That however must be the subject of inquiry.

* Quid enim illo quincunce speciosius est, qui in quam-
cunque partem spectaveris, rectus est. Quinctil. lib. viii.
c. iii.

See also Montesquieu, Fragm. sur le Gout. Addison,
Spectator, No. 414; where he states, as a general position, that, " though there are several wild scenes, that
are more delightful than any artificial shows, yet we find
the works of Nature still more pleasant, the more they
resemble those of art," which he endeavours to account
for philosophically. His natural feelings, however, soon
rise up against his acquired opinions; and, towards the
close of the same paper, he adds, " I do not know whe-

6. The word Beauty is a general term of approbation, of the most vague and extensive meaning, applied indiscriminately to almost every thing that is pleasing, either to the sense, the imagination, or the understanding; whatever the nature of it be, whether a material substance, a moral excellence, or an intellectual theorem. We do not, indeed, so often speak of beautiful smells, or flavours, as of beautiful forms, colours, and sounds; but, nevertheless, we apply the epithet to a problem, a syllogism, or a period, as familiarly, and (as far as we can judge from authority) as correctly as to a rose, a landscape, or a woman. We speak also, and, I believe, with equal propriety, not only of the beauties of symmetry and arrangement, but of those of virtue, charity, holiness, &c. The illustrious author, indeed, of the *Inquiry into the Sublime and Beautiful*, chooses to consider such expressions as improper, and to confine beauty to the sensible qualities of

ther I am singular in my opinion; but, for my own part, I would rather look upon a tree in all its luxuriancy and diffusion of boughs and branches, than when it is thus cut and trimmed into a mathematical figure; and cannot but fancy that an orchard in flower looks infinitely more delightful than all the little labyrinths of the most finished parterre."

This was bold scepticism for so cautious a writer in that age.

things *. But, as an ancient grammarian observed, even Cæsar, though he could command
the lives and fortunes of men, could not command words, nor alter, in a single instance, the
customary idiom of speech; and in this instance
customary idiom has established these expressions, not only in the English, but in all the other
polished languages of Europe, both ancient
and modern; καλος in the Greek, *pulcher* in
the Latin, *bello* in the Italian, and *beau* in the
French, being constantly applied to moral and
intellectual, as well as to physical or material
qualities †. It is in vain, therefore, for individuals to dispute about their propriety or impropriety; for, after all, the ultimate criterion
must be common use—

Quem penes arbitrium est, et jus, et norma loquendi,
and from which he, who chooses to depart, only
makes his meaning less intelligible.

* Part III. f. i. and ix.
† This application of the word καλος has given being to
a saint of signal celebrity in Sicily, and some parts of the
south of Italy, called St. Calogero, the general patron of
all medicinal baths, salubrious springs, excavated rocks,
&c. and much distinguished for his miraculous cures of
all chronical diseases.

Καλος γερων, corrupted in the later times of the Byzantine empire to καλογερος, signified a monk or hermit; and
it is in places inhabited or frequented by such persons,
that we find the relics, or hear of the miracles of St.
Calogero.

7. It may be said, perhaps, that the epithet is used in a plain sense, when applied to objects of sensation; and in a figurative one, when applied to objects of intellect: but no such distinction exists in fact; for, when applied to objects of sight or hearing, it is, in most instances, applied to qualities purely intellectual; such as composition, proportion, expression, fitness, &c. which perpetually distinguish the beautiful from the ugly in the same species; though often totally changed when applied to another species, and sometimes, when applied to a different class in the same species; of both which instances will be given in the sequel. It is true that all epithets, employed to distinguish qualities perceivable only by intellect, were originally applied to objects of sense: for as such objects are the primary subjects of thought and observation, the primary words in all languages belong to them; and are therefore applied *transitively*, though not always *figuratively*, to objects of intellect or imagination. That expression only is properly figurative which employs the image or idea of one thing to illustrate another: but when we speak of the *beauty of virtue*, we mean the pleasing result of well-balanced and duly proportioned affections; and, when we speak of the *beauty of the human form*, we mean the pleasing result of well-balanced and duly proportioned

limbs and features. In both instances the
word is equally applied to the results of proportion, without reference to any other image;
and though, in the one, the *general subject* be
mental, and in the other corporeal, the *particular object,* in both, is an abstract idea, and
consequently, purely intellectual; nor is the
expression more figurative in the one than in
the other*. If we speak, indeed, of any individual human form, the idea is not abstract;
but then it is complex: and of the ideas that
compose it, those of colour only are immediately derived from the sense of sight; the
others being entirely the results of mental operation, employing the evidence of other senses;
as has been abundantly shewn by Locke, Reid,
and other metaphysical writers; and as will
be further explained in the course of this
inquiry.

8. I admit, however, that the word Beauty
entirely changes its meaning with every complete or generic change of its application: that
is, accordingly as it is applied to objects of the

---

* Ἡ συμμετρια των μελων μετα της ευχροιας το καλλος ποιει τȣ
σωματος. Gregor. Nyssen. orat. de anima.

Καλλος εϛι το εν τη συνθεσει των μελων ευαρμοϛον, επανθȣσαν
αυτω την χαριν εχον. Basil. Cæs. in xliv.

Καλλος ψυχης το κατ᾽ αρετην συμμετρον. Id. in Isai. c. v.

Καλος καγαθος—τελιως σπουδαιος, επι γαρ της αρετης το καλον
και αγαθον λεγȣσιν. Aristot. εθικ. μεν. lib. ii. c.ix.

senses, the imagination, or the understanding;
for, though these faculties are so mixed and
compounded in their operations, in the complicated mind of civilized man, that it is extremely difficult to discriminate them accurately;
yet the pleasures of each, though mixed in their
effects, are utterly distinct in their causes. '

9. Perfect beauty, indeed, taking *perfect* in
its most strict, and *beauty* in its most comprehensive signification, ought to be equally pleasing to all; but of this instances are scarcely to
be found: for, as to taking them, or, indeed,
any examples for illustration, from the other
sex of our own species, it is extremely falla-
cious; as there can be little doubt that all
male animals think the females of their own
species the most beautiful productions of Nature. At least, we know this to be the case
among the different varieties of men, whose
respective ideas of the beauty of their females
are as widely different as those of man, and
any other animal, can be. The sable Africans
view with pity and contempt the marked deformity of the Europeans; whose mouths are
compressed, their noses pinched, their cheeks
shrunk, their hair rendered lank and flimsy,
their bodies lengthened and emaciated, and
their skins unnaturally bleached by shade and
seclusion, and the baneful influence of a cold

humid climate *. Were they to draw an image of female perfection, or a goddess of love and beauty, she would have a broad flat nose, high cheeks, woolly hair, a jet black skin, and squat thick form, with breasts reaching to her navel. To us imagination can scarcely present a more disgusting mass of deformity; but perhaps at Tomboctoo the fairest nymph of St. James's, who, while she treads the mazes of the dance, displays her light and slender form through transparent folds of muslin, might make the

---

* See Park's Journey to the Niger. A Birman describing a very ugly race of people to Captain Symes, the English ambassador, mentioned white teeth as a principal characteristic of their ugliness; the inhabitants of that empire, like those of many other countries of the East, staining their teeth black.—Voyage to Ava, c. x. p. 264.

Mr. Hearne, who resided more than twenty years among the nations of the frozen regions of North America, says, " Ask a northern Indian what is beauty, he will answer, *a broad flat face, small eyes, high cheek bones, three or four black lines across each cheek, a low forehead, a large broad chin, a clumsy hook nose, a tawny hide, and breasts hanging down to the belt.*"

The same people were so far from thinking the whiteness of an European skin at all conducive to beauty, that it only excited in them the disgusting idea of dead flesh sodden in water till all the blood and juices were extracted.—Journey from Hudson's Bay to the Northern Ocean, &c. p. 88 and 122.

See various other opposite opinions on this subject, cited by Buffon, Hist. Nat. t. ii. p. 555.

same impression; and who shall decide which
party is right, or which is wrong; or whether
the black or white model be, according to the
laws of nature, the most perfect specimen of a
perfect woman? The late great physiologist,
John Hunter, used to maintain (and I think
he proved it), that the African black was the
true original man, and all the others only
different varieties derived from him, and more
or less debased or improved. If so, what more
infallible criterion can there be for judging of
the natural taste and inclination of mankind,
than the unsophisticated sentiments of the
most natural and original of the species? We
can neither weigh nor measure the results of
feeling or sentiment; and can only judge whether they are just and natural, or corrupt and
artificial, by comparing them with the general
laws of nature; that is, with the general deductions, which we make from the particular operations of nature, which fall under our observation: for of the real laws of nature we know
nothing; these deductions amounting to no
more than rules of analogy of our own forming; by which, we judge of the future by the
past, and form opinions of things, which we do
not know, by things which we do.

10. It was, probably, from observing this
marked difference, and even direct opposition
of tastes, in matters which affect the primary

and innate sentiments of man, that an acute and
ingenious sceptic has ventured to assert, that
all beauty is merely ideal and imaginary, and
not in any case an inherent quality in external
objects. " Beauty," says Mr. Hume, " is no
" quality in things themselves : it exists merely
" in the mind, which contemplates them, and
" each mind perceives a different beauty. One
" person may even perceive deformity where
" another is sensible of beauty ; and every in-
" dividual ought to acquiesce in his own senti-
" ment, without pretending to regulate those of
" others. To seek the real beauty or real de-
" formity is as fruitless an inquiry, as to pretend
" to ascertain the real sweet or real bitter. Ac-
" cording to the disposition of the organs the
" same object may be both sweet and bitter ;
" and the proverb has justly determined it to
" be fruitless to dispute concerning tastes. It is
" very natural, and even quite necessary, to ex-
" tend this axiom to mental as well as bodily
" taste ; and thus common sense, which is often
" at variance with philosophy, especially with the
" sceptical kind, is found, in one instance at least,
" to agree in pronouncing the same decision."
    Whether this subtle philosopher has not, like
many others, applied the analogy of sexual sympathy to things beyond its reach, and made his
negative axiom too general, will, perhaps, appear in the following inquiry. At present I

shall only remark, that the illustration, which
he employs, of the confused sensations of morbid
or vitiated organs, is quite unfair. To
every sound and uncorrupted palate, sugar is
sweet, and gall bitter; and though they may
not be so to an individual labouring under
disease, yet the exception is of that kind,
which confirms instead of invalidating the general principle of discrimination. Even persons of the most vitiated palates, though they
may prefer bitter to sweet, still agree in calling sweet, sweet, and bitter, bitter; and those
who, through disease, find bitter in every
thing, have the bitter really in their mouths,
mixed with the saliva, and consequently in-
corporated with every thing that they taste.
The African, who prefers a black complexion
to a white one, perceives that it is black as
clearly as we do; and black has the same analogy with darkness, in his eyes, as in ours, and
consequently makes a similar impression, notwithstanding that it embellishes the charms,
and increases the attractions, of his mistress.

11. The sexual desires of brutes are probably more strictly natural inclinations, and
less changed or modified by the influence of
acquired ideas, or social habits, than those of
any race of mankind; but their desires seem,
in general, to be excited by smell, rather than
by sight or contact. If, however, a boar can

C

think a sow the sweetest and most lovely of
living creatures, we can have no difficulty in
believing that he also thinks her the most beautiful: for the sense of smell is much more
impartial, and less liable to be influenced or
perverted by mental sympathies, than that
of sight; there being no communications
of thought or sentiment from one mind to
another (at least among human creatures) by
the nose, as there are by the eyes.

12· The sense of taste is equally impartial;
being equally unconnected with, and uninfluenced by, the higher faculties of the mind:
it is also the first that is employed in preserving life by selecting nourishment; and that
which hath consequently given a name to that
rule or criterion of just exertion in all the rest,
which is the subject of the present inquiry: -
wherefore I shall examine it first; and, after
comparing it with those of its two kindred
organs of smell and touch, in order to ascertain the principles of sensation in general, proceed to the examination of the remaining two,
whose objects are the proper objects of taste
in the more general sense of the word, as used
to signify a general discriminative faculty arising from just feeling and correct judgment
implanted in the mind of man by his Creator,
and improved by exercise, study, and medi-
tation.

PART I.

OF SENSATION.

CHAPTER I.

OF TASTE.

1. THE organs of taste, considered merely as the faculty of distinguishing flavours, are the lips, the tongue, and the palate, whose sensibility is preserved by a fluid, with which they are constantly moistened; and which is consequently a medium of communication for every thing applied to them.

2. If any quantity of any other fluid of exactly the same quality and temperature be received into the mouth, it will produce no other sensation than that of pressure; that is, it will merely cause itself to be perceived by its gravitation upon the extremity of the nerves, without otherwise altering the mode or degree of their action. This is the first and simplest kind of sensation; for unless there be some gratification of a want, such as thirst, the perception is merely of contact.

3. But let the liquid, so received, be impregnated with salt, with sugar, with acid, or

CHAP.
I.
Of Taste.

c 2

any other extraneous matter; or let it be of a
greater or less degree of warmth; and its impression will not be mere contact, but will
produce a change in the mode or degree of
action in the nerves; by which we perceive its
flavour. I say a change in the mode or degree of action; because the commencement of
a new sensation is never from absolute inaction; all the organic parts of animal bodies,
and many of those of vegetables, being irritable; and a certain degree of irritation being
always kept up in the former by the mere stimulus of the blood, or by the necessary operation of vital warmth and motion.

4. This irritation may be either increased or
diminished by external impressions, accordingly as they are stimulant or narcotic; or its
modes may be changed according to the different qualities of the substances applied: but
how these changes take place, or what those
different modes are, by which we discriminate
such an infinite variety of different flavours,
smells, tones, colours, &c. is beyond the reach
of human faculties to discover. All that we
know is, that certain modes of irritation produce sensations, which are pleasant, and others,
sensations which are unpleasant; that there
must be a certain degree of it to produce
either; and that, beyond a certain degree, all
are painful. If the irritation be too weak, the

effect is insipidity or flatness:—if it be too
strong, it is pain or uneasiness.

5. The effect, however, of the same things
on different individuals varies according to the
different degrees of irritability in their organs;
from which 'their sensibility arises:—it also
varies in the same individual, as he advances
from infancy to maturity; and from maturity
to decay. Very young children are almost
always fond of pure sweet; but as the palate
grows adult, it requires some mixture of acid
or bitter to vary it, and give it pungency, or it
becomes vapid and disgusting.

6. These mixt flavours continue ever after
to be most grateful; and it is in mixing and
preparing them in the ways best adapted to
excite and prolong appetite by stimulating the
organs, that all the arts subservient to gluttony
consist. Nature, however, has anticipated
most of these arts, and rendered them superfluous further than as they tend to assist and
vary her operations; for we must not imagine
that the food, which we call simple, is in reality so: all the fruits, herbs, and meats, on
which we feed being composed of many simple
elements, blended and tempered by Nature
with a delicacy and exactitude, which art can
but feebly imitate. By the variation and succession of the seasons, too, we are supplied
with all that variety, which, if not necessary to

health, is certainly requisite to pleasure; at least to that of sense; as none can last long without it; there being scarcely any sensations but such as are too violent to be pleasant, that will not, by being very frequently repeated, or very long continued, become so familiar, as to be no longer sensations but mere habits of existence. The organs, by being continually subjected to the same impression, become assimilated and adapted to it, so that the action of the nerves excited by it becomes a sort of spontaneous motion; the irritation being little more perceived or noticed, than that caused by the action of the blood, or the natural operation of any other internal stimulus. Hence we naturally seek for some new impression, that may restore that pleasure, which we originally felt from this sensation, which has thus become stale and vapid.

7. If this desire of change be indulged to excess, men soon begin to require an increase in the degree, as well as variation in the mode, of irritation; whence arises that vicious appetite for strong odours, relishing food, and stimulant liquors, which, if once suffered to prevail, always increases in a constant, and regularly accelerated progression; till at length things, naturally the most nauseous, become most grateful; and things, naturally most grateful, most insipid.

8. This extreme effect, however, only takes place where the palate has become morbid and vitiated by continued, and even forced, gratification; and even then the metaphors taken from this sense, and employed to express intellectual qualities, show that it is always felt and considered as a corruption, even by those who are most corrupted : for though there are many, who prefer port wine to malmsey, and tobacco to sugar, yet no one ever spoke of a *sour* or *bitter* temper, as pleasant, or of a *sweet* one, as unpleasant.

9. Yet the pleasures derived from these vitiated tastes seem to be more exquisite, than any derived from nature : for, when men have once acquired them, they are more constant in the indulgence of them, and find greater difficulty in dispensing with the gratification, after they have been used to it. No one, past the age of childhood, has ever found any permanent pleasure in sucking sugar-candy; but how many do we see, to whom the chewing or smoking of tobacco has become an habitual, and even an indispensable gratification. Ottar of roses and other sweet scents are only occasionally applied to the nose; and, if used too frequently, cloy and satiate : but the use of snuff becomes a permanent and constant habit.

10. The case is, that all those tastes, which are natural, lose, and all those which are un-

natural, acquire strength by indulgence: ,for no strained or unnatural action of the nerves can ever be so assimilated to their constitutional modes of existence, as not to produce, on every re-application of its cause, a change sufficient to excite a pleasing irritation; which, those that are natural and gentle cease by degrees to do; since, by uninterrupted continuance for any long time, they become blended and confounded with those, which belong to the vital motion and constitutional existence of the organ. A man may inhale air impregnated with ottar of roses, or other sweet scents, till he no longer perceives that it is impregnated; as we often find to be the case with those who live in perfumers' shops: but no one can inhale air mixed with effluvia of assafetida or tobacco without perceiving it, unless his olfactory nerves have totally lost their sensibility.

11. It is to be observed, however, that a great part of the pleasure, arising from the use of bitter and nauseous drugs, and fermented liquors, arises from their exhilarating and intoxicating qualities: but these belong to another branch of our inquiry, and shall be examined in the proper place.

CHAPTER II.

OF SMELL.

1. WHAT has been said of tastes may, in almost every instance, be applied with equal propriety to smells; which are caused by the finer particles of bodies being dissolved in the air, which we inhale, and borne by it through the nostrils to the olfactory nerves; as tastes are caused by the same finer particles being diluted in the saliva, and conveyed with it to the palate and other organs of the mouth. The pleasures and pains of each seem to depend on similar modes and degrees of irritation: but, in mankind, to be more limited in their extent, in the sense of smelling, than in that of tasting.

2. In some kinds of animals, however, the sense of smell seems to be connected with certain mental sympathies; as those of hearing and sight are in all that possess them in any high degree: for not only their sexual desires appear to be excited by means of it; but other instinctive passions, which, according to the usual system of nature, should be still more remote from its influence. It has been observed that dogs, though wholly unacquainted with lions, will tremble and shudder at their roar; and an elephant, that has never seen a

tiger, will, in the same manner, show the strongest symptoms of horror and affright at the smell of it. The late Lord Clive exhibited a combat between two of these animals at Calcutta: but the scent of the tiger had such an effect upon the elephant, that nothing could either force or allure him to go along the road, where the cage, in which it was enclosed, had passed; till a gallon of arrack was given him; when, his horror suddenly turning to fury, he broke down the paling to get at his enemy, and killed him without difficulty.

3. The excessive eagerness, which dogs express on smelling their game, seems to be but little connected with the appetite for food, and wholly independent of any preconceived ideas of the objects of their pursuit being fit for it. Hence several kinds of them will not eat the game, which they pursue with such wild impetuosity; and of which the scent seems to animate them to a degree of ecstasy, far beyond what the mere desire of food can produce.

4. Where blood has been shed, particularly, that of their own species, oxen will assemble; and, upon smelling it, roar and bellow, and show the most manifest symptoms of horror and distress. Yet these symptoms could not arise from any associated ideas of danger or death; since they appear in them, that never had any opportunities of acquiring such ideas.

They must therefore be instinctive, like other innate antipathies and propensities; in which sensation appears to operate upon the passions and mental affections more immediately, than it is ever found to do in the human species.

5. An eminent author, who makes terror to be a principal source of the sublime, has thence conceived a notion (upon a principle, indeed, different from that here stated) of stinks being sublime; though he acknowledges that he never could bring his mind to act in unison with his nose, so as to satisfy himself that he had really smelt a sublime stink. Through the medium of description, however, he has no doubt of the sentiment being excited by this sensation; in proof of which he quotes a cele-brated passage of Virgil*. In this, however, as well as in many other instances, this truly great author has most unphilosophically mis-taken a power for a sensation: a mistake, for which no excuse can be made but the early period of life at which *the Inquiry into the Sublime and Beautiful* was written; and his having soon after, unfortunately for his peace of mind, abandoned himself to more active pur-suits, " and to party given up what was meant for mankind." But, nevertheless, at this early

---

* Inquiry into the Sublime and Beautiful. Part II. ſ. xxi,

period, his feelings were generally right, even where his judgment was most wrong; so that he *felt*, though he did not *know* that, in the description, it is the *power* only, and in the reality, the *sensation* only, that affects the mind, or is at all perceived by it. But of this more hereafter: at present I shall merely observe, in justice to his memory, that, in his latter days, he laughed very candidly and good-humouredly at many of the philosophical absurdities, which will be here exposed; and I must add, in justice to myself, that I should not have thus undertaken to expose them, had they not been since adopted by others, and made to contribute so largely to the propagation of bad taste; of which instances will be given in the proper place.

6. In exciting the sexual desires of animals, the sense of smell seems to be no further concerned than in indicating their object; the real principles and incentives of their desires being certain internal stimuli, which operate periodically with a degree of violence far surpassing that of any other appetite. As in other instances, in which the other senses are concerned, the sensation excites the idea, and the idea excites the appetite.

——————— tum sævus aper, tum pessima tigris:
Heu! malè tum Libyæ solis erratur in agris.

Nonne vides ut tota tremor pertentet equorum
Corpora, si tantùm notas odor adtulit auras?
Ac neque eos jam fræna virûm, neque verbera sæva;
Non scopuli, rupésque cavæ, atque objecta retardant
Flumina correptos undâ torquentia montes.

GEORGIC III. 248.

No sooner are these stimuli felt, than every
thing else, even the preservation of their own
existence, seems to be forgotten. Food is neglected ; dangers are encountered ; wounds are
endured without appearing to be felt ; and all
obstacles are borne down or surmounted : the
timid become valiant ; and the valiant, furi-
ously mad.

CHAPTER III.

OF TOUCH.

1. The pleasures of touch, if we omit those arising from the communication of the sexes, are few beyond the variations of warmth and coolness; and even those few are extremely limited in their degree. The elegant author, indeed, before cited, has expatiated upon the gratifications of feeling smooth and undulating surfaces in general: but, I believe, these gratifications have been confined to himself; and probably to his own imagination acting through the medium of his favourite system: for, except in the communication of the sexes, which affords no general illustration, and ought therefore to be kept entirely out of the question, I have never heard of any person being addicted to such luxuries; though a feeling board would certainly afford as cheap and innocent a gratification, as either a smelling-bottle, a picture, or a flute, provided it were capable of affording any gratification at all.

2. This notion of smoothness being beauty seems to have arisen, like many other erroneous notions of the same kind, from the common mistake of a particular sexual sympathy for a general principle. We all know how

11

essential a smooth skin is to the charms of a
desirable woman; and, as, in the other sex,
whatever is desirable is commonly called beautiful, we naturally apply the same term to correspondent qualities in other objects, although
they excite no similar sentiments or feelings.
Those beauties, which owe their existence as
beauties to sexual sympathies, are so much
more powerful and efficient than any others,
that they extend their influence, by means of
trains of associated ideas, to a vast distance
from its source: but, abstracted from such
sympathies, the pleasures of this sense, if pleasures they may be called, seem to arise from
gentle irritation; which, if it be extended beyond a certain degree, proportioned always to
the sensibility of the part, becomes painful;
and as this sense of touch extends over the
whole body, the pain, which it can endure,
knows no limit but the termination of life; a
limit, which enlarges the scale of corporeal
pain far beyond that of corporeal pleasure.

3. The modes of irritation, which the touch,
abstracted from the other senses, is capable
of, are few; since, strictly speaking, all are
senses of touch; the impressions upon all being
made by contact. There is, nevertheless,
one mode of irritation belonging exclusively
to the surface of particular parts of the body,
which has so little analogy with any other

sensation, that it may almost be considered as a sense by itself. This is tickling, which produces that unaccountable convulsion called laughter ; a sort of involuntary expression of joy or pleasure, which, when long continued, and carried to excess, becomes painful. It is peculiar, I believe, to the human race, and to the monkey species; though some other animals, such as horses, seem sensible of the sensation which produces it. A similar effect is produced by the operation of certain trains of ideas upon the mind; but this is never so violent as to be painful.

4. This, indeed, is not the only instance of something like an internal sense of touch ; by means of which the conceptions of the mind operate upon the organs of the body involuntarily and mechanically. It is observed by Sir Joshua Reynolds, that *if a man born blind were to recover his sight, and the most beautiful woman were brought before him, he could not determine whether she was handsome, or not* [*]. The justice of this remark I shall confirm in treating of vision, by reasons either not known to, or which did not occur to, the great artist, when he made it. At present, I shall only add this further remark, by way of corollary, that if a man, perfectly

---

[*] Idler, No. 8.

possessed both of feeling and sight—conversant
with, and sensible to, the charms of women,
were even to be in contact with what he conceived to be the most beautiful and lovely of
the sex; and at the moment, when he was
going to embrace her, he was to discover that
the parts which he touched only were feminine
or human; and that, in the rest of her form,
she was an animal of a different species, or a
person of his own sex, the total and instantaneous change of his sentiments from one extreme to another would abundantly convince
him that his sexual desires depended as little
upon the abstract sense of touch, as upon that
of sight.

5. Are these sexual desires, therefore, governed by any innate images or ideas, according to which the external impressions upon
the organs of sense affect us one way or
another? Certainly not: for the doctrine of
innate ideas has been so completely confuted
and exploded, that no person in his senses can
now entertain it; but, nevertheless, there may
be internal stimuli, which, though not innate,
grow up constitutionally in the body; and naturally and instinctively dispose the desires of all
animals to the opposite sex of their own species. Animal desire or want may exist without
any idea of its object, if there be a stimulus
to excite it; so that a male, who had arrived

D

at maturity without knowing the existence of a female of his own species, might feel it, as a new-born child feels the want of food, without having any determinate notion of what was proper to gratify it.

6. Beauty of form and colour, which act, in these cases, through the medium of the imagination only, have nothing to do with this mere irritation of the nerves, whether it proceed from internal or external stimuli; for this irritability extends in some instances to vegetable substances, which have no power of perception; but of which the organic parts are not only irritable, but require the touch of an insect or other extraneous body to render them effective in reproduction.

7. Many sorts of plants seem, in other respects, capable of sensation, as far as this power consists in the mere aptitude of the organs to receive impressions: but it does not appear that the impressions ever go further than the organs, which receive them; and if they do not, it is evident that they can excite neither pleasure nor pain; nor leave any traces or memorials behind them of any kind. The impressions, therefore, being unperceived, produce only mechanical vibrations in the fibres, of which the sufferer is not conscious, and which, therefore, only differ in their cause or mode from those which impulse or attraction

excites in the component parts of metals: for though the impressions upon the external organs of sense are the primary causes of those sensations, which imprint the ideas of them upon the mind; yet the perception of those sensations, and consequently the pleasures and pains arising from them, as well as the ideas which they imprint, are in the brain; from which, if the organ be separated, though it may retain its irritability, and its apparent sensibility, for a considerable time, it will still be utterly incapable of sensation, and in exactly the same predicament as we have supposed the irritable organs of vegetables to be *. On the contrary, sensations, exactly resembling those produced by impressions on the external organs, will continue to be felt when the organ is no more; it being common for a person, who has lost a limb, to imagine that he feels a pain in the extremity which has been ampu-

* I am speaking only of animals whose organization is perfect, and analogous to our own. I know that butterflies, wasps, &c. do appear to be sensible of pleasure or pain, and even live and linger for a long time after their heads are off; but then it does not appear that the heads of such animals contain any centre of organization or seat of life analogous to the brain in birds and quadrupeds. Many of the cold-blooded amphibious animals also retain life for a long time after the head has been separated from the body; but if there be any sense of pain left, I should conceive it to be in the head only.

tated; that is, really to feel a pain, excited by some internal cause, similar to that which he had before felt in that extremity.

8. For this, as well as for many other reasons, it is evident that neither the sensations, nor the ideas imprinted by them, have any resemblance to the objects, or the qualities of objects, which have produced them; but that the connection between them, howsoever spontaneous and immediate it may seem, is merely habitual, and the result of experience and observation *. Certain sensations constantly accompanying certain objects, we naturally and justly conceive those objects to be the cause of them; and when impressions are made upon two or more different organs, by the same object, at the same time, the evidence of their being so is as strong and certain as any, that does not admit of demonstration, by comparative numbers and quantities, can be. I may have a pain in my hand, produced by some internal cause, so exactly resembling that produced by the puncture of a needle, or

---

* See Locke, Berkeley, Hume, Reid, &c. Locke, indeed, with some hesitation excepted what he calls the primary qualities of bodies, such as figure, extension, &c. and admitted that the ideas of these were resemblances of them, (Essay on Human Understanding, Book II. c. viii.) but Berkeley and Hume found no difficulty in confuting him, and proving that these had no more similitude to their archetypes than any others.

the burning of a caustic, that, if I had no other sense, but that of feeling, I might not be able to distinguish the one from the other : hut if I *see* the needle thrust into it, or the caustic applied to it, and *feel* the pain to commence at the same instant, I naturally connect them as cause and effect; and, having once imprinted them as such in my memory, continue to connect them ever afterwards. Neither the needle, however, nor the puncture ; the caustic, nor the burning, have any resemblance, either with the sensations felt or with the remembrances of them imprinted: but the evidence of two senses to one point becomes that of a parallax * ; and the force of it is

* A *parallax* in astronomy is the difference between the relative situation of any heavenly body, as it *is* seen from the surface, and as it *would be* seen from the centre of the earth : which difference, being ascertained by an angle, the base of which is half the earth's diametre, affords *evidence* of the real magnitude and distance of the body, to which the perpendicular of that angle extends.

The term, though usually employed in astronomy, more properly belongs to optics; and may be equally applied to any visible object, which, by a variation of the point of sight, appears to vary its relative situation ; and the extent of such variation, being ascertained by similar means, will afford similar *evidence* concerning the object.

The author should feel shame in thus obtruding explanations, which, to every reader of liberal education, must appear useless and impertinent, had not a whole synod of professed critics proclaimed their want of them, by petu-

lantly

doubled with every repetition of the same sensation from the same external cause.

9. These remembrances, or retained perceptions or notions, Des Cartes and Locke called
ideas; a name borrowed from the Platonic
philosophy, with which their followers Berkeley and Hume contrived to subvert first the
material, and then the intellectual world.
Plato, indeed, had before attempted to subvert the former; or, at least, to render its
foundations very insecure: for he too perceived that there was no resemblance between
ideas and the material objects that they appear to represent in the mind: but concluding that these notions must be exact copies
from some real existences, he derived them
from the intellectual world; whence the human soul sprang, and where the eternal ideas,
according to which the fleeting and changeable
forms, which we see impressed upon gross matter, remained immutable in the divine mind.
All real knowledge, therefore, according to
this philosopher, was innate; and the improvement of it consisted in recovering and restor-
ing the images, with which the soul had originally been endowed, but which were buried
and obscured in the opaque dross of matter.
These images or ideas were not derived from

lantly reproaching him with their own ignorance.—EDINB.
REVIEW, No. XIV.

any particular forms of substances, either here or elsewhere; but all particular forms of substances, together with our ideas of them, were derived from the general ideas of the intellectual world; so that a triangle was not a triangle, a square not a square, nor a circle a circle, because it had a particular material form, or relative dimensions; but because it partook, in a certain degree, of the qualities of the immutable idea of triangularity, squareness, or rotundity eternally exifting in the divine mind *.

10. When men once renounce the evidence of their senses, either in believing or doubting, there is nothing which they may not believe or doubt with perfect consistency. If we can once persuade ourselves that, because ideas have no resemblance to their material objects, they may have arisen in the mind without them, we may certainly believe or disbelieve the existence of those material objects, as we please: for our feelings and perceptions are certainly internal; nor can we at all tell how they are connected with any thing external; the mode of conveyance, between the organs of sense and those of perception, being beyond the reach of human discovery. That there is some mode of conveyance the constant recurrence

* See Phædon, et de Republicâ, lib, x.

of particular associations proves to the satisfaction of ordinary men: but if learned philosophers choose to doubt it, because it is not
demonstrable, they must doubt on. Scepticism has never attempted to make proselytes
by fire or sword, and is therefore at least an
innocent absurdity compared with its antagonist bigotry.

11. All its wandering clouds of confusion
and perplexity seem to have arisen from employing the Greek word *idea*, sometimes in its
proper sense to signify a mental image or
vision, and sometimes in others the most adverse and remote, to signify *perception, remembrance, notion, knowledge*, and almost
every other operation, or result of operation,
of which mind is capable. Of motion, for
instance, in a particular object, we have a
perception when we see or feel it move, and a
remembrance afterwards: but of the motion
of the earth, either on its axis or in its orbit,
we have neither *perception* nor *remembrance*,
but only a *notion*, acquired by comparative
deductions from other perceptions: while of
motion in general we have no particular *perception, remembrance* or *notion*; but only
general knowledge collected and abstracted
from all. Of neither, however, have we any
idea, if by idea be meant *mental image* or *resemblance*: but, nevertheless, to infer from

thence that we have no adequate *perception,* *remembrance, notion,* or *knowledge* either of *motion* or *body,* seems as adverse to sound philosophy as to common sense; there being no more reason why a *notion* should resemble a *perception*; a *perception,* a *sensation,* or a *sensation* its *object,* than that an *exertion* should resemble an *arm*; an *arm,* a *lever*; or a *lever,* a *weight*; nor is it less absurd to make the want of resemblance between the cause, the means, and the end, a ground for doubting the reality of either, in the one case, than in the other*. I could therefore wish to drop or modify the use of the word *idea:* but it has become too general and established for an individual to attempt it; and I have only to intreat the reader to keep these distinctions in his mind, and apply them occasionally.

12. Among the pleasures of sense, more particularly among those belonging to touch, there is a certain class, which, though arising from negative causes, are nevertheless real and positive pleasures: as when we gradually sink from any violent or excessive degree of action or irritation into a state of tranquillity and re-

---

* Since the above was written, a very able and eloquent advocate of the ideal system has appeared in the Right Hon. W. Drummond, whose " Academical Questions" I have read with much delight and instruction, if not with conviction.

pose: I say *gradually*; for if the transition
be sudden and abrupt, it will not be pleasant;
the pleasure arising from the inverted action
of the nerves, and not from the utter cessation
of action.

13. From this inverted action arises the
gratification which we receive from a cool
breeze, when the body has been excessively
heated; or from the rocking of a cradle, or
the gentle motion of a boat, or easy carriage,
after having been fatigued with violent exercise.   Such, too, is that which twilight, or the
gloomy shade of a thicket, affords to the eye,
after it has been dazzled with the blaze of the
mid-day sun; and such, likewise, is that, which
the ear receives, from the gradual diminution
of loudness of tone in music; and it is by
alternately ascending and descending this scale,
that what is called (by a metaphor taken from
painting) the chromatic in that art, is produced: but why the sensation caused by the
ascent of the scale should be called pleasure,
and that caused by its descent, delight, as distinguished by an eminent writer*, I cannot
discover.

* Sublime and Beautiful, P. I. f. iv.

CHAPTER IV.

OF HEARING.

1. SOUND is produced by the vibrations of elastic air or some other fluid contained in it, and communicated to the interior organs of perception by means of the drum of the ear and auditory nerves; which are formed by nature with a peculiar kind of irritability suited to such vibrations, which have no effect on any other part of the body, how exquisite soever its sensibility may be. They have, nevertheless, a very strong and marked effect upon the hardest substances in nature, provided they are such as are capable of receiving vibrations in unison: whence sound will break a glass, at the same time, that it cannot move a feather or the flame of a candle; nor make any perceptible impression upon the ball of the eye.

2. Its vibrations, indeed, seem to be communicable to every hard and elastic substance; as appears from the ticking of a watch, or any other minute sound being conveyed to almost any distance by a pole or wire extending from the sonorous object to the ear. Where the drum of that organ, too, is diseased; and the sense of hearing consequently lost or impaired, the lowest whisper will, nevertheless, be dis-

tinctly heard, if spoken to one end of a bar of metal or glass, while the other is held between the teeth of the person addressed: but if the disease extends to the auditory nerves; so as to deprive them of their irritability, nothing can be heard by these or any other means. The sound, therefore, appears, in this instance, to be conveyed to those nerves, which communicate with the brain, by means of vibrations received by one solid and elastic substance from another; and thus continued through the bar, the teeth, and the jaw bones.

. 3. Many of these solid bodies, which are so susceptible of the vibrations of sound, such as glass, and different kinds of metal, are impenetrable to air: wherefore I suspect that sound is produced by some finer fluid mixed with air; and pervading elastic, as light does transparent bodies. Of this fluid, however, if such there be, we can never obtain any adequate knowledge: for, as it is only perceived, as the vehicle of impressions to one sense, our ideas of it must always remain in nearly the same state as those which a man born blind can form of the light of the sun by feeling its warmth. That hard and solid substances should transmit this light, which is excluded by the most soft and porous, is equally unaccountable, as that they should transmit sound, In both, probably, there is a peculiar distribu-

tion of the component particles, respectively
adapted to the admission of a particular fluid,
and of that only.

4. But whatever be the nature of the substance, which produces sound, the sensations,
caused by its vibrations upon the organs of
hearing, will depend upon the same principles,
as those produced by other substances on other
organs. Certain modes and degrees of irritation will be pleasant, others painful, and
others insipid; and these will vary in different
individuals according to the different degrees
of sensibility in their respective organs. In
some sorts of dogs, this sensibility is so exquisite, that the sound of a fife or other very
shrill instrument, though perfectly in harmony,
gives them very acute pain, when near to their
ears; as they testify by loud howlings and com-
plainings. The filing of a saw, or other harsh
and discordant sound of that kind, though
not loud, will create a very uneasy and even
painful sensation in the human organs, which
we commonly call *setting the teeth on edge*;
and it seems to be produced by extending the
vibrations from the ears to the teeth, instead
of from the teeth to the ears: as in the experiment of the metal or glass bar before cited.
Extremely loud and jarring sounds, such as
those of kettle-drums or artillery, will extend
this vibration through the whole body; as I

very sensibly felt at the performance of some of Handel's choruses in Westminster Abbey: but, as they were in harmony, the sensation was not at all unpleasant. On the contrary, if I could conceive any sensation to be sublime, I should admit this to be so: but the sentiment of sublimity belongs to the affections of the mind, and not to organic sensation; as I shall fully show in examining that part of my subject.

5. The sensual pleasures of sound, to which I wish at present to confine my inquiries, are in their modes and progress nearly analogous to those of taste. Very young persons almost always prefer the sweet tones of a flute, or the female human voice, unaccompanied and without any technical modulation, to any more complicated harmony: but these simple tones, by being often repeated with little variety, grow vapid and tiresome; while mixtures, when once the relish for them is acquired, give permanent pleasure by varying it through every possible mode of combination; and still further varying these modes of combination by all the diversities of modulation—by swells, cadences, &c.; which render music one of the most delightful of gratifications, even when considered merely as a gratification of sense, independent of character and expression; which belong not to the sensations, which it

11

causes; but to the mental sympathies and associated ideas, which those sensations excite
and renew.

6. For there are certain modulations of
tone, which instinctively express certain mental
sympathies; and, without the intervention of
any determinate notions or ideas, convey the
sentiments of one mind, and awaken those of
another with more unerring precision and em-
·phatical energy, than the artificial medium of
articulation can ever attain.   Such are the various modulations of tone, by which birds and
quadrupeds express their parental and sexual
affections; and their sentiments of anger, resentment, or defiance: expressions, whose
meaning is always clear and unequivocal; and
which are understood as perfectly by those
who have existed but a day, as by them, who
have lived years; no young animal of any kind
ever mistaking the murmur of affection for the
growl of anger, or the cry of joy for the whine
of distress.

7. Similar modulations of tone also serve,
as a natural medium of communication of corresponding sentiments, in the human race,
before the artificial one of articulation is acquired or understood; very young children
always perceiving, by the tone of voice, in
which they are spoken to, whether they are
applauded or reprimanded, long before they

have learned to affix any determinate ideas to
the particular words uttered.

8. To this natural and instinctive effect of
the different modulations of tone is owing, in
a great measure, the effect of what we call expression in music: at least of that which may
properly be called sentimental expression;
since it excites sentiments merely; whereas
another kind of expression excites ideas also:
but this depends upon the principle of association, which will be considered apart. The
primitive music of all nations is, I believe, of
this sentimental kind; music, as well as paint-
-ing and poetry, being in its principle an imitative art*; and, though science may delight
in that various and complicated harmony,
which displays the skill of the composer, and
the dexterity of the performer, without either
pleasing the sense, or touching the heart; yet
the mass of mankind, I believe, never find any
gratification in music, but such as arises either
from sweet tones, pleasing combinations, or
such modulations, as either through instinctive
feeling, or habitual association, awaken pleasing sympathies. The first of these is a sensual, and the second a sentimental pleasure;
while that, which is peculiarly felt by the
learned, may be properly called an intellectual

* Aristot. Poet. f. iii.

pleasure: for this likewise is really a pleasure, and one that may be as reasonably and pro- perly cultivated as either of the others; as I shall show in treating of the pleasures of the understanding.   It is one, indeed, which I am utterly incapable of enjoying: but that is no reason why I should treat it with contempt, according to a too common practice; which, however, always indicates a narrow, or an un- cultivated mind; and generally both.

9. As music consists in the melody of inarti- culate sounds, so does poetry, as far as it can be considered as a gratification of sense, in that of articulate sounds: but as articulation consists in the division and interruption of tones, and harmony in their undulating flow into each other, it must be owned that articu- late and melodious sounds seem to be of very adverse dispositions; and accordingly we find that articulation is almost always partially sup- pressed in singing, even by those, who pro- nounce most distinctly; the pure or mute consonants, which alone mark distinct articu- lation, being softened down into liquids or aspirates.

10. Indeed, it appears to me, that the most melodious versification affords very little, if any at all, of mere sensual gratification; the regularity of metre or rhyme being rather cal- culated to assist memory and facilitate ut-

E

terance,. than to please the ear; which, in music, is always most delighted with irregular combinations: for, though the same closes to particular periods are sometimes repeated at stated intervals, it is generally in lighter compositions, where the music is not principal, but adapted to the verse.

11. Music, too, is still music, upon whatsoever instrument it be performed; nor does that, which was composed for the harp, cease to be melody when performed on the violin. But the metre of one language, when applied to the words of another, ceases to have any effect at all; as has been abundantly proved by the hexameters, Sapphics, Alcaics, &c. which have at different times, and from different authors, appeared in English:—verses less like poetry could scarcely have been produced by the machine of Logado. Nevertheless the metres are exactly the same, as those which are felt to be so musical in the Greek and Latin; and as the tones in both are limited by us to our own habitual pronunciation of the five vowels, there cannot be any great difference in them, as modified to our utterance.

12. The relations of measure and quantity are fixed and determinate, and liable to no variation from the difference of the materials to which they are applied. They must, there-

fore, be the same in Greek, as in English; as they are the same in marble, as in brick; and, as far as the impressions made upon the organs of hearing depend upon measure and quantity, *they* must be the same likewise in both: but still we know that our feelings are very differently affected by the same metrical quantities employed in different languages; wherefore, either the pleasures arising from poetry do not arise from metrical quantity, or metrical quantity makes itself felt by something beyond the mere organs of sense.

13. Indeed, from the manner, in which the verses of the Greek and Latin poets are pronounced in our public schools and universities, it might be reasonably inferred that metrical quantity was of no importance, and not to be considered as a requisite of poetry: for though great pains are taken to teach the mechanism of it; yet, when learnt, it is totally neglected in reading; every word of three syllables being pronounced either as a dactyle or amphibrachys, according to the accentual prosody of our own language. As the ancients, however, did not extend the syllable, upon which they raised the voice, in the manner that we do; and as this mode of pronunciation is peculiar to ourselves, and unintelligible to all the rest of Europe, we may safely conclude it to be wrong; and concur with the general opinion

of mankind that metrical quantity is an essential to poetry, as necessary to be preserved in
reading, as in scanning a verse ; and that much
of the pleasure, which poetry affords, arises
from a just observance of it.

14. It is, nevertheless, evident that this pleasure is not a pleasure of organic sense; though
communicated through the organs of hearing:
for not only the verse of one language ceases
to be verse, and loses all the character of
poetry in another, but the same metre, regulated by the same accentuation, and constituted in every respect upon the same principle,
is in one language appropriated to serious and
tragic, and in another, to ludicrous and frivolous subjects; and the propriety of its use
in each is equally felt by those who are equally
familiar with both.

    " Thus said to my lady the knight full of care,"
And

    " Je chante le heros qui regna sur la France,"

flow exactly in the same time and tune, and
are equally supported by corresponding rhymes
in the lines, that respectively follow ; and yet
to the same ears, and independent of the sense,
there is something, in the flow of the one, light
and ludicrous, and in that of the other, grave
and solemn; though the English language is
certainly much less prone to the light and ludi-

crous, and better adapted to the grave and solemn than the French. There is something, however, in the respective idioms of each, that, in this instance, causes the same modifications of sound to appear ludicrous in the former, and solemn in the latter; wherefore it, is in the nature of idiom, that we must seek for the principle of this difference, as well as for that, which gives its character and effect to all metrical language: but as idiom in language is not a subject of organic sensation, nor any thing immediately pertaining to it, the investigation of it does not belong to the present stage of my inquiry.

15. If the principles of poetical and musical melody were the same, as, I believe, all theoretical writers upon the subject have supposed them to be, similar differences must necessarily arise in the character and effect of the same tune, according as it was played upon instruments respectively differing in the style and character of their tone and modulation: but this is in no instance the case; every composition in music retaining its own original character, upon whatever instrument it be performed, provided the instrument be really musical or in tune, and touched with competent skill and ability. A cracked fiddle may make any composition in music appear ridiculous; as a cracked voice may any composi-

tion in poetry*; but that is upon another principle, which will be hereafter examined.

16. It has been already observed that all
sensation is really produced by contact; the
effluvia, that we smell, and the vibrations, that
we hear, being locally and essentially in the
nose and the ears, just as the food, which we
taste, is in the mouth, or the implements that
we hold, are in the hands. The mere sense
of hearing, therefore, can afford us no information concerning the distance or direction of
a sonorous object, which can only be perceived
by a faculty acquired entirely by habit; though,
by being habitual, the exercise of it has become as spontaneous and instantaneous, as
that of any natural or organic faculty belonging to our constitutions. If this needed any
proof, and was not clearly demonstrated by
the formation of the organs, the common trick
of a ventriloquist, who can make the sound of
his voice appear to come in any direction, or
from any distance within the reach of its being
heard, would be fully sufficient: for this effect
is produced merely by modifying it, as it would
be modified to the ear, if it had really come in
that direction, or from that distance. We,
therefore, judge of the directions of sounds,

---

* Nihil intrare potest in affectum, quod in aure, velut
quodam vestibulo, statim offendit. Quintil. Inst. l. ix.
c. iv.

and the distances of their causes, solely by certain modes of the vibrations affecting the organ, which usually distinguish each respectively, and which are accordingly associated with them in the mind; but which may, nevertheless, be produced by other means so perfectly as to work an entire deception even, in the most acute observers.

17. This is an extremely important consideration in enabling us to estimate properly the grandeur or sublimity of sound; which can no otherwise arise from its loudness, than as that loudness excites an idea of power in the sonorous object, or in some other associated with it in the mind: for a child's drum close to the ear fills it with more real noise, than the discharge of a cannon a mile off; and the rattling of a carriage in the street, when faintly and indistinctly heard, has often been mistaken for thunder at a distance. Yet no one ever imagined the beating of a child's drum, or the rattling of a carriage over stones, to be grand or sublime; which, nevertheless, they must be, if grandeur or sublimity belong at all to the sensation of loudness. But artillery and lightning are *powerful* engines of destruction; and with their *power* we sympathize, whenever the sound of them excites any sentiments of sublimity; which is only when we apprehend no danger from them; or at least no degree of

E 4

danger sufficient to impress fear: for so far is terror from being a source of the sublime, that the smallest degree of fear instantly annihilates it, as far as relates to the person frightened; and to that person only is the object terrible. To all others it is merely powerful, or capable of inspiring terror to those who are more susceptible of it.—But of this more shall be said in the proper place.

CHAPTER V.

OF SIGHT.

1. SIGHT, as well as hearing, is produced
by immediate contact of the exciting cause
with the organ; which exciting cause is the
light reflected, from the objects seen, upon
the retina of the eye; the pictures upon which,
by some impressions or irritations upon the
optic nerves, the modes of which muft be for
ever unknown to us, are conveyed to the mind,
and produce the sense of vision, the most
valuable of all our senses.

2. The sensation, therefore, felt upon opening the eyes for the first time, must necessarily
be that of the objects seen touching them; as
it proved to be in the case of the boy, who,
at the age of fourteen or thereabouts, obtained
his sight, after having been blind from his
birth, by an operation performed upon his
eyes by Cheselden. For a considerable time,
and till the sense of seeing had been aided
and corrected by that of touch, all the objects
seen appeared only as variations of light acting
upon the eye: for the colours of objects are
only different rays of light variously reflected
from their surfaces*; and their visible pro-

---

* See Newton's Theory of Light and Colours.

jection is merely gradation and opposition of light and shadow; which, in round and undulating bodies, are intermixed gradually; and, in those of angular forms, abruptly. It is, therefore, only by habit and experience that we form analogies between the perceptions of vision and those of touch, and thus learn to discover projection by the eye: for, naturally, the eye sees only superficial dimension; as clearly appears in painting and all other optical deceptions, which produce the appearance of projection or thickness upon a flat surface. The faculty, however, when acquired, as it is in all adult persons who have seen from their birth, is exercised as readily and instantaneously as any natural faculty whatsoever *.

3. The perception of visible projection being thus artificial, that of visible distance must necessarily be so likewise: for distance is only projection extended. Accordingly we find that our improved perception of visible distance extends no further than that experience, by which it has been formed and improved: for of the immense distances of the heavenly bodies from each other, and from the earth, we discover nothing by looking at them; they all appearing to occupy the surface of one

---

* See Dr. Reid's Essay on the Mind, where a very clear and full explanation of the theory of vision is given.

blue vault, whose diameter is that of the visible horizon; which the sun, moon, and stars
seem equally to touch at their rising and
setting. Hence the notion of these lumi-
naries setting in, and rising from the ocean
has universally prevailed through all nations:
and it has not been by the evidence of improved sense; but by the calculations and
discoveries of improved intellect, that the
error has been removed.

4. The visible magnitude of bodies depending entirely upon their distance from the eye,
we have, of course, as imperfect and inadequate perceptions of it from the unaided sense
of vision, as we have of distance. The pen,
which I hold between my fingers, occupies a
greater space in the retina, when only a foot
from the eye, than the spire of Salisbury does,
when seen at the distance of a mile; and, consequently, as far as concerns the mere organ
of sense, is bigger: for though the real magnitude of an object, which is perceived by a
computation of its distance, rendered instantaneous by habit, may affect the imagination,
the visible dimensions of it alone are impressed
upon the eye; and, consequently, can alone
affect the sensation excited.

5. Hence we may learn how to estimate
the theory of an eminent writer, who supposes
that objects of large dimensions are sublime,

because the great number of rays, which they emit, crowd into the eye together, or in quick succession, and produce a degree of tension in the membrane of the retina, which, *approaching nearly to the nature of what causes pain, must* (in his own words) *produce an idea of the sublime**. But, to say nothing of this assumed connection between the causes of pain and the ideas of the sublime, the slightest knowledge of optics would have informed him that the sheet of paper, upon which he was writing, being seen thus close to the eye, reflected a greater, and more forcible mass of light; and, consequently, produced more irritation and tension, than the Peak of Teneriffe or Mount St. Elias would, if seen at the distance of a few miles:—yet, surely he would not say that the sheet of paper excited more grand and perfect ideas of the sublime.

6. That the irritation, produced in the membranes of the eye by vision, is proportioned to the quantity of light poured into it, we may perceive by the dilation and contraction of that membrane called the iris; which always expands its circle, as the quantity of light, to which it is exposed, is diminished, and contracts it, as it is increased. In the eyes of animals formed to see with a very small quan-

---

* Sublime and Beautiful, Part IV. f. ix.

tity of light; such as cats, owls, &c. this power is very great; and the membrane affected seems to consist of valves, which open and shut, instead of a sphincter, that dilates and contracts.   Hence, in the night, when these valves are entirely open, the eyes of these animals present a very singular appearance of large luminous circles; which, in the day, are reduced to small horizontal slits; through which the few rays, that they then want, are suffered to pass: for, to organs of such nice sensibility, any great quantity would be painful; and it is probable that the degree of irritation alone regulates the opening and shutting of the membranes, which admit and exclude it, in the same manner as it does the dilation and contraction of the corresponding membranes in our eyes, without the intervention of the will.

7. The pains and pleasures of vision, however, like those of the other senses, depend upon the modes as well as degrees of irritation: for all the different colours may be properly considered as different modes, in which light acts upon the eyes; colours being only collections of rays variously modified, separated, and combined, according to the different textures of the surfaces of the bodies, from which they are reflected, or the substances of those through which they are refracted.

8. There are, indeed, scarcely any human eyes of such extreme sensibility, unless in a morbid state, as to feel any absolute pain from colours composed of reflected rays: for unless the reflection be from the surface of a concave mirror, in which the rays are collected and condensed, the effect of light is necessarily weakened by being reflected; whence the refracted colours of a prism or a rainbow are always more vivid and bright than those which are reflected from any opaque substance. There are, however, some kinds of birds and quadrupeds, such as turkeys and oxen, to whom scarlet is evidently painful; as they will run at it, and attack it with the utmost virulence and fury. Green, on the contrary, appears to be grateful to the eyes of all animals; though colours, as well as sounds and flavours, are more pleasing when harmoniously mixed and graduated, than when distinct and uniform. Indeed, they almost always are graduated and broken in nature; for, though an object be of one colour throughout, unless it present one equal superficies to one equal degree of light, that colour will be variously graduated and diversified to the eye by every undulating or angular projection or indenture of its form. In every individual pink or rose, whether its colour be white, yellow, or red,

there are infinite varieties and gradations of
tint, produced, not only by the different degrees and modifications of light and shadow,
but by the various reflected rays, which one
leaf casts upon another, according to their different degrees of opacity and exposure.

9. When many sorts and varieties of these
rich and splendid productions of nature are
skilfully arranged and combined, as in the
flower-pots of Vanhuysum, they form, perhaps, the most perfect spectacle of mere sensual beauty that is any where to be found.
The magnificent compositions of landscape
are, indeed, spectacles of a higher class; and
afford pleasures of a more exalted kind: but
only a small part of those pleasures are merely
sensual; the venerable ruin, the retired cottage, the spreading oak, the beetling rock, and
limpid stream having charms for the imagination, as well as for the sense; and often
bringing into the mind pleasing trains of ideas
besides those, which their impressions upon the
organs of sense immediately excite. As far,
however, as they do afford sensual pleasure, it
depends upon the same principle as the pleasures of the other senses already treated of;
that is, upon a moderate and varied irritation
of the organic nerves : for, if the irritation be
too strong; that is, if the transitions of colour
be too violent and sudden, and the oppositions

of light and shadow too vigorous and abrupt, the effect will be harsh and dazzling, and the sensation painful, or, at least, unpleasant; while, if they be too monotonous and feeble, the effect will be flat and insipid, and the sensation too languid to be pleasing.

10. In this, however, as in all other pleasures of sense, the scale of the pleasing and displeasing impressions cannot be graduated according to any abstract general rule, but must be adapted to the different degrees of sensibility of different organs; which vary, not only constitutionally, but habitually; the eye, as well as the palate, being liable to be vitiated, and consequently to require such stimulants to give it pleasure, as give pain to those of more refined sensibility. On the contrary, there are persons whose eyes have naturally a sort of morbid irritability, which renders those degrees of light and modifications of colour, which are merely sufficient to be pleasant to others, quite painful to them. In this case, however, as in all others of the kind, the just scale, and criterion of taste, must be taken from the natural feelings of the mass of mankind: for we have here no rules of calculation to appeal to; and rules of analogy are true or false accordingly as they are respectively supported or opposed by the greater number of instances.

1,1. Smoothness being properly a quality perceivable only by the touch, and applied metaphorically to the objects of the other senses, we often apply it very improperly to those of vision; assigning smoothness, as a cause of visible beauty, to things, which, though smooth to the touch, cast the most sharp, harsh, and angular reflections of light upon the eye; and these reflections are all that the eye feels or naturally perceives; its perception of projecting form or tangible smoothness being, as before observed, entirely artificial and acquired; and, therefore, unconnected with pure sensation. Such are all objects of cut glass or polished metal; as may be seen by the manner in which painters imitate them: for, as the imitations of painting extend only to the visible qualities of bodies, they show those visible qualities fairly and impartially—distinct from all others, which the habitual concurrence of other senses has joined with them in the mind, in our perceptions of them in nature. Yet the imitative representation of such objects in painting is far less harsh and dazzling than the effects of them in reality: for there are no materials, that a painter can employ, capable of expressing the sharpness and brilliancy of those angular reflections of the collected and condensed rays, which are emitted from the surfaces of polished metals; so that the only way of imitating them

F

with any tolerable success is to reduce the general tone of the picture to a degree far below
nature; by which means the imperfect imitations of these very bright objects may be
brought into unison with the rest. This artifice is manifest in most of the pictures painted
for effect by the great Venetian and Flemish
masters; particularly Titian and Rembrandt.

12. I do not mean, however, to assert or
insinuate that these brilliant objects are not
really beautiful, especially in composition;
where, to fill the scale of harmony, we must
ascend to the highest pitch of brightness, and
even sharpness, as well as descend to the lowest degree of mellowness and obscurity, that is
compatible with vision. But what I contend
for is, that the visible beauty of such objects
does not consist in their smoothness, according
to the hypothesis of an eloquent writer*, they
being the direct reverse of smooth to the eye.

13. The reflections from the polished coats
of very sleek and pampered animals are also
harsh and angular, though in a less degree;
and the outlines of their bodies sharp and edgy:
wherefore, whatever visible beauties they may
possess, do not consist in their smoothness.

14. Neat new buildings also, and level lawns
intersected by gravel walks marked out in exact

* Inquiry into the Sublime and Beautiful, Part III.
§. xiv.

lines, or winding canals distinctly bounded by
shaven banks, may be properly called smooth,
if we mean smoothness to the touch: but, to
the eye, they present nothing but harsh and
discordant oppositions of colour, distinguished
by crude and abrupt lines, and only diversified
by formal and angular masses of light and shadow. The only quality in visible objects, which
is at all analogous to smoothness in tangible
bodies, is the even monotony of a billiard-table
or bowling-green; and if the bowling-green be
ridged like a corn field, and the ridges covered
with smooth turf, it will be exactly analogous
to the undulating smoothness of tangible surfaces: yet, I doubt much whether even the
love of system, would have power to induce any
person to find much beauty in either of these
objects; though I hold that love to be full as
potent as any other, and perhaps more so: for
I think that affections, which are generated in
the brain, are generally more vigorous, and always more permanent, than those which spring
up in the heart.

15. I do not mean, however, to deny or de-
preciate the charms of neatness, which is so
grateful in itself, and so necessary to the com-
ort and well-being of man, as I shall show in
he proper place: but it forms no part of that
merely visible beauty, abstracted from all men-

F 2

tal sympathies, or intellectual fitness, which is
at present the subject of inquiry.

16. This consists, according to the principles
which I have endeavoured to establish, in harmonious, but yet brilliant and contrasted combinations of light, shade, and colour; blended,
but not confused; and broken, but not cut,
into masses: and it is not peculiarly in straight
or curve, taper or spiral, long or short, little
or great objects, that we are to seek for these;
but in such as display to the eye intricacy of
parts and variety of tint and surface.

17. Such are animals which have loose, shaggy, and curly hair; trees, whose branches are
spread into irregular forms, and exhibit broken
and diversified masses of foliage, and whose
trunks are varied with mosses and lichens, or
enriched with ivy; buildings, that are mouldering into ruin *, whose sharp angles are soft-

---

* " And time hath mouldered into beauty many a
tower," is one of the few happy expressions to be found
in Mr. Mason's " English Garden."

According to Mr. Price, however, beauty, even in architecture, implies the freshness of youth; or, at least,
a state of high and perfect preservation; and buildings
are mouldered out of beauty into *picturesqueness.* Vol. II.
p. 282, &c. and Dialog. Who shall ever understand the
English language, if new and uncouth words are thus to
deprive those sanctioned by long usage of their authorised
and established meaning?

ened by decay, and whose crude and uniform
tints are mellowed and diversified by weather-
stains and wall plants; streams, that flow alternately smooth and agitated, between broken or
sedgy banks, reflecting, sometimes clearly, and
sometimes indistinctly, the various masses of
rock or foliage, that hang over them; in short,
almost all those objects in nature or art, which
my friend Mr. Price has so elegantly described
as picturesque: for painting, as it imitates only
the visible qualities of bodies, separates those
qualities from all others; which the habitual
concurrence and co-operation of the other
senses have mixt and blended with them, in our
ordinary perceptions, from which our ideas are
formed. The imitative deceptions of this art
unmask the habitual deceptions of sight, as
those of the ventriloquist do the habitual deceptions of hearing, by showing that mere
modifications upon one flat surface can exhibit
to the eye the semblance of various projecting
bodies at different degrees of distance from each
other, in the same manner as the mere modifications of one voice could convey to the ear the
semblance of different voices coming in different
directions, and from places differing in their
degrees of proximity: Hence it was with some
difficulty that the nature of painting could be
explained to the boy, restored to sight by Cheselden, even after his eyes had acquired all the

ordinary powers of perception, as well as those of sensation : for when he *saw*, upon a surface, which he *felt* to be flat, all those visible effects produced; by which he had lately been taught to estimate visible projection and distance, he concluded that either his sight or his touch was erroneous, but had not been sufficiently in the habit of comparing their evidence to decide which.

18. In many of the objects of these mixt sensations, there must necessarily occur a mixture of pleasing and displeasing qualities; or of such as please one sense and displease another: or please the senses, and offend the understanding or the imagination. These painting also separates; and, in its imitations of objects, which are pleasing to the eye but otherwise offensive, exhibits the pleasing qualities only; so that we are delighted with the copy, when we should, perhaps, turn away with disgust and abhorrence from the original. Decayed pollard trees, rotten thatch, crumbling masses of perished brick and plaster, tattered worn-out dirty garments, a fish or a flesh market, may all exhibit the most harmonious and brilliant combinations of tints to the eye; and harmonious and brilliant combinations of tints are certainly beautiful in whatsoever they are seen : but, nevertheless, these objects contain so many properties that are offensive to other senses, or to

'the imagination, that in nature we are not pleased with them, nor ever consider them as beautiful. Yet in the pictures of Rembrandt, Ostade, Teniers, and Fyt, the imitations of them are unquestionably beautiful and pleasing to all mankind; and as these painters are remarkable for the fidelity of their imitations, whatever visible qualities existed in the objects must appear in their copies of them; but, in these copies, the mind perceives only the visible qualities; whereas, in the originals, it perceived others less agreeable united with them. Painters, indeed, and persons much conversant with painting, often feel pleasure in viewing the objects themselves: but this is from a principle of association, which will be hereafter explained.

19. A great authority, I know, denies that the imitations of such objects can ever produce " *beautiful, that is, lovely pictures* * ;" and if *beautiful* is thus limited to the sense of *lovely*, I may perhaps not think the point worth contesting; though, even with this arbitrary and unexampled limitation, I can produce at least equal authority in support of a contrary opinion.

> " D'un pinçeau delicat, l'artifice agréable
> Du plus affieux objet, fait un objet *aimable* †."

* Price's Dialog.   † Boileau, Art Poetique, c. iii.

F 4

The same great authority had before admitted that the picturesque, which renders such objects pleasing in pictures, is that which painting can, and sculpture cannot express*; and what is that but colour, and its gradations of light and shade, or distinctness and indistinctness?

20. The beauty of those whimsical and extravagant paintings, called, from the subterraneous apartments in Rome, where the first specimens of them were found, *grottesque*, has never, I believe, been questioned: the brilliance and variety of the tints having afforded pleasure to every eye; and the airy lightness, and playful elegance of the forms, to every imagination, that has been acquainted with them. Yet, were we to meet with such extravagant and disproportioned buildings in reality; or such monstrous combinations of human, animal, and vegetable forms in nature, our understandings would revolt at them, and we should turn from them with scorn and disgust: but, in judging of the imitative representations of them, we do not consult our understandings, but merely our senses and imaginations; and to them they are pleasing and beautiful.

21. I am aware that I am here laying myself open to the cavils of a captious adversary; who

---

* Essays: Preface to Vol. II. p. xiv.

may accuse me of calling the tattered rags and filth of a beggar, or the extravagant monsters of grottesque *beautiful;* because I assert that they contain beautiful variations of tint or light and shadow : but he may, with equal justice, accuse me of calling a dunghill *sweet,* because I assert that it contains sugar ; and that the sugar, when separated from the dross, will be of the same quality as that extracted from the cane. In the same manner, the beautiful tints and lights and shadows, when separated, in the imitation, from the disagreeable qualities, with which they were united, are as truly beautiful as if they had never been united with any such qualities. Properly, those substances only can be called *sweet,* in which the qualities of sweetness predominate ; and those only *beautiful,* in which the qualities of beauty predominate : but, if there be any means, as those above mentioned, of separating the subordinate sweet and beautiful qualities from those of a contrary kind, there can be no reason why they should be less sweet or less beautiful when separated, than if they had never been mixt.

22. The natural consequence of confining beauty to smoothness or undulation, either of form or colour, is, that a person of such just taste and feeling, as my friend above mentioned, should discover it to be insipid, as he has done ; and to remedy this defect, he proposes that a

_ 10

certain portion of the quality, which he calls
picturesqueness, should be mixt with it, in
order to give it the proper relish. Of the word
Picturesque, I shall have more to say in another chapter; and, therefore, shall only observe, at present, that whosoever thinks beauty
insipid, and conceives that the addition of any
other quality is requisite to make it pleasing,
has only involved himself in a confusion of
terms, by attaching to the word beauty those
ideas, which the rest of mankind attach to the
word insipidity; and those, which the rest of
mankind attach to the word beauty, to this
nameless amalgamation, which he conceives to
be an improvement of it. The difference is
merely a difference of words, which three
fourths of those, that have arisen in metaphysics and moral philosophy, as well as in religion, have been; and as long as the disputes
concerning them are confined to the shedding
of ink, and do not extend to the shedding of
blood, they afford a very innocent amusement
to the several disputants, of which I am now
enjoying the benefit.

25. A very remarkable difference of this kind
subsisted between the late President of the
Royal Academy *, and the author of the Inquiry into the Sublime and Beautiful, which it

* Sir Joshua Reynolds.

which he calls
t with it, in
Of the word
to say in ano-
tail only ob-
marks beauty
tition of any
make it pleasing,
a confusion of
d beauty those
ad attach to the
with the rest of
beauty, to this
he conceives to
a difference is
which three
in metaphy-
well as in reli-
as the disputes
on the shedding
the shedding of
amusement
which I am now

anger of this kind
President of the
other of the In-
which I

Is peculiarly pleasant to recall upon the present occasion, because it never cooled the warmth of that friendship, which remained unabated and uninterrupted between those two illustrious persons till death separated them; though both appealed to the public in favour of their respective opinions. The one makes beauty to consist in smooth and undulating surfaces, flowing lines, and colours that are analogous to them*; while the other maintains that beauty does not consist in any particular forms, lines, or colours, but is merely the result of habitual association; by which particular forms, proportions, and colours are appropriated to particular kinds and species, the individuals of which appear beautiful, or ugly, accordingly as they are respectively conformable or adverse to our ideas of the perfection of those particular forms; which ideas have arisen in the mind from a general and comparative view of the whole kind, class, or species †. It will readily appear that these two great critics differ so widely merely from attaching different meanings to the word beauty; which, the one confines to the *sensible*, and the other to the *intellectual* qualities of things; both equally departing from that general use of the term, which is the only ust criterion of propriety in speech.

* Sublime and Beautiful, Part III.   † Idler, No. 8.

CH.
v
Of Si

24. The doctrines of the former concerning beauty have been classed and defined under six distinct heads by the most eminent and distinguished of his disciples; and thus illustrated by a well-known example; which, if it prove nothing else, shows at least to what a degree the most discerning mind may be occasionally deprived even of the ordinary powers of perception by the fascinations of a favourite system.

" No building," says Mr. Price, " is more
" universally admired for its beauty than the
" temple of the Sibyl at Tivoli. Let us then
" consider what are the qualities of beauty
" according to Mr. Burke, and how far they
" apply to beautiful buildings in general, and
" to that in particular. Those qualities are,
" I. to be comparatively small: II. to be smooth:
" III. to have a variety in the direction of the
" parts: but, IV. to have those parts melted, as
" it were, into each other : V. to be of a de-
" licate frame, without any remarkable appear-
" ance of strength: VI. to have the colour
" clear and bright, but not very strong and
" glaring. The temple I have just mentioned,
" has, I think, as much of those chief prin-
" ciples of general beauty, as the particular
" principles of architecture will allow of: it is
" circular, surrounded by columns detached
" from the body of the building; it is light and

" airy; of a delicate frame; in a great mea-
" sure free from angles; and comparatively
" small. I am speaking of it, as it must have
" been in its perfect state, when the tint of the
" stone, and the finishing and preservation of
" the parts, corresponded with the beauty of its
" general form *."

The *ruin* of the temple of Vesta, vulgarly
called the Sibyls' temple, at Tivoli, has unquestionably been very generally admired for its
beauty, and perfectly accords with the principles that I am endeavouring to establish;
though not at all with those of my antagonist,
which can only allow it to be picturesque. What
was the effect of the original temple upon the
minds of those, who saw it entire, we do not
know: but admitting it to have been that of
beauty still more perfect, it remains to be seen
how far, upon a more accurate inspection, and
more detailed examination of its constituent
parts, it will answer the purpose for which it
is cited.

Compared with the Pantheon or the Par-
thenon, it was certainly small; but, compared
with any edifice of similar plan (the proper object of comparison), it was by no means so: for
though smaller in diametre than that of the
same goddess at Rome, it appears to have been

* Essays on the Picturesque, Vol. II. p. 273.

altogether a larger, more massive, and more considerable building, than either that or any other of the kind known.

So far from being smooth, it is all over rough with sculpture, and built of the most rugged, porous, unequal stone, ever employed in a highly wrought edifice.

The parts, instead of having any variety or even difference in their direction, all converge to one centrical point; as they necessarily must in a building completely circular. Even the columns have a horizontal inclination inwards, equal to their perpendicular diminution upwards; which shows a most scrupulous attention to exclude every appearance of such variety.

Instead of being free from angles, every thing is composed of angles: the entablature consists of angles projecting beyond each other; the suffit of angles indented within each other; the capitals are clusters of angles, obtuse in the abacus, and acute in the foliage; while the columns, being fluted, exhibit circles of angles round every shaft, and stand upon a basement surrounded by a cornice composed chiefly of angular mouldings.

So far from being of a delicate frame, or with little appearance of strength, it is remarkable for nothing more than the compact firmness of its construction, which nothing but some convulsion of nature, or the mischievous ex-

ertions of man could have destroyed; nor is
its superiority in beauty over all the numerous
imitations that have been made of it, owing to
any thing more than to its superior size, strength,
and variety of rough angular enrichments. It
is founded on a projecting point of rock enlarged into a square area by vast substructions
of arches, supporting a basement of solid stone,
above forty-five feet in diametre, and nearly
eight feet thick; on which was placed a circle
of columns, each shaft of one stone, upwards
of twenty feet long, and two feet and a half
thick, supporting a massive stone roof, and
surrounding a tower of rough masonry of about
twenty-eight feet in diametre.

The colour is that of the rough Tiburtine
stone, which could never have been other than
a dingy brown; and though a circular Corinthian portico surrounding a circular tower, and
thus appearing, by the laws of perspective, to
retreat from the eye, is extremely light and
airy, upon a principle, which shall be considered in the proper place, this is a species of
lightness no way connected with any of Mr.
Burke's characteristics of beauty; nor at all
incompatible with the most manifest firmness
and stability of construction. The temple of
Vesta at Rome appears to have been after the
same design, with twenty columns instead of
eighteen, of larger size, though slenderer pro-

CHA
IV.
Of Hea

ɑan could have destroyed; nor is
ty in beauty over all the numerous
ɩat have been made of it, owing to
ɔre than to its superior size, strength,
of rough angular enrichments.   It
ɔn a projecting point of rock en-
a square area by vast substructions
upporting a basement of solid stone,
y-five feet in diametre, and nearly
hick; on which was placed a circle
, each shaft of one stone, upwards
feet long, and two feet and a half
porting a massive stone roof, and
ɩg a tower of rough masonry of about
ht feet in diametre.
lour is that of the rough
ich could never have b
rown; and though
tico surrounding ɑ
        the

portions; and probably without the stone roof,
as well as massive basement and substructions;
defects, which, on the principles in question,
should have enhanced rather than diminished
its beauty: yet this temple having become a,
dirty church in a city, instead of a beautiful
ruin in a romantic situation, has scarcely been
noticed: a plain indication of the real causes,
of the celebrity of the other.

The buildings most consonant to the above,
definitions of beauty are the Hindoo domes,
shaped like bee-hives, and composed of a thin
shell of half burnt brick, encrusted in a smooth
coat of the plaster called chinam, which is
white, delicately tinged with red, blue, or yellow. Their undulating flow of outline tapered
to a point; their frail and delicate structure;
their clear bright colours, neither strong nor
glaring; their smooth unbroken surface; their
small size, comparative to that of the buildings
to which they usually belong, all exactly accord; nor is any thing wanting but a variety in
the direction of the parts; and *that* the buildings themselves always abundantly supply. Yet
I do not believe that either Mr. Burke or his
commentator ever found such a building beautiful: for, in practice, their natural good taste
triumphed over their theories, and prevented
them from applying the characteristics of beauty
belonging to a rose, a violet, a bead, or a bon-

net, to any object of so different a kind, as a piece of architecture; in which, either Addison's principle of decoration, Montesquieu's of contrast, or Reynolds's of congruity, might afford a much juster criterion, than either frailty of frame, undulation of outline, or delicacy of colour; as I shall endeavour to show in the sequel.

25. I have already stated a position of the latter writer, *that if a man born blind were to recover his sight, and the most beautiful woman were brought before him, he could not determine whether she was handsome or not*; which is unquestionably true: for till he had verified and ascertained the evidence of his sight by that of touch, he could not discover that she was a being of his own species; or, indeed, any thing more than a fleeting vision—a diminutive picture or impression upon the pupil of his eye. The author, however, grounds it upon a different reason; namely, *that no man can judge whether an animal be beautiful or deformed in its kind, who has not seen many of that kind:* wherefore, he adds, *that if two women, the one the most beautiful, and the other the most deformed, were placed before this blind man restored to sight, he could no better determine to which he should give the preference, having seen only those two.* I believe, however,

G

CHAP.
IV.
Of Hearing.

c mankir
til to poe
rading a
o the pl
fim a ju
14. It i
sre is no
cmmunic
fr not or
t be ver
petry in
lted by
tted in e
im one
tigic, ar
vlous. su
i each i
fmiliar

" Thus
nd

" Je c
fiw ex
æ equ
i the
t the
tere
ad l
ad
ert

ent a kind, as

ch, either Addi

, Montesquieu'

congruity, migh

ion, than eithe

outline, or deli

deavour to sho

position of th

born blind wer

most beautifu

e him, he coul

vas handsome o

true: for till b

the evidence c

could not disco

his own species

than a fleetin

or impressio

The author, how

different reason

judge whether a

rmed in its kinc

that, supposing (as the author evidently does
suppose) the man by this time to be so far perfected in the perception of vision as to discover
them to be females of his own species, or even
animals of any species, the observation will be
found to be extended beyond the truth: for,
in all the higher ranks of animals, particularly
in the human race, the highest of all, there are
certain characters and dispositions of features
better adapted than others to express the sentiments of the mind; and the expression and
intelligence of those sentiments by the features,
particularly by the eyes, is not acquired, but
constitutional and inherent in our natures. In
this way animals communicate their sentiments
to each other; and in this way men communicate their sentiments to animals, and to
young children; who all understand, or rather
feel the language of the looks, as far as they
express anger or approbation, loathing or desire, menace or conciliation, long before they
can have formed any determinate ideas, by the
association of which they could become acquainted with the respective meanings of these
several modes of expression. I am, therefore,
persuaded, that, in the case here stated, the
preference would, without hesitation, be given
to her, whose features were best adapted to
express mild and pleasing sentiments; and, if
there were no difference between them in this

respect, to her whose colour made the most agreeable impression on the eye: for I readily assent to the great artist that a man, in this predicament, could form no judgment of sym-metry, grace, elegance, or any other beauty of form. Grace is, indeed, perceived by mental sympathy; but, nevertheless, the exercise of mental sympathy, in this instance, is as much through the association of ideas, as the ope-ration of the understanding, by which we discover symmetry; as will be hereafter ex-plained.

26. Both colours and forms, however, so far as they exhibit pleasing masses of light and shadow to the eye, are beautiful in animals, as well as in other productions of the creation; and, consequently, may render one animal more beautiful than another, considering its beauty as addressed to the sense of seeing only. We cannot, indeed, determine whether or not a particular animal be beautiful in its kind without having seen many of that kind; for this is a result of comparison: but we can readily decide which is most beautiful of two animals of different kinds; or which is beau-tiful, and which is ugly, though we have seen but one of each kind. I never saw but one zebra, and one rhinoceros; and yet I found no difficulty in pronouncing the one to be a very beautiful, and the other a very ugly

animal; nor have I ever met with any person that did.

We continually find, however, the most decided differences, and even direct oppositions of opinion, concerning the respective beauty of different animals of the same species, not only between different individuals, but between whole classes and generations of men. Ask a modern grazier what constitutes a beautiful bull or cow, and he will tell you, *a small neat head, a round neck, a large long and straight body, supported by very short and slender legs.* But how different is such an animal from that

> " —— cui turpe caput, cui plurima cervix ;
> Et crurum tenus à mento palearia pendent *."

Long palearia or dewlaps are also enumerated among the beauties of the bull that captivated Europa †; and perhaps, not only a painter, but any impartial and uninformed person might agree with the princess and her poet : but, to the real judge of horned cattle, there can scarcely be a greater deformity. The case is that the poet and the painter are looking for those forms and proportions, which are best

---

* Georgic. iii. 52.—The description is of a cow; but of a cow, whose form is best adapted to breed fine male calves.

† Ovid. Metamorph.

adapted to exhibit ease, elegance, and dignity
of gesture and action, and pleasing varieties of
light and shade; while the grazier is only calculating the quantity of eatable and nutritive
flesh, which the animal, in the least possible
time, and with the least possible quantity of
food, may bring into the shambles; and this
consideration forms the scale of his preference.
Habit, however, has taught him to think the
forms and proportions, upon which he can cal-
culate to most advantage, real and essential
beauties; and to hold in the utmost contempt
the taste and judgment of any person, who
should doubt their being so. The beauties of
ease, elegance, and dignity are equally addressed to the mind, and independent of organic sense; as will be more fully shown
hereafter: wherefore who shall presume to
decide that the one are more truly and properly
beauties, than the other? The beauties of
light, shade, and colour are all that affect the
eye, or make any impression upon organic
sense and perception; wherefore, as far as
mere visible beauty is meant, a water spaniel
of the kind which Weenix so often painted,
and of which Golzius has made so fine a print,
seems to me to be a still more beautiful animal
than a zebra; or, perhaps, than any existing:
for his long curling hair affords more play and
variety of light and shadow; and the brown

and white colours, with which that hair is
diversified, are distributed into irregular masses
instead of regular stripes; and irregularity is
certainly an ingredient of beauty, so far as it
affects the organs of sense only; whence
painters delight not only in irregular trees,
but irregular buildings, and buildings irregularly mixed with trees; which afford more
varieties of tint, and a more luxuriant play
of light and shadow, than any regular combination of parts can produce; though these
may be required by the understanding in other
instances.

27. We must not, however, attempt to
apply these principles of abstract beauty to the
charms of the other sex, or imagine that we
can prove or illustrate them by instances drawn
from that source: for though the person,
hypothetically stated above to be restored to
sight, would give the preference in beauty to
the female, whose colour made the most agreeable impression on his eye, provided there was
no difference in expression to influence his
choice, yet this preference would be of a very
cold kind, and utterly void of all the warmth
of sexual desire. It would also be guided by
principles totally different from those, which
direct the choice of men, who have been accustomed to employ the sense of vision, as the
criterion of their sexual predilections: for such

a person would not be able to distinguish the
blush of modesty or glow of sensibility, from
the redness caused by intemperance, or morbid inflammation : nor would the delicate fair-
ness, or cadaverous whiteness of a skin make
any other impressions respectively upon his
feelings, than the same different degrees or
modifications of the same tint, seen in other
substances. All the fascinating attractions of
these charms of the sex owe their influence to
sympathy and habit; as being symptoms of
mental and bodily perfections, the meaning of
which is only known by experience and observation ; so that it could neither be felt nor
understood by a person, who saw them for the
first time. The redness of any morbid inflammation may display a gradation of tint, which,
in a pink or a rose, we should think as beautiful as the *purple light of love and bloom of
young desire*; and the cadaverous paleness of
death or disease, a degree of whiteness, which,
in a piece of marble or alabaster, we should
deem to be as pure, as that of the most delicate skin of the fairest damsel of the frigid
zone : consequently, the mere visible beauty is
in both the same ; and the difference consists
entirely in mental sympathies, excited by certain internal stimuli, and guided by habit. The
African black, when he first beholds an European complexion, thinks both its red and

white morbid and unnatural, and of course disgusting. His sun-burnt beauties express their modesty and sensibility by variations in the sable tints of their countenances, which are equally attractive to him, as the most deli-cate blush of red is to us. Were it possible for a person to judge of the beauty of colour in his own species, upon the same principles and with the same impartiality, as he judges of it in other objects, both animal, vegetable, and mineral, there can be no doubt but that mixed tints would be preferred; and a pimpled face have the same superiority over a smooth one, as a zebra has over an ass, a variegated tulip over a plain one, or a column of jasper or por-phyry over one of common red or white mar-ble. It does, however, sometimes happen that men of quick sensibility and vivid imaginations fall seriously and violently in love, at first sight, and without any other knowledge of the object than what is, at the moment, acquired through the sense of vision: but nevertheless, it is not any merely organic pleasure, felt by this sense, that attaches them; but mental sympathies acting through the medium of the imagination; as shall hereafter be explained.

28. As light is the sole medium of vision, the effects of visible objects upon the eye must depend, not only upon the quantities reflected from them, and the modes of its reflection or

refraction, but, likewise, upon the degree of force with which it acts; and this, as well as the quantity, depends, in a great measure, upon the degrees of proximity between the object and the organ.   Hence in proportion as bodies are near, their outlines appear more sharp, their colours more vivid, and their lights and shadows more forcible and distinct; and, in proportion as they recede from us, all these gradually fade away, till at length they entirely vanish.   Hence there are visible variations in the eye according to the distance of the object, to which it is directed; which seem to be produced by the greater or smaller degrees of irritation caused by impressions more or less vivid *.

* It has been calculated that objects are visible at the distance of 3436 times their diametre, if viewed by eyes perfectly organized, and through the common medium of common daylight equally diffused from the organ to the object: but in proportion as the comparative degree of light is greater upon the object than upon the eye, this power of seeing it at a distance will be extended; and in proportion as it is less, it will be shortened.   We can see a burning coal by night at least 100 times as far as we can see the same coal extinct by daylight; and the dif--ference is proportionately great between looking out of an obscure room upon objects in sunshine, and looking from sunshine at objects in an obscure room.

The above calculation relates of course to the powers of the human eye; there being many kinds of birds of prey, such as eagles, kites, &c. which manifestly possess them in a much greater extent.

29. Similar variations are produced, as before observed, by different quantities of light
thrown directly upon the eyes; the membrane
of the iris contracting with its increase, and
dilating with its decrease, in proportion as the
irritation is more or less violent. When extended beyond a certain degree, it becomes
absolutely painful; and in that case, the eloquent author, already so often cited, by mistaking as usual a power for a sensation, con-
cludes it to be sublime *; though if he or any
other person had been compelled to expose
their eyes to *unsufferable light* for a few
moments, they would have felt how totally
void of all sublime ideas their minds would
have become, how much soever the power and
magnificence of such light, surrounding the
throne of Omnipotence, might have exalted or
expanded their imaginations, when described
in the verses of Milton.

30. Darkness is the entire cessation or ab-
sence of light; and, of course, utterly negative, and producing no sensation at all of
itself: but, nevertheless, when we go suddenly
out of a very strong light into it, the transition, like all other very violent and quick transitions, may be painful to very tender eyes; as
there will ensue a sudden change in the internal state of the fibres; which, notwithstanding

* Sublime and Beautiful, Part II. f. xiv. et seq.

that it be from tension to relaxation, and from irritation to repose, may nevertheless, in the first sensation of it, be unpleasant to some organs, though I could never feel it so.   But to imagine that darkness is painful to the sight, because we sometimes strain our eyelids to such a degree as to produce pain, in the efforts which we make to see in the dark*, is one of the most unaccountable fancies that ever arose in the mind of any man : for if darkness be in itself painful, a person with his eyes shut in a dark room must be in an agony; and yet so widely does the practice of mankind differ from the theories of philosophers, that this is the state, in which we all usually go to sleep; and is probably that, in which this great philosopher and statesman slept as well as the meanest of the swinish multitude.   It is to darkness, like-wise, that men fly for relief, when their eyes, through weakness or inflammation, cannot bear the irritation of light : but I never yet heard of any one, whose eyes were so heterogeneously organized, or so strangely morbid, that they could not bear the effect of darkness, whatever it may be : for as to the uneasiness, which the boy, couched by Cheselden, felt at the first sight of a black object, it arose either from the harshness of its outline, or from its appearing

* Part IV. f. xv. &c.

to act as a partial extinguisher applied to his
eyes; which, as every object, that he saw,
seemed to touch them, would, of course, be its
effect. It could not possibly have been, as
the author supposes, on account of his finding
darkness painful; as it was not till long after
the operation that he could bear to have his
eyes exposed to the light, or endure any thing
but darkness for any considerable time together. All very sharp, broken, or angular objects were disagreeable to him, as they are to
all eyes of very nice sensibility.

31. But it will be said, perhaps, that the
painful sensations, of which this author speaks,
are no common pains; but such as render the
sensations, to which they belong, sublime, and
therefore only capable of being felt by minds
capable of exaltation to sublimity. Such his
unquestionably was, in the highest degree; and
if ever man had a just claim to the privilege of
being visited by sublime visions, whether sleep-
ing or waking, he was undoubtedly the man:
but, if we admit this privation to be a source
of the sublime, I do not know how we shall be
able to exclude silence, which is a privation of
sound, as darkness is of light; and, for its being
sublime upon his own principles, we have the
high authority of Virgil—" simul ipsa silentia
terrent:" but, nevertheless, even his ingenuity
would have found some difficulty in proving

silence a sensation; though he certainly felt it painful on many occasions. There are other privations, however, which it is surprising that he has omitted; since they make themselves most sensibly, and in some instances, most painfully felt throughout all the animal creation; and when personified as powers, and described in poetry, are as truly sublime, as any of the other powers, which he mistook for sensations.

Close by the regal chair,
Fell Thirst and Famine scowl
A baleful smile upon their baffled guest.

Yet no one, I believe, ever found either hunger or thirst to be a sublime sensation; or found his mind elevated or expanded by suffering them. On the contrary, they have been generally esteemed to be most debasing and humiliating to the pride of human nature; as they not only level the highest with the lowest —the prince with the beggar, and the philosopher with the idiot, but man with the brute,

32. The example of this great author proves how difficult it is to keep the operations of the different faculties of the mind distinct from each other; so as to consider sensation singly and alone, unmixed with, and uninfluenced by the ideas previously imprinted in the memory, or the deductions made from them by the understanding; both of which have become, in

almost all adult persons, habitual perceptions, constantly confounded with those immediately resulting from the impressions on the same organs of sense; with which, perhaps, they are no otherwise connected than by continued association.

33. This is peculiarly the case with our perceptions of all objects of sight; *the visible appearance of which*, as an acute and accurate investigator has observed, *is scarcely ever regarded by us, or made a subject of reflection, but serves only as a sign to introduce to the mind something, which may be as distinctly conceived by those, who never saw**. But, nevertheless, the mere sensual pleasures of vision, which are at present exclusively the subject of inquiry, depend entirely on the primary impressions, unimproved and undisguised by the intermixture of other notions and ideas, acquired by means of the other senses: for as they consist in different modes and degrees of organic irritation, they are of a totally distinct class from those which result from the operations of mind.

34. I am aware, however, that they are scarcely ever felt separate and unmixed, except in such extraordinary cases as that of the boy couched by Cheselden, or in very young

---

* Reid on the Mind, c. vi. f. xi.

children; who, of course, do not retain, in their maturer age, any remembrance of the progress of these perceptions; by which the means of exercising both memory and understanding were acquired, and, consequently, the consciousness, of their possessing any such faculties. We may, nevertheless, observe the process, by which these artificial and improved perceptions are formed out of simple sensations, in the manner, in which they handle and turn about all objects which they can lay hold of; now putting them to their mouths, and now placing them at different distances from their eyes; by all which they are rectifying, correcting, and improving the testimony of one sense by that of another; and acquiring the habit of associating their ideas, as they receive them; from which habit the best and principal part of their subsequent knowledge is to be derived.

35. The habit, which we at the same time acquire, of spontaneously mixing associated ideas with organic perceptions in contemplating objects of vision, is the principal reason why the merely sensual pleasures of this organ are, in adult persons, very limited and feeble. Children are delighted with every gay assemblage of colours: but, as the intellect and imagination acquire strength by culture and exercise, they obtain so much influence

over the sense, as to make it reject almost every gratification, in which one of them does not participate. But, nevertheless, the sense acquires a similar negative power, in its turn, by the same habit of association; and if there be any thing, in the object of contemplation, to offend or disgust it, effectually mars the gratification of every other faculty. Thus, in the higher class of landscapes, whether in nature or in art, the mere sensual gratification of the eye is comparatively so small, as scarcely to be attended to: but yet, if there occur a single spot, either in the scene or the picture, offensively harsh and glaring—if the landcape gardener, in the one, or the picture cleaner in the other, have exerted their unhappy talents of polishing, all the magic instantly vanishes, and the imagination avenges the injury offered to the sense. The glaring and unharmonious spot, being the most prominent and obtrusive, irresistibly attracts the attention, so as to interrupt the repose of the whole, and leave the mind no place to rest upon. It is in some respects the same with the sense of hearing. The mere sensual gratification, arising from the melody of an actor's voice, is a very small part, indeed, of the pleasure, which we receive from the representation of a fine drama: but, nevertheless, if a single note of the voice be absolutely cracked and out of tune, so as to offend and disgust the ear, it will completely destroy the effect of the most skilful acting, and render all the sublimity and pathos of the finest tragedy ludicrous.

In objects of vision, however, this influence of organic sensation is much more prevalent in the imitation than the reality: for painting being no ways connected with utility, but intended merely to please, mental habits, prejudices, and associations have much less controul over it than over the objects which it represents. In building and gardening, and still more in dress and furniture, the charms of neatness, propriety, richness, splendor, &c. often reconcile us to those harsh and discordant oppositions of colour, which, if imitated by painting, in all their native crudity, and without being softened and melted together by tender gradations of shadow, become glaringly offensive to every eye, and quite intolerable to those accustomed to the art. In the reality, also, much will depend upon the kind and degree of light to which objects are exposed; whence we can bear, and even require, much more brilliance and opposition of colour in the insides than on the outsides of buildings; and more in articles, that are to be seen by candle-light, than in those which are to be exposed to day-light: for candle-light, moon-light, and twilight melt every thing into one mild hue;

H

through the harmonising medium of which, things the most offensively glittering, gaudy, and harsh, become beautifully rich, splendid, and mellow. Rembrandt seems to have drawn all his landscapes by twilight, and to have given himself no trouble in the selection of subjects. Extensive plains of barren down, bog, or fallow, intersected by rows of pollard trees, straight canals, mounds, and ditches, are so melted and blended together by this light, and so animated by the magic of his pencil, as to exhibit effects the most beautiful; though if seen or represented in the glare of a mid-day sun, they would be most disgustingly ugly. It is the influence of the same kind of light, or of candle-light, which renders gems, brocades, and tissues so beautifully mellow, rich, and splendid in his imitations; while in those of others, even of the greatest painters, they are either harsh or insipid, and not unfrequently both.

PART II.

OF THE ASSOCIATION OF IDEAS.

CHAPTER I.
OF KNOWLEDGE OR IMPROVED PERCEPTION.

1. THE faculty of improved or artificial perception, being acquired in the manner stated
in the concluding sections of the last Chapter
of the first Part, continues to improve through
the subsequent stages of our lives as long as
our minds retain their vigour; and becomes so
far independent of the organs of sense, from
which it is derived, and through which it continues to be exercised, that it often exists in its
highest state of perfection, when those organs
are enfeebled by age, and verging to decay. A
musician can tune an instrument, after his hearing has become defective, more accurately than
a person with the nicest ear, who has not been
used to discriminate sounds; and a vintner,
who has been in the constant habit of tasting
wine, and attending to its flavour, though his
organs be blunted by age and vitiated by intemperance, will distinguish the genuine juice
of the grape, or point out the modes and de-

H 2

grees of its adulteration, with more certainty and precision than an unexperienced person, who enjoys the utmost sensibility of palate; but who never having accustomed himself to discriminate the impressions upon his organs and observe them separately; nor having any analogous ideas pre-existing in his mind, by which to measure and examine them, considers every compound sensation collectively and alone; and consequently, if the irritation be not very harsh and discordant, finds it pleasant, whatever may have been the causes, which excited it.

2. All refinement of taste, therefore, in the liberal arts, arises, in the first instance, from this faculty of improved perception : for painting, sculpture, music, and poetry are all in their principles, as Aristotle has observed, imitative arts *; whence the only pleasures, which the ignorant and unexperienced receive from them, except those of sensation and mental sympathy before explained, are derived from mere imitation.

3. Man, as the same great philosopher observes, is by nature an imitative animal †; and, as those faculties of his mind, by which he has risen so much above the rest of the creation, are owing in a great degree, to one individual

* Poetic.   † Ibid.

imitating another, and still adding something
to what he had acquired, imitation is both naturally and habitually pleasing to him *. Hence
there is no effort of painting or sculpture so
rude, no composition in music or poetry so artless, as not to delight those, who have known
no better; and, perhaps, the pleasures, which
the ignorant feel from mere imitation, when it
has arrived at any degree of exactitude, are
more keen and vivid, though less exquisite and
exalted than those which the learned in art receive from its noblest productions : at least, I
have seen more delight expressed at a piece of
wax-work, or a painting of a mackarel upon a
deal board, or a pheasant on a table, than I ever
observed to be produced by the Apollo of the
Belvidere, or the Transfiguration of Raphael.
It is true that the vulgar express their feelings
more boisterously and impetuously than the
learned; but it is also true that the feelings of
nature have universally more of rapture in them
than those which are excited through the
medium of science.

4. These feelings of nature, however, are of
short duration: for when the novelty of the
first impression is over, and the interest of
curiosity and surprise has subsided, mere imitation of common objects begins to appear trifling

* Ibid. c. vi.

H 3

and insipid; and men look for, in imitative art,
something of character and expression, which
may awaken sympathy, excite new ideas, or expand and elevate those already formed.

5. To produce this requires a knowledge of
mind, as well as of body; and of the interior,
as well as exterior construction of the human
frame, or of whatever else be the object of imitation; whence art becomes engrafted upon
science; and as all the exertions of human skill
and ingenuity are indefinitely progressive, and
never stop at the point, which they originally
aimed at, this art of science or science of art
has been extended, particularly in painting and
music, to the production of excellencies, which
are neither of imitation nor expression; but
which peculiarly belong to technical skill, and
which can only be relished or perceived by those,
who have acquired a certain degree of knowledge in those arts.   Such are, in general, the
compositions of Bravura, as they are called, in
music; and such, in painting, are the works of
the great Venetian painters; whose style of
imitation is any thing but exact; whose expression is never either dignified or forcible; and
whose tone of colouring is too much below that
of nature to please the mere organs of sense;
but whose productions have, nevertheless, always held the highest rank in the art; and, as
far as the mere art and science of painting are

11

concerned, are unquestionably among its most

perfect productions.

6. The taste for them, however, is, as Sir Joshua Reynolds has observed, entirely acquir-ed*; and acquired by the association of ideas: for, as great skill and power, and a masterly facility of execution, in any liberal art, raise our admiration, and consequently excite pleas-ing and exalted ideas; we, by a natural and imperceptible process of the mind, associate these ideas with those excited by the produc-tions of these arts; and thus transfer the merit of the workman to the work. There is, how-ever, another reason why we value facility of execution in works of this kind, which shall be explained hereafter.

7. It is upon the same principle that we pre-fer an original to a copy: for a copy may be equally exact in imitation, equally correct and dignified in expression, and display a tone of colouring and distribution of light and shade equally pleasing to the sense; whence none but the most acute and experienced judges of the art can distinguish the one from the other: but the copy will never have that masterly intelli-gence in the execution—that union between the conceptions of the mind and the operations of the hand, which constitute the superior merit

CHAP.
I.

Of improved
Perception.

* Discourses.

H 4

of the original in the estimation of the real judge of art: for to all others it is imperceptible; and, indeed, unlooked for.

8. This intelligence is often more prominent and striking in a drawing or slight sketch, than in a finished production : whence. persons, who have acquired this refined or artificial. taste, generally value them more; since finishing often blunts or conceals this excellence : but then the drawings or sketches so valued must be the works of great painters, who knew how to finish; for, from their perfect knowledge, is derived the intelligence, which they are enabled to display in their imperfect exertions of it. The drawings of a mere draftsman are never highly esteemed, however excellently designed or brilliantly executed; a loose incorrect sketch of Rembrandt or Salvator Rosa being always preferred by persons conversant in the art, to the most elaborate productions of the light and brilliant pens of Pietro Testa and La Fage.

9. Collectors of pictures and drawings are often ridiculed for paying great prices for slight or juvenile productions of great artists; and it must be owned that vanity, and a silly desire of possessing what is rare, are often the motives for such purchases. But, nevertheless, they are, in many instances, of a more liberal and more reasonable kind: for, by the association of ideas, we often trace a connection between

the earliest and the latest—between the most
imperfect and the most perfect productions of a
great master, which makes, not only his slight
sketches, but his boyish studies interesting. The
question, therefore, which is often insultingly
put to such collectors, " would you give such a
sum for this, if the artist had done nothing better?" does not rest upon a full or fair statement of the case: for the collector might very
candidly answer, no—without incurring any
just imputation of false taste, or servile defe-
rence to the authority of great names.

10. When I say that the colouring of the
great Venetian masters is too much below the
tone of nature to please the mere organs of
sense, I mean, of course, the unimproved organs
of sense: for I am well aware that even the
mere pleasures of sense are so far under the influence of mind, and liable to be modified by
habit, that they may, in some instances, be made
to descend by an inverted scale, from a higher
to a lower stimulus, instead of ascending, in
their natural progression, from a lower to a
higher. But of this, however, I recollect no
instance but in those of hearing and sight,
which are so intimately connected with mental
sympathies that they naturally fall under the
influence of the mind. No person, I believe,
unacquainted with music, ever preferred the
tone of a violoncello to that of a flute :—yet,

when it is perceived to be so much more copious, and so much better adapted to all the
scientific as well as expressive compositions in
music, which require a more extensive scale of
harmony, and a more refined display of ebro-
matic variation, the understanding so far in-
fluences the ear, that I have frequently met
with persons, who had learned to think even the
tones of it pleasanter. Upon the same principle, I believe that no person unacquainted
with the art of painting ever preferred the colouring of Titian to that of Denner or Vander
Werf: but, nevertheless, when it is discovered
how much better adapted it is to fulfil all the
great purposes of the art, the eye by degrees
assents to the testimony of the mind, and learns
to feel it more pleasant.

11. Though the pleasures, which painting
affords to the mass of mankind, be derived entirely from the artifice and trick of imitation;
yet to refined judges, who have accustomed
their minds to seek for merits of a higher kind,
all this artifice and trick, and even extreme
attention to exactitude, if it be ostentatiously
displayed, are offensive: for experience, by
detecting the artifice, teaches us to despise it;
and how much soever we may be delighted with
the results of care and labour, we do not like
that the means, by which they are produced,
should be displayed with them; as they not

only divide the attention, and obstruct all sympathy with the expression, but proclaim *that* to have been done with toil and difficulty, a principal part of whose merit should consist in a masterly display of ease and intelligence; such as might be supposed to proceed from supernatural inspiration.

12. If, however, the defects of exactitude in imitation appear to proceed from want of knowledge or power, instead of want of care and attention, they are more glaringly offensive to the learned than to the ignorant; especially if they extend to those parts or properties of the object, which belong to its general nature, or to the particular character, which the artist means to give it; and are not variable with the transient fluctuations of fashion.   The Grecian painter, who altered the shoe of his figure at the suggestion of a cobbler, showed, perhaps, a superfluous degree of attention to exactitude : but the criticism of the Turkish emperor upon the work of the Venetian artist was as reasonable as it was just; for the shrinking of the skin from the wounded part of the neck, in a decollated head, is the peculiar circumstance, which shows the head to have been cut from a living body; and the omission of it, in a picture of the decollation of St. John the Baptist, entirely breaks that association of ideas, by which the story is connected with the representation

of it, and the subject of the picture made known.

13. Exactitude of imitation is much more requisite in sculpture than in painting : but, nevertheless, even in this art, if it display itself in ostentatious trick or artifice, such as colouring statues to imitate life, it becomes offensive and disgusting to all experienced and intelligent persons : for such persons never look for deception; which they know to be mere trick, the pleasure of which ends with the surprise that it has once occasioned. To attempt to produce it, therefore, by mixing two separate arts, is to weaken the proper effects of both; as the trains of ideas, which severally belong to each, have arisen separately in the mind, and do not therefore readily or properly unite. The great sculptors of Greece, however, often composed one figure of different splendid materials; such as ivory and gold, marble and brass, &c.; but this was not for the purpose of any deception, or greater exactitude of imitation; but to produce an imposing effect of splendor and magnificence in the ideal or allegorical images of supernatural beings. They also frequently made the eyes of silver, gems, or some other shining material; but never, I believe, exactly to resemble the life; and, certainly, not for the purpose of deception; but merely to keep up that energy and vivacity of

expression, which characterized the other features, in which it could be exhibited in forms;
whereas, in the eyes, it could only arise from
brightness or colours.   The effect is, accordingly, the most animated and striking, that can
be conceived, in the instances which we have
remaining of bronze statues with silver eyes;
of which there are many, and some of exquisite work, but all of a small size.   From these,
nevertheless, we may form some ideas of the
imposing and commanding effects, which those
of heroic or colossal dimensions must have had,
when exhibited as objects of devotion in the
temples.   Those of Phidias and Lysippus must
have been sufficient to reconcile even a Jew or
a Mahometan to idolatry.

14. Sculpture, being properly a simple imitation of form, does not seem intended to afford
any merely sensual pleasure to the eye: for
such pleasure can only arise from colour, or
variation of light and shadow; whereas sculpture, considered abstractedly, has no colour,
and the lights and shadows, in which it most
delights, are regular, feeble, or harsh; so as to
be always either too much, or too little broken
to suit painting; and, therefore, certainly not
in themselves pleasing to the eye.   Rembrandt
laughed at those artists, who talked of improving themselves in painting by studying the antique sculptures; and showed, as his cabinet

of antiques, a room furnished with cloaks, hats, turbans, &c. of various stuffs and tissues. As a mere painter, whose object was to please the eye, Rembrandt was quite right; and, indeed, no man ever understood that branch of the imitative art better, or practised it with more delicacy and success; his works arriving nearer to abstract perfection, in what they pretend to, than those of any other modern artist in any branch of art.

15. As sculpture is to painting, so, in some respects at least, is the melody of poetry compared with that of music. Sculpture and poetry require order and regularity: painting and music delight in wild and irregular variety: sculpture and poetry, too, are addressed entirely to the imagination and the passions; while painting and music are, in a degree, addressed to the organs of sight and hearing, and calculated to produce pleasures merely sensual.

16. Articulate language is entirely artificial and acquired; as appears from the case of deaf persons, who never learn to speak; and as has been further proved by the learned author, who has written expressly upon the subject *. But, nevertheless, inarticulate notes are natural to men, as well as to other animals; wherefore music is, in its principle, natural, while poetry

* Lord Monboddo.

is wholly artificial: for though the tones of the voice be from nature, the division of them into syllables and words is from acquired habit *.

17. In the habitual modes of distribution and combination of words into sentences, in order to express the sentiments and operations of the mind, the idiom of language consists; which thus depending upon accidental habit, is different in every different tongue. Rhythm is the disposition and arrangement of the long and short syllables in the order most easy and plea-sant to the speaker, and most grateful and har-monious to the hearer; while prosody is a similar disposition and arrangement of the high and low syllables; that is, of those which the habitual idiom of the language has decreed to be respectively pronounced in a high or low tone of voice; which words *high* and *low* may mean either acute and base, as in the Greek prosody; or loud and its contrary, as in the modern.

18. In a just and skilful application of the variations of rhythm and prosody, such as arises from just feeling only, does the melody of lan-guage consist: but, nevertheless, this melody affords no gratification to the mere organs of hearing; but is solely perceived and felt by mental sympathy, as appears from our feeling

* See Origin and Progress of Language, by Lord Mon-boddo.

it; when we read inwardly, and without any
utterance of sound; and also from its varying
with the habitual variations of idiom in different languages: for, if it were a pleasure of organic sensation, it must necessarily, as before
observed, be the same in all languages.

19. Articulation is merely division of tone;
which division may be either entire interruption,
or only partial suppression, accordingly as the
respective organs, by which it is produced, are
entirely compressed, or only approximated to
each other. The entire compression of the
organs is signified in writing by the mute consonants, and the partial approximation by the
liquids and aspirates; neither of which admit
of any variation in mode or degree beyond
that respectively produced by the compression
or approximation of the respective organs
of speech; or the different degrees of force or
emphasis, with which they are compressed or
approximated, which different degrees constitute the differences between the consonants B
and P, D and T, and G and K; which are
commutable in all flexible tongues.

20. Verse, therefore, considered as a metrical and accentual arrangement of syllables,
independent of any chant or melody of tone,
with which it is uttered, has nearly the same
relation to prose, as dancing has to walking, or
other irregular exercise of the limbs. Both,

considered thus abstractedly, are merely regulated divisions of motion; one of the organs of
the mouth, and the other of the members of
the body; and, as both are regulated by musical divisions of time, and graduated according
to the emphasis, by which those divisions are
marked, both are intimately connected with,
and naturally accompanied by music; though
both be in principle essentially different from
it.

21. Articulation, being the means by which
sound is made the vehicle of thought as well as
of sentiment, the modulation of the tone, by
which its intervals are filled up, is, in a great
degree, regulated by the meaning, which it con-
veys; wherefore the melody of verse can neither be expressed nor felt by those, who do not
understand the language: for, upon that modulation, the prosody depends entirely, and the
rhythm in a great measure.

22. Poetry, so far as it consists in language,
is the division of rhythm and prosody into certain limited and regular portions, so modified
as to express, in the most appropriate sounds,
and with the utmost facility and energy, that
the respective idioms of the particular languages
allow, the various affections, sentiments, and
passions of the mind; and those images in
nature or art which are the proper subjects and
motives of its various passions, sentiments, and

affections.   There are, as before observed,
certain modifications of tone adapted by nature
to excite certain sympathies in the mind: consequently . the greater proportion of tone, a
language has, and the less of articulation, the
greater variety of such modifications will it
admit of, and the better adapted will it be to
the purposes of poetry.   Hence arises the
superiority of the Italian over all·modern languages, both for poetry and music, and the
superiority of the Greek, particularly the primitive Homeric Greek, over all others both
ancient and modern.

23. Attempts have been made, both in ancient and modern times, to give to the articulate harmony of poetry the diversity and irregularity of, musical composition ; and similar
attempts were made in the seventeenth century
to give to sculpture the airy and fantastic variety.
of painting; but neither the one nor the other
succeeded.   Of the ancient dithyrambics, indeed, we have no entire specimens: but their
being all lost proves that they were not very
popular productions ; and as for the promis-
cuous mixtures of verses of different metres,
only one instance of it is recorded *, which
sufficiently shows the sort of reception which it
met with.   In modern lyrics, indeed, verses of

* That of Chæremon, in a poem called The Centaur.—
·Aristot. Poet. c. iii.

unequal lengths have been irregularly mixed;
and, in the productions of Dryden and Gray
certainly with happy effect: but then there are
always correspondent rhymes, which preserve a
certain degree of that regularity, which has, in
all nations, been the general characteristic of
poetry. This alone is sufficient to prove that
the pleasures which it affords, are not of the
ear, but of the intellect: for the combinations
of tone, which delight the ear; as well as the
combinations of tints, which delight the eye,
are irregular. The sweetness and modulation
of the voice, indeed, with which poetry is recited, may be pleasing to the mere organs of
sense: but this is a pleasure independent of
the versification; and one, which, I believe, is
never felt in any great degree: for I never
heard of any person who found delight in
listening to the recitation of verse in a language,
which he did not understand; though, as far
as the mere sensual pleasure is concerned, his
understanding it or not can make no difference.
An ingenious, but fanciful writer has, I know,
imagined that he should have enjoyed the versification of Virgil more, if he had not understood the meaning of the words *: but, probably, had he tried the experiment with any
Persian or Arabian poet celebrated for the

* Lord Orford.

I 2

melody of his versification, he would have listened in vain for this melody, or for any thing else that could have afforded enjoyment; and would only have perceived a greater or less degree of roughness or smoothness in the flow of the lines, accordingly as the proportionate quantities of articulation or tone respectively predominated in the utterance: but this mere perception, unaccompanied by any musical chant or singing, would not have been of a kind to afford him any pleasure.

24. It is remarkable that the best versifier in our language should have had no taste or liking for music of any kind; and that he, who possessed the most skill, and had the truest relish for that art, should have left more uncouth and unharmonious verses, than any other poet of eminence. I know, indeed, that there are critics, who have pretended to discover refinements of melody in the most rugged anomalies of Milton, and, of course, a total want of it in the polished elegance and regularity of Pope * : but, to such critics, I have nothing to say. If they be serious and sincere, they are as extraordinary anomalies as any of those which they admire, and afford ample illustration of the proverb, that there is no disputing concerning tastes.

* See Webb on Poetry.

25. English verse arises from a limited and regulated distribution of accents and pauses, as well as of quantities; and, as Pope has observed *, in the heroic verse of ten syllables, a pause naturally falls upon the fourth, fifth, or sixth syllable; besides that at the end of every verse; which equally takes place in every kind of metre in every language; since, without it, the verse is only a distinct portion of measure to the eye, but not at all to the ear.   Milton has, however, frequently no pause at the end of the verse, but occasionally upon every other syllable, from the first to the ninth; and this licence has been applauded, as adding endless variety to the harmony of his versification †. That it must add variety either to the harmony or dissonance of language, I admit: but the very essence of verse consists in the variety of its harmony not being endless, but being limited to the changes, that certain divisions of articulate sound, determinate in their quantities, regulated in their modes of utterance, and corresponding to, or succeeding each other, are capable of.   Language may have more variety of cadence without these limitations or regulations; but then it will not be versified language, although it be duly and correctly measured out into lines of ten syllables each:

* Fourth Letter to Walsh.   † Webb on Poetry.

I 3

neither will it have that elastic energy and rapidity of movement, which give a character of
enthusiasm; and, in fact, make it poetry* : for
it is this character of enthusiasm, 'that marks
the poetical language of all nations'; and to this
a metrical division, strongly marked by limited
pauses or accents,' or similar terminations of
the verses, as in the Greek and Latin hexa-
meter, or English couplet, is certainly most
appropriate.

26. The principle of harmony, as Dionysius
of Halicarnassus has observed, is the same in
prose as in verse; it consisting in certain ar-
rangements of quantities, accents, and pauses
in both; which, in the one, are without limitation or restraint; but, in the other, are restricted
by rules, and measured out into given portions;
which succeed each other, either immediately,
as in our heroic metre; alternately, as in our
elegiac and lighter lyric; or after certain
periods, as in our pindaric or graver lyric. It
is possible that a person may prefer free and
unrestrained language, in all cases, to that
which is restricted to rule and measure; as it

---

* The critic above cited says, in praise of a line, *that
the breast actually labours to get through it.* Dial. i. p. 46.
To employ labour in writing may be a merit, if it be employed with taste; but to require labour in reading is a
species of ponderous excellence, that never yet found
favour in the ears of any but a systematic critic.

3

is possible that he may prefer ale to champagne;
but let him not, therefore, hold up licence as the perfection of rule, or malt liquor, as the only pure wine. Hall, Donne, Hobbes, and Crashaw are as licentious in their pauses as Milton; and distribute them, with the same irregularity, through the verse, from the first to the ninth syllable; and, if this licence be so exquisite a beauty, and add so much to harmony, their versification ought to be preferred to that of Dryden, Pope, or Goldsmith: but, unfortunately, they have not deserved or acquired so great a name, in other respects, as Milton; and the authority of a name is a medium, through which critics of this class discover innumerable excellencies, which otherwise would have remained as imperceptible to them as to the rest of mankind. The great and transcendent merits of Milton's poetry may excuse even greater blemishes and defects than are to be found in it: but to hear these defects and blemishes, the stains of negligence and rust of antiquity, extolled and recommended as refinements of taste and artifice, cannot but excite the indignation of every writer, whose indignation is not stifled by contempt.

27. Poetry is the language of inspiration, and consequently of enthusiasm; and it appears to me that a methodical arrangement of

I 4

the sound into certain equal or corresponding
portions, called verses, the terminations of
which are distinctly marked to the ear; and the
subdivisions or pauses of which are limited
within certain bounds, is absolutely necessary
to sustain that steady rapidity of utterance and
exaltation above the ordinary tone of common
speech; which can alone give a continued character of enthusiastic expression to any extensive composition. It is only by a constant
preconception of what is to follow, that the
poetical flow of utterance and elevation of tone
are sustained: for unless the reader be generally apprized of what is to come, by what has
gone before, he is like a person walking blind-
folded over an uneven road; and knows as
little how to modulate his voice, as such a
person does how to regulate his steps: both
march timidly, and consequently without vehemence or enthusiastic animation, in the just
expression of which poetry consists; and to
free it from metre and rhyme; restraints, with
which, it has been said, *that only the ignorance
or necessities of a rude age have shackled it* *,
would be in fact to deprive it of its essence.

28. It is observed by Dr. Johnson, *that the
Paradise Lost is one of the books, which the
reader admires and lays down, and forgets to*

* See Alison's Essays on Taste, p. 318.

take up again. None ever wished it longer than it is. Its perusal is a duty rather than a pleasure. We read Milton for instruction, retire harassed and over-burdened, and look elsewhere for recreation !* If we dip into the Iliad, we are immediately borne along by the enthusiastic vehemence of the poet's diction, as it were by a torrent; and even in the Odyssey, the Æneid, or Jerusalem, we glide down the stream without labour or effort; but, in the Paradise Lost, we are perpetually tugging at the oar; and though we discover, at every turn, what fills us with astonishment and delight, the discovery is, nevertheless, a work of toil and exertion: consequently we can only enjoy it, when the powers of attention are fresh and vigorous; no man ever flying to the Paradise Lost, as he does to the works of other great epic poets, as a refuge from lassitude or dejection. Yet surely the first and most essential merit of poetry is to be pleasing—to exhilarate and exalt the spirits by brilliant imagery and enthusiastic sentiment, rather than to overawe and depress by gloomy grandeur and sour morality.

" On peut être à la fois et pompeux et plaisant,
    Et je hais un sublime ennuyeux et pesant."

29. This great defect, the want of the power to please and amuse, I cannot but think as

* Life of Milton.

CHAP.
I.
Of improved
Perception.

much owing to the nature of his versification,
as to that of his subject: for we feel no such
lassitude or depression from the same subjects,
when treated by Tasso or Vida; though, except
in the lightness and elasticity of their versification, we cannot but allow that Milton has treated
them more poetically, as well as more properly.
In the scenes, too, of Paradise, and the loves
of Adam and Eve, Milton's imagery is gay and
beautiful, and his sentiments warm and rapturous; but, nevertheless, that very irregularity of the pauses, which certain critics have
so much commended, gives the character of
prose to his verse, and deprives it of all that
fire and enthusiasm of expression, which Pope
has happily preserved in his translation of the
corresponding passages of the Iliad.

> But come, so well refreshed, now let us play,
> As meet is, after such delicious fare;
> For never did thy beauty, since the day
> I saw thee first, and wedded thee, adorn'd
> With all perfections, so inflame my sense
> With ardour to enjoy thee; fairer now
> Than ever, bounty of this virtuous tree.
>
> PARADISE LOST, ix. 1026.

> These softer moments, let delight employ,
> And kind embraces snatch the hasty joy.
> Not thus I loved thee, when, from Sparta's shore,
> My forced, my willing, heavenly prize, I bore;

When first entranced in Cranäe's isle I lay,
Mix'd with thy soul, and all dissolved away!

POPE'S ILIAD, iii. 549.

Adam's argument, in this case, is certainly more pointed and logical, than that of the young Trojan; but pointed and logical argument is not what the case required.   The rapturous glow of enthusiastic passion, with which the latter addresses his mistress, would have much more influence upon the affections of an amorous lady, though it may be' less satisfactory to the understanding of a learned critic. The language of Homer and of Pope is such as Paris might have really used, and used with effect; but had he made love to Helen in the language of Milton, Menelaus might have trusted him with perfect security.

In such passages, as the following, the admirers of the irregular variety of Miltonic pauses, will find some difficulty in discovering any thing like verse; since even scanning the syllables upon their fingers will scarcely enable them to measure the lines.

" To whom the angel.   Therefore what he gives, whose praise be ever sung, to man, in part spiritual, may, of purest spirits, be found no ungrateful food : and, food alike, those pure intelligential substances require, as doth your rational; and both contain, within them, every lower faculty of sense, whereby they hear, see, smell, touch, taste; tasting concoct, digest assimilate, and corporeal to incorporeal turn."

Here are ten lines taken from one of the most admired books of the poem: but it ap_pears to me (perhaps for want of taste and discernment) that any ten lines transcribed from his history of the Heptarchy, might with equal propriety be ranked with poetry *. That they may be excused, however, in a long work, on account of the beauties, by which they are counterbalanced, I readily admit;

" sed emendata videri,
Pulchráque, et exactis minimùm distantia, miror."

30. The blank verse of Thomson and Cowper is much more strictly verse than that of Milton: but the complete failure of the latter in his translation of the Iliad is at least a presumptive proof that this species of verse is not suited to such compositions; for when Cowper has failed,

---

* The ancients seem to have had much more nice and accurate powers of discrimination in verse than we have. " In versu quidem theatra tota exclamant, si fit una syllaba aut brevior aut longior. Nec vero multitudo pedes novit, nec ullos numeros tenet; nec illud, quod offendit, aut cur, aut in quo offendat, intelligit: et tamen omnium longitudinum, et brevitatum in sonis, sicut acutarum graviumque vocum judicium ipsa natura in auribus nostris collocavit."—Cic. de Orator.

The most learned and refined of a modern audience show no such quickness of perception or nicety of judgment.

who shall hope to succeed? The case is, that where it is not stiffened and elevated by some peculiar dignity and elevation of subject, as in the more splendid parts of the Paradise Lost, it requires so many inversions and transpositions to keep it out of prose, as render it quite unsuitable to the enthusiastic spirit, and glowing simplicity of heroic narrative, which is perfect only " cum ita structa verba sunt, ut numerus non quæsitus sed secutus esse videatur —quod indicat non ingratam negligentiam, de re hominis magis quam de verbis laborantis.". Cic. Orator.

31. Not, however, that I would wholly exclude from poetry, or even from animated prose, what are, according to our idiom, inversions and transpositions: for, in many instances, such a collocation of the words is the natural and original order of speech; and when we address the imagination or the passions, the natural and original order will be found the most impressive, though it may differ from that established by ordinary use. To explain this, I shall take the liberty of quoting the words of one of the latest and ablest writers upon philosophical criticism; whose words, in this instance, cannot be altered without being injured.

32. " Let us figure to ourselves," says Dr. Blair *, " a savage, who beholds some object,

* Lect. vii.

" such as fruit, which raises his desire, and
" who requests another to give it to him. Sup-
" posing our savage to be unacquainted with
" words, he would, in that case, labour to make
" himself be understood, by pointing earnestly
" at the object, which he desired, and uttering,
" at the same time,. a passionate cry. Sup-
" posing him to have acquired words, the first
" word, which he uttered, would, of course,
" be the name of that object.   He would not
" express himself according to our English
" order of construction, ' Give me fruit,' but
" according to the Latin order, ' Fruit give
" me,' Pomum da mihi : for this plain reason,
" that his attention was wholly directed towards
" fruit, the desired object.   This was the ex-
" citing idea; the object which moved him to
" speak; and, of course, would be the first
" named.   Such an arrangement is precisely
" putting into words the gesture, which nature
" taught the savage to make, before he was
" acquainted with words; and, therefore, it
" may be depended upon as certain, that he
" would fall most readily into this arrange-
" ment.

     " Accustomed now to a different method of
" ordering our words, we call this inversion,
" and consider it as a forced and unnatural
" order of speech.   But, though not the most
" logical, it is however, in one view, the most

" natural order; because it is the order sug-
" gested by imagination and desire, which al-
" ways impel us to mention their object in the
" first place. We might, therefore, conclude,
" *à priori*, that this would be the order, in
" which words were most commonly arranged
" at the beginnings of language; and accord-
" ingly we find, in fact, that, in this order,
" words are arranged in most of the ancient
" tongues; as in the Greek, and the Latin;
" and, it is said, also in the Russian, the Scla-
" vonic, the Gaelic, and several of the Ame-
" rican tongues *."

* * * * * * * * * * * *
* * * * * * * * * * * *

" All the other modern languages of Europe
" have adopted a different arrangement from
" the ancient. In their prose compositions,
" very little variety is admitted in the colloca-
" tion of words: they are mostly fixed to one
" order; and that order is what may be called
" the order of the understanding. They place,
" first, in the sentence, the person or thing,
" which speaks or acts; next its action; and
" lastly, the object of its action. So that the
" ideas are made to succeed to one another,
" not according to the degree of importance,

* P. 135, 8vo. ed.

" which the several objects carry in 'the ima-
" gination, but according to the order of na-
" ture, and of time *."

* * * * * * * * *. * * *
* * * * * * * * * * * *
* * * * * * * * * * * *

" It appears that, in all the successive
" changes, which language has undergone, as
" the world advanced, the understanding has
" gained ground on the fancy and imagination.
" The progress of language, in this respect, re-
" sembles the progress of age in man. The
" imagination is most vigorous and predo-
" minant in youth; with advancing years the
" imagination cools, and the understanding
" ripens. Thus language, proceeding from
" sterility to copiousness, hath, at the same
" time, proceeded f$_{ro}$m vivacity to accuracy;
" from fire and enthusiasm to coolness and
" precision † !"

33. The collocation of words, according to
the order of desire or imagination, it is easy to
perceive, must have been much better adapted
to the purposes of poetry, than the collocation
of them according to the order of the understanding; but a variety of flexible terminations
is absolutely necessary to make-words, so ar-

* P. 138.   † P. 143.

ranged, intelligible; and, in these, all the polished languages of modern Europe are defective: wherefore it is impossible that they should ever rival those of the Greeks and Romans in poetical diction and expression. No language is more inflexible than the English; and none, except perhaps the French, requires its words to be arranged more strictly according to the order of the understanding: but, nevertheless, when glowing sentiment or passion is to be expressed; or when the mind of the speaker is so agitated as to be more under the influence of feeling, than of thought, it often reverts to the primitive order; and' allows, without any violation of idiom, the words to be arranged by natural impulse instead of artificial reflection or acquired habit.

> That, which should accompany old age,
> As honour, love, obedience, troops of friends,
> I must not look to have ———

says Macbeth, when agitated by remorse and despair; and the passage would lose all its energy and beauty, were the words arranged according to the regular process of thought, with the agent first, the action next, and the object last—" I must not look to have honour, love, obedience, troops of friends, &c. which ought to accompany old age *." Shakspeare,

---

* " Videsne, ut ordine verborum paulum commutato,
iisdem

K

who' wrote from feeling, has many happy instances of the same kind; as " *me* of my
lawful pleasure, she bereft, &c. ;" but Milton,
and other epic and moral writers in blank
verse, who viewed nature through the medium
of books, and wrote from the head rather than
the heart, have often employed this inverted
order merely to stiffen their diction, and keep
it out of prose; an artifice, of all others, the
most adverse to the 'genuine purposes of a
metrical or poetical style; which, though
known to be the result of study and labour,
should always appear to flow from inspiration.
In matters of taste, it is of little importance
what the understanding knows by inference or
analogy; but it is different with what the imagination perceives by immediate impression.

34. The pleasure, which we receive from
verse, in light or didactic compositions; or
such as are not capable of exciting or sustain-
ing enthusiasm, arises from the charms of
neatness, point, and emphasis; all of which
are improved and invigorated by the regularity
of a metrical style, which facilitates the flow
of utterance, and directs and fixes the attention to the particular idea, which the author
wishes to impress most strongly. By these
means, as well as by the periodical recurrence

iisdem verbis stante sententia, ad nihilum omnia recident,
cum sint ex aptis dissoluta."—Cic. Orator.

of similar quantities or modifications of sound, it also greatly facilitates remembrance; and to facilitate remembrance seems to have been the original use and purpose of verse: whence the muses were fabled to be the daughters of memory; and the oldest metrical writer extant addresses his most earnest and emphatical prayer to them, not to obtain their inspiration in developing the counsels of the gods, or in relating the actions of Diomede or Achilles, but to procure their assistance in compiling the catalogue of the Grecian army.

35. In the accentual pronunciation of the different languages of modern Europe, each pronounces the Greek and Latin words accordingly as words of the same number of syllables are usually pronounced in their own respective languages.   Thus an Englishman pronounces the first syllable of the verb *cano*, and of the adjective *canus*, equally long; and a Frenchman, equally short; though it be invariably long in the latter, and invariably short in the former.   In conformity to the idiom of our own language, we also arbitrarily alter the quantity of the first syllable of a word, when another is added to the end of it; as in virum and virus; which are always pronounced as trochees; while *virumque* and *virusque* are as invariably turned into amphibrachys. The first

K 2

syllable of the one is, however, uniformly short, and of the other, uniformly long.

36. But notwithstanding these violations of quantity, which all the nations of Europe commit, in different modes and degrees; each finds melody in the verses of the Greek and Latin poets, when pronounced after its own fashion; and the ears of each are equally offended at hearing them pronounced after any other fashion. This alone, were there no other instance, abundantly proves the great influence of habit and imagination, and the little influence of sensation, in matters of this kind. All agree in fixing a pause at the end of the line or stanza; and in giving it a regularly marked termination of some kind or other; and this instantly constitutes verse, which each nation puts into tune according to the particular habitual pronunciation of its own language; and with this tune or mode of reading, be it ever so anomalous, all, who speak that language, are satisfied, and even delighted. Every deviation from it, though strictly according to the laws of metre, offends them; because, when their own pronunciation has been familiarized, and, as it were, naturalized, to their ears, every other sounds foreign, and consequently ridiculous, upon a principle, that will be explained, when we come to treat of ridicule.

37. As each of these various modes of reading preserves the character of verse, though
all in different ways, and all differing from the
metrical laws of the original language, that
character may nevertheless be capable of an-
swering its purposes, both in maintaining the
character of enthusiasm by giving an uniform
exaltation to the style above that of common
speech, and in enhancing the charms of point,
neatness, and emphasis, in compositions of
another kind. Where the sense of the lines is
vigorous and impassioned; and strongly expressive of enthusiasm and inspiration, we
naturally endeavour to recite them with a correspondent tone of utterance; and how anomalous soever the particular divisions of it may
be, the general flow will be sufficiently maintained, by the effort itself, to preserve the
character and spirit of poetry. To pretend
that the ear is more delighted with the versification of Virgil than with that of Manilius,
when every principle of metre is violated in
the pronunciation, may seem like affectation:
but, nevertheless, the glowing animated sense
and polished periods of the one will inspire the
reader with a flow and facility in his tone of
utterance, which the other can never obtain;
and thus dupe the ear through the medium of
the imagination. Hence I have known persons really and sincerely delighted with the

versification of the Latin poets, and capable
of discriminating accurately their respective
merits; who have all violated the metre in
different, and even opposite ways; one by corrupting it to the English, another to the
French, another to the German, and another
to the Italian standard of pronunciation. It
is common, too, in each of these nations, and
in none more common than our own, to meet
with learned persons, who, while they pronounce without any regard to quantity, are
extremely acute in discovering any error or
defect in the structure or formation of a verse:
but, though they attribute this faculty to nicety
of ear, it is in fact merely accuracy of memory,
and readiness of discernment, in which the
perfection of the organ has no concern; it
being employed merely as the instrument of
perception. They *know* the respective quantities of every word in the language, and of
every foot in the verse; and therefore immediately perceive a syllable out of its place;
but this perception is the result of acquired
knowledge, and not of organic refinement. I
remember a copy of Latin verses being shown
to some learned men, in which the word
gladius was employed as a dactyle; and they
all instantly exclaimed against the writer for
having *no ear*; at the same time that each of
them pronounced the first syllable of the word,

longer than almost any in the language. Had

they accused the writer of want of knowledge

or memory, and themselves of want of ear,

their censures would have been just.

CHAPTER II.

OF IMAGINATION.

1. THE habit of associating our ideas having commenced with our earliest perceptions, the process of it, whatever it was in its beginning, has become so spontaneous and rapid in adult persons, that it seems to be a mechanical operation of the mind, which we cannot directly influence or control: those ideas, which we have once associated, associating themselves again in our memories of their own accord; and presenting themselves together to our notice, whether we will or not. Hence agreeable and disagreeable trains of thought and imagery are often excited by circumstances no otherwise connected with them than by having before occurred to our minds at the same time, or in the same place, or in the same company; and these trains of thought will continue to haunt us in spite of all that we can do to free ourselves from them; so that we feel ourselves in a situation not unlike that of a moth fluttering round a candle. At other times the contrary takes place; and pleasant and brilliant trains will succeed each other in the most rapid and delightful transitions; though, perhaps, excited at first by circum-

stances and situations by no means pleasing
in themselves; and continued without any intentional effort, or other cause that we can
assign.

2. In proportion as persons are respectively
liable, by the natural constitutions of their
minds and bodies, to associate their ideas in
these several trains, their dispositions are melancholy or gay; and if either be carried to
such excess as to break the natural connection,
or derange the natural order of them, the
effect is lunacy; whence that malady is often
partial, affecting some particular trains of
ideas, which have been connected with violent or long-continued emotions of affection
or passion; whilst all the others proceed with
the utmost regularity without manifesting any
signs or symptoms of perturbation even in the
most complicated evolutions of thought.

3. Intoxication is a temporary lunacy arising from a similar derangement in the trains
of ideas, caused by the irritation, produced in
the stomach by wine or other intoxicating
liquors or drugs, extending itself to the brain;
as it does almost instantaneously, when large
quantities are taken at a time. If taken gradually, it at first only stimulates and quickens
the action of the mind, so as to produce sudden
gleams or coruscations, either of wit or folly,
either of imagery or conceit, accordingly as the,

natural vigour or acquired furniture of the understanding may be calculated to supply either the one or the other. But, as the irritation is increased, the action is increased too; so that, at length, it becomes so rapid and violent, that it can no longer be limited or regulated by any principles of logical connection or coherence; and the most wild and extravagant combinations, both of thought and imagery, ensue.

4. Similar effects of excessive and irregular action also take place in dreams, which equally proceed from the irritations of the stomach being extended to the brain: whence that degree of intemperance, which does not cause absolute intoxication, is almost always followed by turbid and incoherent dreams. The infusions also of exhilarating plants and drugs, such as tea, coffee, opium, &c., which are all intoxicating in different modes and degrees, will produce similar effects, if taken to excess: for all exhilaration of the spirits produced by stimulants is a degree of intoxication.

5. As the irritations of the stomach, in cases of intoxication, disorder the mind through the medium of the brain; so do all violent irritations of the mind, such as those of excessive grief, anxiety, or vexation, disorder the stomach through the same medium; loss of digestion and atrophy being generally the

proximate, or, more properly speaking, the
instrumental causes of ·death in those persons,
who die of what is called a broken heart: a
malady, which, I suspect, kills a great many
more than it has credit for.

6. Some persons have constitutionally such
a vivacity of spirits—such a restlessness rather
than fertility of imagination, ever showing
itself in new combinations of imagery, sometimes just and pleasing, and sometimes the
reverse, that they may be properly said to live
naturally in a state bordering on intoxication;
their spirits being as much the effect of stimulants as those which are given by wine; but of
natural and constitutional stimulants, which
rise and operate occasionally, and then leave
them low and vapid till the nerves have re-
covered their irritability or power of action:
for such persons have always their ebbs and
flows of spirits; the fit of vivacity being invariably followed by one of dejection. Hence
wit and madness are said to be nearly allied:
since, if these constitutional and inherent stimulants act upon machinery too weak to bear
them, they will of course break it. In minds
of adequate vigour, endued with just feelings,
and enriched with various imagery, the combinations, which they excite, though unusual
and diversified, will always be just and cohe-
rent; and, in the readiness and facility of such

combinations, wit properly consists. But, if the proportionate strength of the stimulants be too great, and the action, in consequence, too violent, though the readiness and facility of combination may remain, or even be increased, the justness and coherence of it is gone, and madness, of course, becomes the result.

7. As madness arises from the association of ideas being deranged, so does idiotcy from its being defective; the powers of intellect being, in the one, either totally, or in part, disordered; and, in the other, in a greater or less degree, deficient. Hence, while madmen reason wrongly on particular points, idiots reason feebly and imperfectly on all: for reason, when not employed upon number or quantity is purely association; as will be explained in the next Chapter. The primary perceptions of both lunatics and idiots appear to be as correct and perfect as those of the most discreet and wise of the species: for, unless where the external organs of sense are defective, they all can perceive and discriminate flavours, odours, colours, and sounds, clearly and distinctly; though, in idiots, the power of retaining, as well as that of combining the ideas excited by them, is generally defective; whilst, in lunatics, it is often rendered useless, either by the violent emotions to

which they are subject, or the entire possession, which the disordered trains of ideas have
obtained, of their minds.   Hence only the natural, and not the acquired, or improved perceptions of either, are correct.

8. In proportion to the vigour and extent
of this retaining faculty; and to the number
and variety of images, with which observation,
study, and experience, have enriched it, will
the powers of association be multiplied, and
their operations varied and extended.   Memory, may, indeed, exist without imagination;
but imagination can never act without the aid
of memory; no image or idea having ever been
formed or conceived by the most fertile or
extravagant fancy, the component elements of
which had not been previously received into
this storehouse of the mind through the external organs of sense.   We may compose,
paint, and describe monsters and chimeras of
every extravagant variety of form: but still,
if we analyse them, we shall always find that
the component parts, how much soever they
may be distorted or disguised, have been taken
from objects, or qualities of objects, with which
we have previously become acquainted through
the organs of sensation.

9. As the same perfection of organization,
which produces a vigorous memory, must, in
the common course of nature, produce a vigo-

rous imagination, I suspect, that, wherever
there is much appearance of memory and little
of imagination, the memory is artificial; and
the ideas, with which it is stored, only such as
have been imprinted upon it by dint of, labour
and application; whence they have become
fixed and inflexible, so that they can only be
brought forth in the order in which they were
received. Men, whose minds have been thus
formed, can often go through the minutest
details of a prolix narrative, or the most complicated subtleties of a perplexed argument,
with circumstantial accuracy and unerring precision: but it is only when they have an opportunity of narrating or arguing methodically.
That promptitude of illustration, facility of
transition, and rapidity of application, which
require a memory, that can, at any time, supply
materials for new, as well as retain old combinations, they are ever incapable of acquiring: whence, though they may excel in the
schools, the pulpit, or the college, they are
wholly unfit for desultory debate or familiar
conversation.

10. There is another class of persons, who
are directly the reverse of these—whose memories are naturally retentive, and who are
always furnishing them with new images and
ideas, which they can, at all times, bring forth
with the utmost promptitude and facility: but

having no discernment or judgment to guide
them in the selection of what they amass, nor
feeling to regulate them in the use and application of it, they encumber without enriching
their memories, and stimulate without feeding
their imaginations; whence they pour out, at
random, whatever suggests itself, without considering whither it tends, how it is connected,
or to what it may be applied. ·

11. Of these two classes of talkers, the first
are commonly called prosers, and the second
prattlers. In the one, the manure thrown
upon the mind is without soil, and therefore.
only continues to stink. In the other, it is
without culture, and therefore only produces
weeds.·

12. As all the pleasures of intellect arise
from the association of ideas, the more · the
materials of association are multiplied, the
more will the sphere of these pleasures be enlarged. To a mind richly stored, almost every
object of nature or art, that presents itself to
the senses, either excites fresh trains and combinations of ideas, or vivifies and strengthens
those which existed before: ·so that recollection enhances enjoyment, and enjoyment
brightens recollection. Every insect, plant,
or fossil, which the peasant treads upon unheeded, is, to the naturalist and philosopher,
a subject of curious inquiry and speculation,—

first, as to its structure, formation, or means of existence or propagation;—and then, as to its comparative degree, or mode of connection with others of the same or different kinds; and the respective ranks and situations, which they all severally hold in the graduated system of created beings. To the eye of the uninformed observer, the sublime spectacle of the heavens presents nothing but a blue vault bespangled with twinkling fires: but, to the learned and enlightened, it displays unnumbered worlds, distributed through the boundless vacuity of unmeasurable space; and peopled, perhaps, with different orders of intelligent beings, ascending, in an uninterrupted scale of gradation from the lowest dregs of animated matter to the incomprehensible throne of Omnipotence itself.

13. In the same manner, when we descend to a lower and more limited sphere of observation, and contemplate the artificial productions of social life, we shall find that the trains of association in our ideas will be multiplied and extended, as the circles of our knowledge are expanded; and that the scale of our enjoyments resulting from them will be enlarged in the same proportion. If we mention London or Paris to a person only distantly and generally acquainted with them, a confused mass of ideas of multitudes of houses,

churches, and inhabitants, will present itself: if to one, who has visited these capitals, the confusion will be dispelled, and the distinct ideas of spacious streets, sumptuous palaces, and all the various objects of wealth and grandeur, which he saw there, will spontaneously arise, in the order of their association, to his imagination :—if to one, who has resided long in either of them, in addition to these ideas, and prior in order to them, the more interesting remembrances of the social connections, which he formed there, the companions, with whom he lived, and the friends, in whom he confided, with the various events of prosperity or adversity, which have since befallen them, will present themselves in the same order, and excite their correspondent emotions of solace or regret—of gratulation or sorrow.

14. To descend into a still lower and more confined sphere, let us apply this principle to the subjects of our present inquiry ; and we shall find that much of the pleasure, which we receive from painting, sculpture, music, poetry, &c. arises from our associating other ideas with those immediately excited by them. Hence the productions of these arts are never thoroughly enjoyed but by persons, whose minds are enriched by a variety of kindred and corresponding imagery; the extent and

I.

compass of which, allowing for different de‑
grees of sensibility, and habits of attention,
will form the scale of such enjoyment. Nor
are the gratifications,.which such persons re‑
ceive from these arts limited to their mere
productions, but extended to every object in
nature or circumstance in society, that is at
all connected with them: for, by such con‑
nection, it will be enabled to excite similar or
associated trains of ideas, in minds so enriched,
and consequently to afford them similar plea‑
sures.

15. Of this description are the objects and
circumstances called *picturesque :* for, except
in the instances, before explained, of pleasing
effects of colour, light, and shadow, they afford
no pleasure, but to persons conversant with
the art of painting, and sufficiently skilled in
it to distinguish, and be really delighted with
its real excellences. To all others, how acute
soever may be their discernment, or how ex‑
quisite soever their sensibility, it is utterly
imperceptible : consequently there must be
some properties in the fine productions of this
art, which, by the association of ideas, com‑
municate the power of pleasing to certain ob‑
jects and circumstances of its imitation, which
are therefore called picturesque.

16. No word corresponding to this, or of
exactly similar meaning, is to be found in any,

of the languages of antiquity now extant; nor
in any modern tongue, as far as I have been
able to discover, except such as have borrowed
it from the Italian; in which, the earliest authority, that I can find for it, is that of Redi,
one of the original academicians of la Crusca,
who flourished towards the end of the sixteenth
century. The Spanish does not appear to
have yet received it: at least it is not to be
found in the great authorized dictionary of
that language, the completest work of the kind
that has been hitherto executed, and far ex-
ceeding those of the French and Italian academies in every respect. In our own language,
it has lately been received into very general
use : but, nevertheless, it has not been considered as perfectly naturalized among us : for
Johnson has not admitted it into his dictionary,
though he has received the word *pictorial,* as
the Spaniards have the word *pictorico*; both
of which answer in meaning to the Greek adjective γραφικος ; except that, in the Greek, the
arts of writing, painting, and engraving being
expressed by the same verb, any adjective or
metaphor taken from it must, of course, have
a more extensive, and less determinate signification. The Abbé Winkelman, who understood nothing of the Greek language, translates
γραφικον, in a passage of Strabo, *picturesque*;
and my friend Mr. Price has received his inter-

pretation without examining it ; though, as the
object, to which the epithet relates, is an
Ægyptian temple of plain architecture, of
which the geographer merely says that it had
ꙅδεν χαριεν, ꙅδε γραφικον, it does not afford much
either of illustration or confirmation to his
hypothesis. Had the German antiquary
chanced to stumble upon such an expression
as γραφικον ρεεθρον, we cannot doubt, from the
specimen, which we have already had of his
learning and sagacity, but he would have trans-
lated it *picturesque stream* ; and this would
have exactly suited my friend's purpose. Unfortunately, however, had his usual accuracy
of research, or any suspicions of the infallibility of his guide, led him to look at the context, or even to consult his lexicon, he would
have found that this sonorous phrase only means
ink, more commonly called μελαν γραφικον.

17. According to the idiom of the Italian
language, by which the meaning of all ad-
jectives ending in *esco* is precisely ascertained,
pittoresco must mean, *after the manner of
painters :* whence we may reasonably infer that
painting had, at that time, appropriated to
itself certain descriptions of objects for representation ; or had adopted some peculiar mode
of representing them different from simple or
common imitation ; which peculiar mode would
naturally give them a peculiar character in the

eyes of persons familiar with, and skilled in
that art.

18ˀ At its first revival, as at its first commencement, painting, like sculpture in its first
stage, pretended only to exact imitation; the
truth and precision of which formed the scale
of its merit, as they do still in the estimation
of the ignorant.   In the human figure it attempted to distinguish the several hairs of the
head, and the pores of the skin; and when it
aimed at producing any thing like landscape,
it was by copying distinctly every blade in the
grass, every leaf in the trees, and every stone
or brick in the buildings, which it tried to
represent.

19. It was soon, however, discovered that
this was rather copying what the mind knew
to be, from the concurrent testimony of another sense, than what the eye saw; and that,
even had it been practicable to the utmost extent and variety of nature, it would not have
been a true representation of the visible appearance of things : for the eye, when at a
sufficient distance to comprehend the whole of
a human figure, a tree, or a building, within
the field of vision, sees parts so comparatively
minute as the hair, the leaves, and the stones
or bricks, in masses, and not individually.

20. Hence the mode of imitation was changed; and, as this *massing* gave breadth to the

lights and shadows, mellowed them into each
other, and enabled the artist to break and blend
them together ; all which add much to the tenderness, lustre, and beauty of the productions
of- this art, the great painters of the Venetian
and Lombard schools ; and afterwards those
of the Flemish and Dutch, carried this principle of *massing* to a degree beyond what
appears in ordinary nature ; and departed
from the system of strict imitation in a contrary extreme to that of their predecessors.
Instead of making their lines more distinct,
and keeping their tints more separate, than
the visible appearance of the objects of imitation warranted, they blended and melted
them together with a playful and airy kind
of lightness, and a sort of loose and sketchy
indistinctness not observable in the reality,
unless under peculiar circumstances and modifications of the atmosphere ; and then only
in those objects and combinations of objects,
which exhibit blended and broken tints, or
irregular masses of light and shadow harmoniously melted into each other.

21. Such are the objects and compositions
of objects, which we properly call *picturesque* ;
and we find that the style of painting, which
distinguished them as such, was invented by
Georgione about the beginning, and perfected
by Titian about the middle of the sixteenth

century; soon after which the word made its first appearance in the Italian, and, I believe, in any language.

22. Indeed, if we consider the natural and necessary connection between words and ideas; and the progressive order, in which the former arise out of the latter, it will appear impossible that it should have existed sooner: for till painters had adopted some distinct manner of imitating nature, appropriate to their own art, men could never have thought of distinguishing any object or class of objects by an epithet signifying *after the manner of painters :* since, unless painters had some peculiar manner, such epithet could mark no peculiar discrimination, nor have any distinct meaning.

23. Tints happily broken and blended, and irregular masses of light and shadow harmoniously melted into each other, are, in themselves, as before observed, more grateful to the eye, than any single tints, upon the same principle that harmonious combinations of tones or flavours are more grateful to the ear or the palate, than any single tones or flavours can be. They are therefore more properly beautiful, according to the strictest meaning of the word beauty; when applied to that which is pleasing to the sense only; and not, as it usually is, to that, which is alike pleasing to the senses, the intellect and the imagination;

according to which comprehensive signification of the word, many objects, that we call
picturesque, certainly are not beautiful ; since
they may be void of symmetry, neatness, clean-
ness, &c. ; all which are necessary to constitute that kind of beauty, which addresses itself
to the understanding and the fancy.

24. The sensual pleasure arising from viewing objects and compositions, which we call
picturesque, may be felt equally by all mankind
in proportion to the correctness and sensibility
of their organs of sight ; for it is wholly independent of their being picturesque, or *after*
the manner of painters. But this very relation to painting, expressed by the word *pic-*
turesque, is that, which affords the whole
pleasure derived from association ; which can,
therefore, only be felt by persons, who have
correspondent ideas to associate ; that is, by
persons in a certain degree conversant with
that art. Such persons being in the habit of
viewing, and receiving pleasure from fine pictures, will naturally feel pleasure in viewing
those objects in nature, which have called forth
those powers of imitation and embellishment ;
and those combinations and circumstances of
objects, which have guided those powers in
their happiest exertions. The objects recall
to the mind the imitations, which skill, taste,
and genius have produced ; and these again

recall to the mind the objects themselves, and show them through an improved medium— that of the feeling and discernment of a great artist.

25. By thus comparing nature and art, both the eye and the intellect acquire a higher relish for the productions of each; and the ideas, excited by both, are invigorated, as well as refined, by being thus associated and contrasted. The pleasures of vision acquire a wider range, and find endless gratifications, at once exquisite and innocent, in all the variety of productions, whether animal, vegetable, or mineral, which nature has scattered over the earth. All display beauty in some combinations or others; and when that beauty has been selected, imitated, and embellished by art, those, who before overlooked or neglected it, discern at once all its charms through this discriminating medium; and when the sentiment, which it excited, was new to them, they called those appearances of things, which excited it, by a new name, *picturesque* :—a word, that is now become extremely common and familiar in our own tongue; and which, like all other foreign words, that are become so, is very frequently employed improperly.

26. The skilful painter, like the skilful poet, passes slightly over those parts of his subject, which neither the compass of his art, nor the

nature of his materials, allow him to represent with advantage; and employs all his labour. and attention upon those, which he can adorn and embellish. These are the *picturesque* parts; that is, those which nature has formed in the style and manner appropriate to paint-ing; and the eye, that has been accustomed to see these happily displayed and embellished by art, will relish them more in nature; as a per-son conversant with the writings of Theocritus and Virgil will relish pastoral scenery more than one unacquainted with such poetry. The spectator, having his mind enriched with the embellishments of the painter and the poet, applies them, by the spontaneous association of ideas, to the natural objects presented to. his eye, which thus acquire ideal and imaginary beauties; that is, beauties, which are not felt by the organic sense of vision; but by the intellect and imagination through that sense.

27. To attempt to analyze, class, or enume-rate the objects in nature, which are, in this proper sense of the word, *picturesque*, would be vain and impracticable; as they compre-hend, in some degree, every thing of every kind, which has been, or may be represented to advantage in painting: and, if the scale of imitation in that art should be hereafter ex-tended, the boundaries of the picturesque will be extended in the same proportion. Lately,

too, the word has been extended to criticism, and employed to signify that clear and vivid style of narration or description, which paints to the imagination, and shows every event or object distinctly, as if represented in a picture *. But, according to my friend Mr. Price's system, this employment of it must be improper; and it ought to signify that middle stile, which is not sufficiently smooth to be beautiful, nor sufficiently rough and elevated to be sublime. In objects of imitative art, we properly call *picturesque*, not only those of the most opposite kinds, but those which mark the opposite extremes of the same kind. The boors of Ostade, the peasants of Gainsborough, and the shepherds of Berghem, are picturesque; but so likewise are the warriors of Salvator Rosa, the apostles of Raphael, and the bacchanalians of Poussin: nor is the giant oak of Ruysdael, or full-grown pine or ilex of Claude, less so than the stumpy decayed pollard of Rubens or Rembrandt: nor the shaggy worn-out hack or cart-horse of Morland or Asselyn, than the pampered warhorse with luxuriant mane, and flowing tail, which we so justly admire in the pictures of Wovermans. The dirty and tattered garments, the dishevelled hair, and general wild appear-

* See Blair's Lectures,

ance of gipsies and beggar girls are often pic
turésque.: but the flowing ringlets, fine shawls,
and robes of delicate muslin thrown into all
the easy, negligent, and playful folds of antique
drapery by polished grace and refined elegance,
are still more so. The first, indeed, are merely
picturesque; that is, they have only the painter's
beauties of harmonious variety of tint, and
light and shade, blended with every thing else,
that is disgusting; while the others have these
in an equal, or even superior degree, in addition to the charms of lightness, neatness, and
purity. The mouldering ruins of ancient temples, theatres, and aqueducts, enriched by such
a variety of tints, all mellowed into each other,
as they appear in the landscapes of Claude,
are, in the highest degree, picturesque: but
the magnificent quays and palaces, adorned
with porticos and balustrades, and intermixed
with shipping, which enrich the seaports of the
same master, are likewise picturesque; though
in a less degree: for new buildings have an
unity of tint, and sharpness of angle, which
render them unfit for painting, unless when
mixed with trees or some other objects, which
may break and diversify their colour, and gra-
duate and harmonize the abruptness of their
lights and shadows.

28. Are not, therefore, new buildings beautiful? Unquestionably they are; and pecu-
13

liarly so : for neatness, freshness, lightness,
symmetry, regularity, uniformity, and propriety,
are undoubtedly beauties of the highest class ;
though the pleasure, which they afford, is not
simply a pleasure of the sense of seeing; nor
one received by the mind through the medium
of painting.   But, upon the same principle,
as the association of ideas renders those qualities in visible objects, which are peculiarly
appropriate to painting, peculiarly pleasing to
those conversant in that art ; so likewise does
it render those qualities, which are peculiarly
adapted to promote the comforts and enjoyments of social life, pleasing to the eye of
civilized man ; though there be nothing, in the
forms or colours of the objects themselves, in
any degree pleasing to the sense ; but, perhaps, the contrary.   Hence neatness and freshness will always delight, if not out of character
with the objects, in which they appear ; or
with the scenery, with which they are connected : for the mind requires propriety in
every thing ; that is, it requires that those properties, the ideas of which it has been invariably habituated to associate, should be associated in reality; otherwise the combinations
will appear to be unnatural, incoherent, or
absurd.

29. For this reason we require, immediately
adjoining the dwellings of opulence and lux-

ury, that every thing should assume its character; and not only be, but appear to be
dressed and cultivated. In such situations,
neat gravel walks, mown turf, and flowering-
plants and shrubs, trained and distributed by
art, are perfectly in character; although, if
the same buildings were abandoned, and in
ruins, we should, on the same principle of consistency and propriety, require neglected paths,
rugged lanes, and wild uncultivated thickets;
which are, in themselves, more pleasing, both
to the eye and the imagination, but, unfit accompaniments for objects, not only originally
produced by art, but, in which, art is constantly
employed and exhibited. Nevertheless a path
with the sides shaggy and neglected, or a picturesque lane between broken and rugged
banks, may be kept as clean, and as commo-
dious for the purpose of walking, as the neatest
gravel walk; wherefore it is not upon any principle of reason, that the preference is, in such
situations, justly given to the latter; but merely
upon that of the habitual association of ideas,
which is, indeed, in effect, reason.

30. This sort of neatness should, on the
same principle, be confined to the immediate
appendages of the house; that is, to the
grounds, which are so connected with it, as
to appear necessary adjuncts to the dwelling,
and therefore to be under the influence of the

same character, which is a character of art.
On this account, I think the avowed character
of art of the Italian gardens preferable, in
garden scenery, to the concealed one now in
fashion; which is, in reality, rather counter-
feited than concealed; for it appears in every
thing; but appears in a dress, that does not
belong to it: at every step we perceive its exertions; but, at the same time, perceive that it
has laboured much to effect little; and that
while it seeks to hide its character, it only, like
a prostitute who affects modesty, discovers it
the more.   In the decorations, however, of
ground adjoining a house, much should depend upon the character of the house itself:
if it be neat and regular, neatness and regularity should accompany it; but if it be rugged and picturesque, and situated amidst
scenery of the same character, art should
approach it with more caution : for though it
be, in itself, an avowed work of art; yet the
influence of time, with the accompaniments
of trees and creepers, may have given it a character of nature, which ought to be as little
disturbed, as is consistent with comfort : for,
after all, the character of nature is more pleasing than any that can be given by art.

    31. At all events the character of dress and
artificial neatness ought never to be suffered
to encroach upon the park or the forest;

where it is as contrary to propriety as it is to
beauty; and where its introduction, by our
modern landscape gardeners, affords one of
the most memorable instances of any recorded
in the history of fashions, of the extravagant
absurdity, with which an insatiate passion for
novelty may infect a whole nation.

32. That this sense of propriety or congruity is entirely artificial, and acquired by the
habitual association of ideas, we need no other
proof, than its being wholly dependent upon
variable circumstances: in the pictures of
Claude and Gaspar, we perpetually see a mixture of Grecian and Gothic architecture employed with the happiest effect in the same
building; and no critic has ever yet objected
to the incongruity of it: for, as the temples,
tombs, and palaces of the Greeks and Romans
in Italy were fortified with towers and battlements by the Goths and Lombards in the
middle ages, such combinations have been
naturalized in that country; and are, therefore,
perfectly in harmony with the scenery; and
so far from interrupting the chain of ideas,
that they lead it on and extend it, in the pleasantest manner, through different ages, and
successive revolutions in tastes, arts, and
sciences.

33. Perhaps, we are becoming too rigid in
rejecting such combinations in the buildings of

our own country: for they have been, in some degree, naturalized here, as well as in Italy; though in a different order of succession, the Gothic having here preceded the Grecian. Nevertheless, the effect is the same; the fortresses of our ancestors, which, in the course of the two last centuries, were transformed into Italianized villas, and decked with the porticos, balustrades, and terraces of Jones and Palladio, affording, in many instances, the most beautiful compositions; especially when mellowed by time and neglect, and harmonized and united by ivy, mosses, lichens, &c. Perhaps, however, as we always attach some ideas of regularity, neatness, or congruity to the word *beauty*, they may more exactly accord with what is generally expressed by the word *picturesque*; that is, the beauty of various tints and forms happily blended, without rule or symmetry, and rendered venerable by those imposing marks of antiquity, which the successive modes of decoration, employed by successive ages, and each become obsolete in its turn, afford.

34. This air of venerability (which belongs to the sublime, and not to the beautiful, and which will therefore be considered hereafter) cannot, it is true, be given to any new structures of this mixed kind: but, nevertheless, all the beauties of lightness, variety, and intricacy of

M

form, and light and shadow, may be carried to a degree, which no regular or homogenial building (if I may use the expression) will admit of. After all, too, this congruity, or strict historical unity of plan and design, is only felt by the learned ; or, at least, by those who imagine themselves to be so : for, upon this point, I believe, the pleasures and disgusts, which men feel, are, in a great measure, founded in error ; so that both would probably vanish, were they undeceived.

35. At this time, when the taste for Gothic architecture has been so generally revived, nothing is more common, than to hear professors, as well as lovers, of the art, expatiating upon the merits of the pure Gothic ; and gravely endeavouring to separate it from those spurious and adscititious ornaments, by which it has lately been debased : but, nevertheless, if we ask what they mean by *pure Gothic*, we can receive no satisfactory answer :—there are no rules—no proportions—and, consequently, no definitions : but we are referred to certain models of generally acknowledged excellence ; which models are of two kinds, entirely differing from each other ; the one called the castle, and the other the cathedral or monastic ; the one having been employed in the fortresses, and the other in the churches and convents of those

nations, which divided the Roman empire, and erected the states and kingdoms of modern Europe upon its ruins.

36. In tracing back these nations, however, to the countries from which they came; and examining the arts, which they exercised prior to their emigration, we can find no vestiges of either of these kinds of architecture; nor, indeed, of any architecture whatever; their fortresses having been mounds of earth, or piles of timber, sometimes driven into the ground, and sometimes clumsily framed together; and their temples, circles of massive stones, rude from the quarry. It is, therefore, manifest that they either invented, or adopted both these styles of architecture after their settlement in the Roman empire; and, consequently, after they had become acquainted with the buildings of those civilized nations, which they subdued.

37. That the military architecture of the Greeks and Romans consisted, from the earliest to the latest times, of walls and towers capped with battlements, is certain *; but in what manner those battlements were formed and finished, is not so easily ascertained; there being no perfect specimen of them extant. It is probable,

---

* The Greeks appear to have had private houses so fortified even in the time of the Peloponnesian war. οἱ δε Αθηναιοι ημυνοντο τε εκ φαυλε τειχισματος, και απ᾽ οικιων επιαλξεις εχεσων. Thucyd. l. iv. f. 114.

however, that they differed in different ages, accordingly as the modes of attack and defence were varied. The overhanging battlements, now called Gothic, were certainly known to the Romans, as early as the reign of Titus: as there are, among the paintings of Herculaneum, representations of walls and towers completely finished in this way *; and it is probable that this fashion continued down to the subversion of the empire, and was then adopted by the conquerors. It is, indeed, the natural mode of fortification for any people, skilled in masonry, and not acquainted with artillery, to employ; as it afforded the most obvious and effective means of at once guarding the defendants, and annoying the assailants: wherefore it might have been used by different nations, which had no communication with each other; and which might, with equal justice, claim the invention of it. The forms, proportions, and distribution of the towers, and their respective height, compared with that of the walls, as well as the general plans of the castles, to which they belonged, depended entirely upon circumstances and situations; and were confined by no rules or systems of architecture.

38. In like manner, the villas or country houses of the Romans were quite irregular—

* Pittura d'Herculan. tom. i. tav. xlix. and tom. iii. tav. xli.

adapted to the situations, on which they were
placed—and spread out in every direction,
according to the wants or inclinations; the
taste, wealth, or magnificence of the respective
owners. In those of great splendor and extent,
such as that of the Emperor Hadrian at Tivoli,
every species of decoration, then known, was
employed in some part or other ; and though
we have no precise accounts of military architecture having a place in these edifices of luxury,
we can scarcely doubt that it was employed in
them for defence, if not for ornament, in the
declining state of the monarchy; when the
hordes of barbarians, which menaced the fron-
tiers, and the gangs of robbers, which infested
the interior, were little more terrible to the
peaceful and wealthy inhabitants, than the
legions of undisciplined soldiers employed to
defend them.

39. That style of architecture, which we call
cathedral or monastic Gothic, is manifestly a
corruption of the sacred architecture of the
Greeks and Romans, by a mixture of the
Moorish or Saracenesque, which is formed out
of a combination of the Ægyptian, Persian, and
Hindoo. It may easily be traced through all
its variations, from the church of Santa Sophia
at Constantinople, and the cathedral of Mon-
treale near Palermo, the one of the sixth, and
the other of the eighth century, down to King's

M 3

were meant to be ornamental, were intended to
adorn streets and squares, rather than parks or
gardens. The Greek temples were, almost
always, of an oblong square; and, as the cells
were, in general, small and simple, their magnificence was displayed in the lofty and spacious
colonnades, which surrounded them; consisting,
sometimes of single, and sometimes of double
rows of pillars; which, by the richness and
variety of their effects, contributed, in the
highest degree, to embellish and adorn the
cities; and, by excluding the sun and rain, and
admitting the air, afforded the most grateful
walks to the inhabitants: where those, who
could afford to be idle, passed the greatest part
of their time in discussing the common topics
of business or pleasure, politics or philosophy.

41. These regular structures being the only
monuments of ancient taste and magnificence
in architecture, that remained, at the resurrec-
tion of the arts, in a state sufficiently entire to
be perfectly understood, the revivers of the
Grecian style copied it servilely from them,
and applied it indiscriminately to country, as
well as town houses: but, as they felt its
incongruity with the surrounding scenery of
unimproved and unperverted nature, they endeavoured to make that conform to it, as far
as it was within their reach, or under their
control. Hence probably arose the Italian style
13

of gardening; though other causes, which will
be hereafter noticed, may have co-operated.

42. Since the introduction of another style
of ornamental gardening, called at first oriental,
and afterwards landscape gardening (probably
from its efficacy in destroying all picturesque
composition) Grecian temples have been employed as decorations by almost all persons,
who could afford to indulge their taste in objects
so costly: but, though executed, in many instances, on a scale and in a manner suitable to
the design, disappointment has, I believe, been
invariably the result.   Nevertheless they are
unquestionably beautiful, being exactly copied
from those models, which have stood the eriti-
cism of many successive ages, and been constantly beheld with delight and admiration.   In
the rich lawns and shrubberies of England,
however, they lose all that power to please
which they so eminently possess on the barren
hills of Agrigentum and Segesta, or the naked
plains of Pæstum and Athens.   But barren
and naked as these hills and plains are, they
are still, if I may say so, their native hills and
plains—the scenery, in which they sprang; and
in which the mind, therefore, contemplates
them connected and associated with numberless
interesting circumstances, both local and historical—both physical and moral, upon which it
delights to dwell.   In our parks and gardens,

on the contrary, they stand wholly unconnected
with all that surrounds them—mere unmeaning
excrescences; or, what is worse, manifestly
meant for ornament, and therefore having no
accessory character, but that of ostentatious
vanity: so that, instead of exciting any interest,
they vitiate and destroy that, which the naturalized objects of the country connected with them
would otherwise excite. Even if the landscape
scenery should be rendered really beautiful by
such ornaments, its beauty will be that of a vain
and affected coquette; which, though it may
allure the sense, offends the understanding;
and, on the whole, excites more disgust than
pleasure. In all matters of this kind, the imagination must be conciliated before the eye can
be delighted.

43. Many of the less important productions
of ancient art; such as coins, &c. owe much of
the interest, which they excite; and, consequently, much of the value, which they have
acquired, to the same principle of association.
Considered individually, as detached specimens
of art, their value may seem inadequate to the
prices sometimes paid for them: but, nevertheless, when viewed in a series, and considered
as exhibiting genuine though minute examples
of the rise, progress, perfection, and decay of
imitative art, employed upon the noblest subjects, the images of gods, heroes, and princes,

among those nations, from which all excellence
in art and literature is derived, they stand connected with subjects so interesting and important, that they become truly interesting and
important themselves; as far at least as any
objects of mere elegant taste and speculative
study can be interesting and important.   It is
true, that, in this, as in all other pursuits of the
kind, the province of taste and science has been
sometimes usurped by vanity and affectation
displayed in the silly desire of possessing, at
any price, that which has no other merit than
being rare: but, nevertheless, I believe that
instances of it are much less common, than they
are generally supposed to be:—at least very
few have come to my knowledge, during a very
long and extensive acquaintance with such pursuits and their votaries, through most parts of
Europe.   As for the hacknied tales of Othos, &c.
so often employed to ridicule collectors, they
are, I believe, entirely fictitious; every collector, who has any knowledge of the subject,
being well aware that no such coin as the Latin
one of Otho, supposed to be the ultimate object
of his hopes and desires, ever did exist; and as
for those struck in the eastern provinces of the
empire, they are neither rare nor valuable in
any high degree.   Rareness certainly adds to
the value of that, which is in itself valuable and
interesting, either as an object of taste or

science; but the mere frivolous distinction of possessing that, which others have not, is such as no man of common sense can reasonably be supposed ambitious of.

44. Nearly connected with propriety or congruity, is symmetry, or the fitness and proportion of parts to each other, and to the whole: —a necessary ingredient to beauty in all composite forms; and one, which alone entitles them, in many instances, to be called beautiful. It depends entirely upon the association of ideas, and not at all upon either abstract reason or organic sensation; otherwise, like harmony in sound or colour, it would result equally from the same comparative relations in all objects; which is so far from being the case, that the same relative dimensions, which make one animal beautiful, make another absolutely ugly. That, which is the most exquisite symmetry in a horse, would be the most gross deformity in an elephant, and *vice versâ:* but the same proportionate combinations of sound, which produce harmony in a fiddle, produce it also in a flute or a harp.

45. In many productions of art, symmetry is still more apparently the result of arbitrary convention; that is, it proceeds from an association of ideas, which have not been so invariably associated; and which are, therefore, less intimately and firmly connected. In a Grecian

building, in which the relative proportions of the different orders of columns were not observed, a person skilled in architecture would instantly discover a want of symmetry; which, to another of even more correct taste, as far as correct taste depends on just feeling, may be utterly imperceptible: for there is no reason whatever in the nature of things, or in the analogy of the parts, why a Corinthian capital should be placed on a slenderer shaft than a Doric or Ionic one.   On the contrary, the Corinthian, being of the largest, and consequently of the heaviest proportion, would naturally require the column of the largest dimensions, proportioned to its height, to sustain it.

46. The appropriation of particular proportions to the columns of particular orders is, I believe, of no higher antiquity than the practice of placing one order over another; of which, I know of no instance anterior to the theatres and amphitheatres of the Romans; the first of which, excepting temporary structures of wood, was that of Pompey*. In the arrangement of

* I am aware that Pausanius describes a temple at Tegea, said to have been designed by Serpas, in which a range of Corinthian was placed over one of Ionic columns: but as this temple was built on the site of one burnt in the second year of the xcvi[th] Olympiad, we may fairly conclude, considering the usual slow progress of these expensive structures in inferior cities, and the

the different orders in buildings of this kind, the plainest was naturally placed lowest, and the most enriched, highest; and hence the plainest was made the most massive; and the most ornamented, the most light and slender: but as this distinction of proportions arose merely from the relative positions, which they held, when thus employed together, and not from any inherent principle of propriety; there can be no other reason, than that of established custom, why it should be observed, when they are employed separately, and independent of each other.

47. In the Grecian buildings, which are anterior to any customary rules of this kind, the proportionate thickness of the columns, in each of the three orders, which are properly Grecian, appears to have been diminished gradually as the art advanced towards refinement: and, as the Doric was the earliest, and the Corinthian the latest invented, the proportions of the first are, of course, the most massive, and those of the last the most slender. It was only by repeated experiment, and long observ-

state into which those parts of the Peloponnesus soon after fell, that the upper range was added under the Roman emperors. See Pausan. Arcadie, xli.

In all the temples, known to be of remote antiquity, both in Europe and Asia, the two ranges of columns are of the same order.

ation, that men learned the power of a vertical shaft to bear a perpendicular weight; and therefore, in the infancy of the art, made their columns unnecessarily large and ponderous; which is observable, not only in the primitive efforts of the Greeks and Egyptians, but also in the imitations made, at the revival of the art, by the Saxons, Goths, Franks, Lombards, &c.   In all, the progress has been from excessive ponderous solidity to excessive lightness; though as the Greeks and Romans bound themselves by certain rules of proportion, before they had run into the latter extreme, they never indulged themselves in the extravagant licence of the Gothic architects, who recognized no rules, but worked merely for effect.

48. Under the Macedonian kings and first Roman emperors, the refinements of accurate proportion appear to have been carried to a frivolous excess *: for though they may have contributed to preserve that elegance and purity of taste, which distinguishes all the works of those periods, yet they certainly tend to restrain genius, and prevent grandeur of effect, which can only be produced by contrast, which is the direct opposite of proportion. Contrast appears to have been the leading principle of the Gothic architects, and as its operation upon the mind,

* Vitruv. lib. iii.

as well as that of proportion, is by the association of ideas, it is impossible to limit it to any precise rules or restrictions; since the acquisition of new ideas may at any time produce new associations, or change those previously existing. The Gothic architects varied the proportions of their columns from four, to one hundred and twenty diametres, and contrasted the ornaments and the parts with equal licence; and though a column so slender, employed to support a vaulted roof of stone, may offend the eye of a person, who suspects it to be inadequate to its purpose, and therefore associates ideas of weakness and danger with it; yet, to those who know it to be sufficient, it will appear extremely light and beautiful; as is proved by the columns in the cathedral of Salisbury, which are of this proportion, and which have been universally admired for many centuries.

The contrivers of this refined and fantastic Gothic seem to have aimed at producing grandeur and solemnity, together with lightness of effect; and incompatible as these qualities may seem, by attending to effect only, and considering the means of producing it as wholly subordinate, and in their own power, they succeeded to a degree, which the Grecian architects, who worked by rule, never approached.

49. The eye always measures the whole of an edifice by a scale taken from the parts; and,

particularly, those parts, with which it is most familiar; and for which the common observation of nature has supplied the memory with models; such as statues, foliage, and other imitations of natural productions.

50. In the cathedral of St. Peter at Rome, all these are of a gigantic size, taken from a given scale, proportionate to that of the build-ing; and I have often heard this rigid adherence to uniform proportion admired as a very high excellence; though all allow that the effect of it has been to make the building appear much smaller, than it really is; and if it be a merit to make it appear small, it certainly was extreme folly to incur such immense expence in building it large.

51. Our Gothic architects worked upon prin-ciples diametrically opposite, and made all these subordinate parts, and incidental decorations, of as small a proportion as was compatible with their being distinctly seen; and, in this, they appear to me to have judged wisely; for the ornaments appear more light and elegant, by being small: and the very profusion, with which they were scattered, in order to diffuse them over a large space, still extended the scale, which they afforded to the eye, for the admea-surement of the whole.

52. This grandeur of effect was rendered more solemn, and consequently more grand, by

N

large masses of dim and discoloured light, diffused, in various directions, and at different
intervals, through unequal varieties of space,
divided but not separated, so as to produce
intricacy without confusion: the room was
evidently one, and the general form and dimensions of it were easily discernible through the
successive ranges of arches, piers, and columns,
with which the view was interrupted; but there
was no point, from which the eye could see the
whole of it at one glance; so that, though much
was seen, something still remained to be seen,
which the imagination measured from the scale
of the rest.—Thus effects more imposing have
been produced, than are, perhaps, to be found
in any other works of man.

53. That visible effect, which we call lightness, proceeds, like all other beauties of this
kind, from the association of ideas: for the
specific gravity of bodies is not measured by
the eye; and we all know, from experience, that
neither statues of brass or marble, nor buildings of brick or stone, are, in reality, light:
but, nevertheless, there are certain relative
proportions, and combinations of forms, to
which, the same habitual experience has taught
us to associate ideas of motion and elasticity,
which are naturally connected with lightness;
and the same spontaneous and mechanical operation of the mind makes us apply these to

bodies, which we know, at the same time, to be
neither elastic nor capable of motion. Sculpture, indeed, generally imitates bodies in motion
or capable of motion and action; wherefore an
appearance of lightness and elasticity in its
forms is among the most appropriate and indispensable of its excellences: but buildings are
meant to appear, as well as to be stationary;
and their proper characteristic is massive
strength and solid stability. Attempts at lightness, unless supported by extreme richness,
either of material or ornament, either of colour
or form, almost always produce meagreness,
poverty, and weakness of effect; such as is but
too manifest in most of the works of Grecian
or Roman architecture lately executed in this
country; where spindle columns, bald capitals,
wide intercolumniations, and scanty entablatures form a sort of frippery trimming fit only
to adorn a house built after the model of a
brick clamp: which is, indeed, the usual application of them. In the magnificent structures
of the Roman emperors, the entablatures continued full, and the intercolumniations moderate, after the proportions of the columns had
become slender; at the same time that the cost-
liness and brilliancy of the materials, and the
variety and elegance of the sculptures were
alone sufficient to suppress any ideas of poverty
or meanness, which a want of **substance** might

otherwise have excited. In the Gothic churches, too, a profusion of elaborate ornament, how licentiously soever designed or disposed, seldom failed to produce a similar effect: but the modern fashion of making buildings neither rich nor massive, and producing lightness of appearance by the deficiency rather than the disposition of the parts, is of all tricks of taste the most absurd, and the most certain of counteracting its own ends. The ponderous extravagancies of Vanbrugh, how blamable soever in the detail, are never contemptible in the whole; and amidst all the unmeaning absurdities, which the learned observer may discover in the parts of Blenheim and Castle Howard, the general mass in each has been universally felt and acknowledged to be grand and imposing: but in later works of the same kind, which it might perhaps be invidious to name, equal expence has been incurred to produce objects similar to what we may reasonably suppose a cabinet-maker of Brobdignag would have made for Gulliver's nurse.

Even where the genuine Grecian order, that is, the old Doric, has been employed, it has been by a mere servile and mechanic imitation of its existing remains, without any attention to the principles which directed their authors; whence many absurd and perverse fashions have arisen. It was the constant practice of the

ancient Greeks to leave the exterior surface of
the stones rough, both in the walls and columns,
till after the building was erected ; and only to
hew them round the edges in the one, and to
finish them at intervals in the other, that the
workmen might have points of reference for
accurately completing them afterwards : but as
wars, revolutions, or other public calamities
often intervened, many important edifices remained in this imperfect and unfinished state;
the accidental defects of which have been studiously and elaborately copied, and called *rustic
work*, of which I know of no example in any
finished building of antiquity, except in under-
ground substructions, where finishing was dispensed with.   Every Greek temple was raised
upon a basement which served as a general
pedestal for all the columns, and obviated the
necessity of obstructing the intercolumniations
with separate plinths or bases to each : but
when columns are erected upon an even plain,
without any support under them, they seem as
if they had sunk into it; and thus give a building an appearance of heaviness without stability,
and of weakness without lightness.

54. The fundamental error of imitators in
all arts is, that they servilely copy the effects,
which they see produced, instead of studying
and adopting the principles, which guided the
original artists in producing them; wherefore

they disregard all those local, temporary, or
accidental circumstances, upon which their
propriety or impropriety—their congruity or
incongruity wholly depend : for principles in
art are no other than the trains of ideas, which
arise in the mind of the artist out of a just and
adequate consideration of all such circumstances; and direct him in adapting his work
to the purposes for which it is intended : consequently, if either those circumstances or purposes change, his ideas must change with them,
or his principles will be false, and his works
incongruous. Grecian temples, Gothic abbeys,
and feudal castles were all well adapted to their
respective uses, circumstances, and situations :
the distribution of the parts subservient to the
purposes of the whole ; and the ornaments and
decorations suited to the character of the parts ;
and to the manners, habits, and employments
of the persons who were to occupy them : but
the house of an English nobleman of the
eighteenth or nineteenth century is neither a
Grecian temple, a Gothic abbey, nor a feudal
castle; and if the style of distribution or decoration of either be employed in it, such changes
and modifications should be admitted as may
adapt it to existing circumstances ; otherwise
the scale of its exactitude becomes that of its
incongruity, and the deviation from principle
proportioned to the fidelity of imitation. Com-

mon practitioners think every objection answered, when some respectable authority is
adduced; though perhaps the only point proved
by such authority is that the person, who uses
it, does not understand it, or know how to
apply it.

55. In painting an appearance of lightness
depends, not only on the forms, and proportions of the objects delineated, but on the mode
of imitation, which the artist employs; a slow
pencil, and heavy manner of execution, will
make almost any object appear heavy in the
picture; and, on the contrary, a brilliant, free,
and sketchy one will always make the same
appear light; although the imitation be equally
exact in both.   This difference is, however,
more easily discernible in drawings than in
paintings; and in slight, than in finished per
formances; for the more is left to the imagination, the more free and spontaneous will the
association of ideas, between the style of the
imitation, and that of the thing imitated, be;
and the more readily will the mind transfer the
properties, which it observes in the former, to
the notions, which it has formed of the latter.

Objects, that are not circumscribed by
straight, or very determinate outlines, but of
which the forms are loose and flowing, are
peculiarly well adapted to this free and sketchy
style of imitation; and are, therefore, properly

to be considered as *picturesque*. Rubens, who of all the painters, was most eminent for this facility or *bravura* of execution, has shown himself most attached to these kinds of forms; the columns of his buildings being generally twisted and fluted; and the limbs of his figures always bent, and the muscles charged and prominent: upon the same principle was, probably, his fondness for painting fat and flabby women; whose shapeless bodies were entirely freed from those regular and determined outlines which he seemed to consider as insurmountable enemies of his art. It is curious to observe how he has twisted and distorted them in his attempts to improve the drawings of the old Roman and Florentine masters; whose meagre upright figures have their muscles swoln, and their limbs bent into all those flowing and undulating lines, which have been called the lines of grace and beauty; how truly, the compositions of Rubens, in which they always predominate, and those of Raphael, in which they are never employed, but incidentally, may decide *. They may,

---

* See Idler, No. 76; where Sir Joshua Reynolds has introduced, with much humour, a systematic connoisseur just returned from Italy with his head full of harmonic proportions, flowing lines of grace and beauty, pyramidal principles of grouping, &c. &c.; by which he criticises the cartoons of Raphael, and laments that no traces of them are to be found in those celebrated works of so extraordinary a genius; thus, as the author observes, pretending

however, be justly called picturesque, in the most limited and proper sense of the word, as being peculiarly appropriate to painting.

56. Corregio has employed similar outlines, as uniformly, but with more of the modesty and moderation of nature than Rubens ; his women being always desirable, and the expression of their countenances, and character of their attitudes, elegant and pleasing : whence they have been thought handsome ; though their general forms have as little of that beauty, which arises from correct and just symmetry, as those of any of the Flemish painters ; and this beauty, perhaps, is the only one in the human figure, whether male or female, which can strictly and philosophically be considered as a beauty : for all the others depend, in a great measure, upon sexual or social sympathies ; and therefore belong as much to the peculiar properties of the minds, which feel, as to those of the persons, which display them.

57. I am aware, indeed, that it would be no easy task to persuade a lover that the forms, upon which he dotes with such rapture, are not really beautiful, independent of the medium of affection, passion, and appetite, through which

great admiration for a name of fixed reputation, and, at the same time, raising objections against those very qualities, by which that great name was acquired.

·he views them. But before he pronounces
either the infidel or the sceptic guilty of blas-
phemy against nature, let him take a mould
from the lovely features or lovely bosom of this
master-piece of creation, and cast a plum-pud-
:,ding in it ʻ(an object by no means disgusting to
most men's appetites) and, I think, he will no
longer be in raptures with the form, whatever
·he may be with the substance. Display,. too,
the most beautiful of the sex, in all the freshness
of youth and bloom of health, to any animal of
another kind,· and she will be viewed with per-
feet indifference ; though many ,of them show
the nicest and most discriminating ʻ sensibility
to different colours; green being, as before
observed, grateful to all,ˋ and scarlet evidently
offensive and painful to some. Even in· the
·females of their own species, they seem to be
quite insensible to the charms ,of this freshness
of youth and bloom of health, which we value
so much in ours : for it has been observed that
a. ram always gives the preference to the oldest
of his flock; his appetites being excited by that,
whichˊis one of the most effectual extinguishers
of ours.

ʻ58. Men, it is true, often fall violently in love
ʻat first sight ; and when the momentary impression, made by the object on the organ of vision,
is all that they can know of her : but, nevertheless, this· organic impression is, as before ob-

served, no further the cause of love, than as it
serves to communicate the object to the mind;
the mere sensual pleasure of sight having little
or nothing to do with it.

59. That love, which arises from an union of
rational esteem, sympathetic sentiment, and
animal desire, is, I believe, peculiar to civilized
man ; brutes seeking for nothing more in their
females than the gratification of their periodical
appetites; and savage men considering them
merely as slaves, whose only valuable qualifications are those, which befit them for useful
labour or sensual pleasure. · The sexual affections, indeed, of some kinds of birds seem to be
productive of something like mental attachment;
especially in their co-operation in fostering their
eggs and nourishing their young: but, nevertheless, its principle appears to be merely a
natural and instinctive propensity ; whereas
that of rational and sentimental love is entirely
artificial and acquired, otherwise such love
would not be limited to men in an artificial
state of society.

60. When, however, the propensity is acquired, it may exist, like all other propensities,
without any determinate object: for when, at
the age of puberty, animal desire obtrudes itself
on a mind already qualified to feel and enjoy
the charms of intellectual merit, the imagination
immediately begins to form pictures of perfec-

tion by exaggerating and combining in one
hypothetic object every excellence, that can
possibly belong to the whole sex ; and the first
individual, that meets the eye, with any exterior
signs of any of these ideal excellences, is
immediately decorated with them all by the
creative magic of a vigorous and fertile fancy.
Hence she instantaneously becomes the object
of the most fervent affection, which is as instantaneously cooled by possession : for, as it
was not the object herself, but a false idea of her
raised in a heated imagination, that called forth
all the lover's raptures, all immediately vanish
at the detection of his delusion ; and a degree
of disgust proportioned to the disappointment,
of which it is the inevitable consequence, instantly, succeeds.—Thus it happens that what
are called love matches are seldom or never
happy.

61. Mere animal desire is a natural or physical affection of the mind, excited by corporeal
stimuli, and therefore existing, in a greater or
less degree, in every individual of the human
species, whose organization is complete : but
the sentiment of love, being a social passion
acquired by social and artificial habits, is never
felt at all by persons of very cold and phlegm-
atic tempers; nor by those, whose attention is
steadily fixed, or their minds deeply absorbed,
either in the active pursuits of worldly business,

or the silent meditations of abstract study.
Neither is it ever felt in any violent degree,
unless by persons, whose imaginations are naturally warm and vivid ; and who have, at the
same time, leisure to indulge, and society to
exercise them.   Such persons, when they have
no other pursuits, are always in love, from the
age of puberty to that of decrepitude ; so that
their whole lives may be said to be passed in a
perpetual renovation of hope, and a constant
succession of disappointment : for whether the
object prove attainable or not, disappointment
equally ensues, though in different ways.   No
real charms either of mind or body ever reach
the visionary perfections, which a lively and
glowing imagination stimulated by keen sensibility bestows on an admired object : and
though we may read, in poems and romances,
of chaste or unsuccessful love continuing during
long periods of years, and only ending with the
lives of the parties, it may reasonably be presumed that such love, if it ever existed at all,
partook more of the nature of a sophism, than
a sentiment ; and was rather a metaphysical
delusion of the understanding, than an energetic
affection of the soul.

62. Such appears to have been the love of
Petrarch, Cowley, Waller, and other such lovers
in verse ; whose quaint illustrations, analytical
definitions, and metaphysical explanations of

their passion abundantly prove that they never really felt it; but only chose it as a fashionable subject, on which to display their talents and obtain distinction.

63. There is another and very different description of erotic poets, who, combining the refinements of sentimental love, which they have acquired amidst the elegancies of the most polished society; with the manners of primæval simplicity, and the imagery of pastoral life, have called into being a race of mortals utterly unknown to nature; such as love-sick sentimental savages, shepherds, and ploughmen. Of this description are the cyclops and swains of the elegant Theocritus; who, bred in the polished city of Syracuse, and writing in the still more polished court of the second Ptolemy, gave a new character to his own delicate sentiments of love, by expressing them in the archaic simplicity of dialect, or with the native rusticity of imagery of Sicilian-peasants; and the novelty of that character, the simplicity of that dialect, and the beauty and gaiety of that imagery naturally rendered the sentiments expressed more pleasing and impressive: but, if any of the courtiers of Alexandria had gone among the mountains of Sicily in quest of a Thyrsis or Amaryllis, they would have felt the same disappointment, as a London cockney would feel, were he to seek, in the mountains of Scotland

S

or Wales, for such shepherds and shepherd-
esses, as he sees in an opera.

64. It has of late been very much the fashion
of the English as well as the French and German theatres, to bring examples of the most
pure heroic love, and disinterested sentimental
gallantry from the lowest-ranks of society—
from common soldiers, mendicants, robbers,
and slaves; and not only the courtiers and
cockneys of London and Paris, but scholars
and philosophers of the first eminence gave
themselves up to the delusion; which seems to
be not entirely cured even by the events of the
French revolution; though that has afforded
such abundant instances of the delicate sentiments and tender affections of men, whose
minds are neither exalted by situation, enlarged
by science, nor refined by culture. Narrow
sordid selfishness is, with few exceptions, the
universal principle of action in such men; and
not less so in the pursuits of love than in those
of interest or ambition. Personal beauty, as
an incentive to appetite, and a capacity for
labour and household management, are the
qualifications generally sought for: but as to
any of that refinement of mental affection or
sympathy of soul, which makes beauty an object
of more pure and exalted love in the higher
orders of society, it is, as far as I have been
able to observe, wholly unknown.

65. But to return to the proper subjects of the present inquiry; the art of sculpture is a much fairer and more impartial representer of beauty of form, than that of painting: for, as it exhibits form only, it can employ no tricks of light and shade to give preternatural distinctness to one part, or preternatural obscurity to ano-. ther; and, as its imitations are complete, as far as they extend, it can leave nothing to the imagination, nor employ any of that loose and sketchy brilliancy of execution, by which painting gives an artificial appearance of lightness to forms, which, in nature, always appear heavy.

66. The forms, therefore, both of the human figure and countenance, which are peculiarly appropriate to sculpture, are directly the reverse of the picturesque forms above mentioned; this art requiring exact symmetry in limb and body, muscles and joints strongly indicated, regular and distinct features, full lips, prominent brows, and curly elastic hair, more accurately divided into masses, than it ever is by the unassisted hand of nature. Even the most regular arrangement of it into locks and ringlets has been employed, by the great sculptors of antiquity, with the happiest effect, which it never could be in painting.

67. This character, though very different from any that is commonly esteemed beautiful, has, nevertheless, peculiar beauties for eyes

conversant with the fine productions of ancient sculpture: whence we may reasonably infer, that, had this art been as generally and familiarly understood, and as universally practised, as that of painting, we should probably have heard of a *sculpturesque*, as well as a *picturesque* *, since the one exists in nature just as much as the other; and my friend Mr. Price might have found another distinct character to occupy another place in his scale of taste, with those of the sublime, the picturesque and the beautiful. But the imitations of sculpture being less mannered, and more confined than those of painting; its process more slow and laborious; and its materials either costly, ponderous, or cumbersome; the taste for it has never been sufficiently diffused among the mass of mankind to give rise to a familiar metaphor.

68. One particular style of painting has, however, produced such a metaphor, and given

---

* We may write either *picturesque* and *sculpturesque*, from *pictura* and *sculptura*; or *pictoresque* and *sculptoresque*, from *pictor* and *sculptor*; the first signifying *after the manner of the arts*, and the latter *after the manner of the artists*. The latter is most strictly etymological; but as the word *pictor* has not been adopted into the English language, and the words *pictura* and *sculptura*, in an anglicised form, have, the former appears to be the most proper; and, in words not yet naturalized, propriety may be preferred to etymology.

O

its name to such descriptions of objects and such modes of composition, as appear to have some similitude to those, from which it sprang. Thus we often hear of *grottesque* figures, *grottesque* countenances, and *grottesque* groupes ; which, according to the system of my friend above mentioned, should be such as bear somewhat of the same relation to the *picturesque*, as he supposes the *picturesque* to bear to the *beautiful* : for the *grottesque* is certainly, a degree or two at least, further removed from the insipid smoothness and regularity of beauty, than he supposes the picturesque to be. In tracing, however, the word to its source, we find that *grottesque* means *after the manner of grottos,* as *picturesque* means *after the manner of painting.* The one is just as much a separate character as the other.

69. Indeed, if my friend will attentively look around him, his sagacity will readily discover many other distinct characters of the same kind, which he may employ, in any future editions of his work, **to** season the insipidity of beauty to any extent that pleases him ; and thus give it such various modes and degrees of relish, as must suit every appetite. A few of these, I shall here point out, as concisely as possible ; leaving the task of describing them more accurately, or applying them more systematically, to him, or any other person more competent than myself.

70. Ruined buildings, with fragments of
sculptured walls and broken columns, the
mouldering remnants of obsolete taste and
fallen magnificence, afford pleasure to every
learned beholder, imperceptible to the ignorant, and wholly independent of their real
beauty, or the pleasing impressions, which they
make on the organs of sight; more especially
when discovered in countries of ancient celebrity, renowned in history for learning, arts,
or empire. The mind is led by the view of
them into the most pleasing trains of ideas;
and the whole scenery around receives an accessory character; which is commonly called
classical; as the ideas, which it excites, associate themselves with those, which the mind
has previously received from the writings called
classic.

71. There is another species of scenery, in
which every object is wild, abrupt, and fantastic;—in which endless intricacies discover,
at every turn, something new and unexpected;
so that we are at once amused and surprised,
and curiosity is constantly gratified, but never
satiated. This sort of scenery we call *romantic*;
not only because it is similar to that usually
described in romances, but because it affords
the same kind of pleasure, as we feel from
the incidents usually related in such of them

CHAP.
II.
Of Imagina-
tion.

O 2

as are composed with sufficient skill to afford any pleasure at all.

72. In other scenes, we are delighted with neat and comfortable cottages, inhabited by a plain and simple, but not rude or vulgar peasantry; placed amidst cultivated, but not ornamented gardens, meads, and pastures, abounding in flocks and herds, refreshed by bubbling springs, and cooled by overhanging shade. Such scenery we call *pastoral*; and, though the impressions, which it makes upon the sense, be pleasing; yet this pleasure is greatly enhanced, to a mind conversant with pastoral poetry, by the association of the ideas excited with those previously formed.

73. In the same manner, marts thronged with the bustle of commerce, seaports crowded with shipping, plains enriched by culture and population, all afford pleasures to the learned and contemplative mind, wholly independent of the impressions, which the scenery makes upon the eye; though that, from its richness and variety, may be in the highest degree pleasing.

74. All these extra pleasures are from the minds of the spectators; whose pre-existing trains of ideas are revived, refreshed, and re-associated by new, but correspondent impressions on the organs of sense; and the great fundamental error, which prevails throughout

the otherwise able and elegant *Essays on the Picturesque,* is seeking for distinctions in external objects, which only exist in the modes and habits of viewing and considering them. The author had viewed nature, and examined art with the eye of a painter, the feelings of a poet, and the discernment of a critic: but not having been accustomed to investigate and discriminate the operations of mind, he unfortunately suffered himself to be misled by the brilliant, but absurd and superficial theories of the *Inquiry into the Sublime and Beautiful.* Show either picturesque, classical, romantic or pastoral scenery to a person, whose mind, how well soever organized, is wholly unprovided with correspondent ideas, and it will no otherwise affect him than as beautiful tints, forms, or varieties of light and shadow would, if seen in objects, which had nothing of either of these characters. Novelty will, indeed, make mountainous scenery peculiarly pleasing to the inhabitant of a plain; and richly cultivated scenery, to the inhabitant of a forest; and *vice versâ;* but this is upon another principle which will be hereafter explained.

All this, indeed, is admitted; and it is further stated that ugliness itself may be picturesque; and through the power of painting, be gazed on with delight by those, who have been accustomed to be charmed with it in the

imitative productions of that art*: an observation, which could not but have led its
author to the true cause and source of that
delight, had not the natural clearness of his
discernment been pre-occupied by a system :
for where objects in themselves ugly, that is,
displeasing to sight, become *pleasing objects
of sight,* to persons skilled in a particular art,
and to no others, by means of ideas derived
from that art, it surely did not require his
sagacity to perceive that the pleasure must
proceed from those ideas, and not from the necessary and inherent qualities of the objects †.

75. Man, both from his natural and social
habits, is so accustomed to respect order and
regularity, that it may properly be considered,

---

* Vol. I. p. 28, 231, 241, 404. Vol. I. pref. xiii. Vol. I.
p. 221.

† A set of northern critics defend this distinction of
picturesqueness by an auxiliary, which they create for
the purpose, and call by a name still less intelligible
and more uncouth, *unexpectedness.* Edinburgh Review,
N° XIV.

It would be amusing to hear them define, after the example which they illustrate, the particular modifications
of colour, shape, and size, under which this *distinct character* appears to those, who *do expect* the objects, to
which it is attributed: since if it really belong to the
objects, and not to the *minds of the observers,* it must
be equally perceptible to those who *do,* as to those who
do not expect them; unless indeed prescience destroy
perception, instead of rendering it more acute.

both physically and morally, as a principle of his existence. All our limbs and organs serve us in pairs, and by mutual co-operation with each other : whence the habitual association of ideas has taught us to consider this uni- formity as indispensable to the beauty and perfection of the animal form. There is no reason to be deduced from any abstract con- sideration of the nature of things why an animal should be more ugly and disgusting for having only one eye, or one ear, than for having only one nose or one mouth: yet if we were to meet with a beast with one eye, or two noses or mouths, in any part of the world, we should, without inquiry, decide it to be a monster, and turn from it with abhorrence : neither is there any reason, in the nature of things, why a strict parity, or relative equality, in the correspondent limbs and features of a man or a horse, should be absolutely essential to beauty, and absolutely destructive of it in the roots and branches of a tree. But, ne- vertheless, the Creator having formed the one regular, and the other irregular, we habitually associate ideas of regularity to the perfection of the one, and ideas of irregularity to the perfection of the other; and this habit has been so unvaried, as to have become natural.

76. Hence, though irregularity of appearance is generally essential to picturesque beauty, no

painter has ever thought of making a man or
animal more picturesque, by exhibiting them
with one leg shorter than the other, or one eye
smaller than the other; and, though men have
cut off the ears and tails of their horses, and
cropped their manes, to make them more beautiful, no one has ever thought of cutting off
only one ear, shearing the tail on one side, or
cropping the mane in one part and not in
another, in order to produce this effect. Nevertheless men do commit similar violations of
nature in the vegetable creation; and with the
happiest effect: for we often see trees of the
fir kind cropped and mutilated in order to
make them grow irregularly, and the beauty,
which they thus acquire, is universally felt and
acknowledged.

77. But it must be remembered that irregularity is the general characteristic of trees,
and regularity that of animals; so that the
mutilations, in one instance, tend to render a
single species more, and in the other less, conformable to its kind; and consequently, in the
one, to connect and extend, and in the other
to interrupt and destroy the association of
ideas. It must be remembered, also, that our
mental sympathies extend, in some degree, to
every thing, which seems to participate of
mind; or in any degree to possess the faculties
of feeling and thinking: whence the mutilation

of an animal, and that of a plant, excite very
different sentiments; and it is to be lamented,
for the honour of human nature, that these
sentiments are not still more different than they
appear, from the general practice of mankind,
to be.

78. The regular conformation of animals,
however, is rather perceived by the mind than
the eye : for there is no object, composed of
parts, either in nature or art, that can appear
regular to the eye, unless seen at right angles;
and this is the point of sight, which a painter
of any taste always studiously avoids : consequently, in his compositions, the forms of men
and animals, as well as those of trees, are irregular, in their appearance to the eye; at the
same time, that he takes care to represent
them, in such a manner, as to inform the mind,
that their conformation is according to the
laws of nature.   Even when the point of sight
is at right angles with the limbs of the figure,
the form will not appear regular to the eye,
unless each corresponding limb be exactly in
the same posture; and the position of the
whole be perpendicularly erect, with the weight
distributed, exactly in due proportions, on the
parts intended to bear it : still, however, the
painter has a resource; for if he should be
compelled, by the nature of his subject, to
introduce, into his composition, a figure in

this stiff and unpicturesque attitude, he can at
all times vary it, in the human form, by irregular, draperies; and, in horses and cattle, by
the casual and irregular movements of the
ears, the mane, and the tail. Of the features,
the eyes only, by the converging of their axes
in vision, are always uniform and concordant.
with each other in every expression; all deviation from it being, in a greater or less degree,
that morbid disposition called squinting. The
brows, the cheeks, and the lips assume irregular forms in expressing the passions, sentiments, and affections of the mind; and this
irregularity is varied, increased, or diminished
by the distribution of the hair adjoining the face,
which the artist may dispose as he chooses.

79. My friend, Mr. Price, indeed, admits
squinting among the irregular and picturesque
charms of the parson's daughter; whom (to
illustrate the picturesque in opposition to the
beautiful) he wishes to make appear lovely
and attractive, though without symmetry or
beauty *: He has not, however, extended the

* " The good old parson's daughter is made upon the
model of her father's house: her features are as irregular,
and her eyes are inclined to look across each other, like
the roofs of the old parsonage; but a clear skin, clean,
white teeth, though not very even, and a look of neatness and cheerfulness, in spite of these irregularities,
made me look at her with pleasure; and I really think,

10

details of this want of symmetry and regularity further than to the features of the face;
though to make the figure consistent and complete, the same happy mixture of the irregular
and picturesque must have prevailed through
her limbs and person; and consequently she
must have hobbled as well as squinted; and
had hips and shoulders as irregular as her
teeth, cheeks, and eyebrows. All my friend's
parental fondness for his system is certainly
necessary to make him think such an assemblage of picturesque circumstances either lovely
or attractive; or induce him to imagine, that
he should be content with such a creature, as

if I were of the cloth, I should like very well to take the
living, the house, and its inhabitant." Dialog. p. 135.—
" Here is a house and a woman without symmetry or
beauty; and yet many might prefer them both to such as
had infinitely more of what they and the world would
acknowledge to be regularly beautiful." Ib. p. 136.

It is presumed that, by *symmetry, conformity* is here
meant: for symmetry is the mutual proportion of com-
mensurate parts; and in all animals nature has fixt
certain relative proportions for each kind and species,
according to the perfection or imperfection of which,
each individual of that kind or species is more or less
perfect: but an individual wholly without such proportion, that is, without symmetry, can only be a monster.

A building, indeed, being a work of mere art and
invention, can have no natural proportions; and may
therefore, as before observed, be rendered pleasing, both
to the eye and imagination, by contrast, without symmetry in its correlative parts.

a companion for life; and I heartily congratulate him ,that this fondness did not arise .at
an earlier period, to obstruct him in a very
different choice. Indeed, he seems to have
still some remains of his former prejudices
lurking about him : for he soon after uses the
epithets beautiful and lovely, as synonymous;
and defines the one by the other, in spite of
all his philosophy of the picturesque *.

80. This philosophy has, I confess, long
puzzled me, in spite of the many discussions,
which we have had to explain it. A single
sentence, however, in his last publication, has
given me a complete key to it. " All these
ideas," says an interlocutor, who, on this occasion, sustains his own part in his dialogue,
" are originally acquired by the touch ; but
from use they are become as much objects of
sight as colours †," When there is so little
discrimination between the operations of mind
and the objects of sense, that ideas become
objects of sight, all the rest follows of course ;
and the different classes of beauty may be
divided into as many distinct characters, as
there are distinct ideas ; and be still progres-
sively augmented with the augmentation of
science, and extension of art. Beauty may

---

* " The most beautiful, that is, the most lovely,"
Dialog. p. 149.

† Dialog. p. 107.

also, in one page, be synonymous with love-
linesss; and yet, in another, loveliness may
exist without beauty or symmetry, by means
of certain qualities, which are analogous to
beauty; such as a clear skin, and clean white
teeth *. These, however, in every other part
of the work, are considered as real and positive beauties, not depending upon habit, as
Sir Joshua Reynolds has supposed them to
be; and as the facts, before cited, prove them
to be †. When a squinting woman, however,
without symmetry or beauty, was to be invested
with a sufficient portion of sexual charms to
render her capable of exciting affection and
desire, those charms suddenly become *qualities
analogous to beauty*; and, in this disguised
and undefinable form, are slipped into a composition, with which they would otherwise have
been found incompatible.

81. I do not mean, however, to deny that a
woman, with even greater personal defects
than either hobbling or squinting, may, by the
influence of sexual and social sympathies, be

---

* Dialog. p. 107. Essays, vol. i. p. 126, &c. In all these
passages, my friend equally mistakes ideas for things;
and the effects of internal sympathies, for those of external circumstances; as he does through both his preceding volumes; and thence grounds the best practical
lessons of taste upon false principles, and false philosophy.

† See Part I. c. iii. f. 4. and c. v. f. 24.

extremely interesting and attractive. The lovely and amiable Duchess of La Valiere is said, not only to have had bad teeth, but also, in consequence of an accident in her childhood, to have limped or hobbled in her gait; which, nevertheless, *seemed* to add to, rather than take away from the graces of her person *. Probably, however, it *seemed* so only to those, who, like her royal lover, were predisposed, by the influence of those graces, to approve every thing that she did : for this passion of love, how blind soever it may be, can at all times discover charms and graces, where ordinary discernment can only see faults and defects †. Imitative art separates these faults and defects from the magic, which recommends them in real life : for figures in stone or on canvass, excite too little either of social or sexual sympathy to engage the feelings of the man in support of the theories of the philosopher. The irregular movements of

---

* " Elle boitoit un peu, mais il sembloit, qu'au lieu de nuire, ce defaut ajoutoit à ses grâces."—Fragm. de Lett. de Madame, &c.

" Illuc prævertamur, amatorem quod amicæ
Turpia decipiunt cæcum vitia, aut etiam ipsa hæc
Delectant." , HORAT. Serm. l. i. f. iii. v. 38.

† ——————— η γαρ ερωτι
πολλακις, ω Πολυφαμε, τα μη καλα καλα πεφανται.
TIIEOCRIT. Idyl. vi. 18.

the monarch's lovely mistress, or the irregular
looks of the parson's blooming daughter, may
have been very charming to those, who were
predisposed by other charming qualities of tint,
form, or expression, to be pleased with them;
and as these irregular charms belong neither
to the sublime nor the beautiful, my friend,
consistently with his system, seeks for them in
his general intermediate repository of the picturesque; though they are not at all after the
manner of painting.   Other philosophers have
sought for them in the minds of the spectators,
where, I believe, all the charm will ultimately
be found.

But, though all these distinctions be but
mental or ideal modifications for different
classes of visible objects, which cannot be
classed by any characteristic distinctions inherent in themselves, I am not aware that any
thing, that I have ever written or said on the
subject, can fairly be construed to imply that
I ever considered the words *beautiful* and *picturesque* to be synonymous or convertible terms,
as has been supposed.   In the " *Essays on the
Picturesque,*" indeed, it is merely stated *that
there are persons, who, in reality, hold the
two words to be synonymous; though they do
not say so in express terms; and others, who
allow that the words have a different meaning,
but that there is no distinct character of the*

picturesque*. Of this latter sect I have always *meant* to profess myself; and even if I have expressed that meaning so ill, as to give just cause for being placed in the other, I cannot but think that the interlocutor in the dialogue, who makes me, *in express terms,* say *that there is no distinction between them : in other words, that they are, in respect to visible objects, synonymous†*, adopts rather an inquisitorial mode of proceeding; which howsoever sanctioned by authority in the trials of heretics, has not yet been acknowledged in the courts of philosophy, or by the judicature of common sense.

82. To express that perfect serenity of mind, which was attributed to deities, and deified personages, the ancient artists exhibited the features perfectly regular ; and made one side of the face an exact counterpart of the other : but, where passion or affection is expressed, they are always varied, as in nature. In the infancy of art, the figure was always represented with its weight equally poised upon both legs; so that its position was regularly and rigidly erect. The Ægyptians, with that superstitious reverence for established customs, which distinguished them in every thing, adhered to this mode down to the latest times ; but the

* Vol I. p. 229.　　† P. 182.

Greeks departed from it, even in the figures of
their deities, as early as the age of Polycletus[*],
and probably much earlier in subjects, which
allowed the artists more liberty. Then the
weight of the body, in standing figures, was
thrown almost entirely upon one leg, by which
means the muscles were, in some parts dilated,
and in others, contracted; and the whole outline of the figure became loose and irregular.

88. Hence arose that ease, grace, elegance,
and dignity of attitude and gesture, which we
so much admire in the Greek statues: not that
these qualities consist in any lines of beauty, or
depend upon the impressions, which any specific
forms make on the organs of sight. On the
contrary, they arise wholly from mental sympathies and the association of ideas: wherefore
the forms which appear easy, graceful, elegant,
or dignified in a horse, are totally different from
those which appear so in a man; and even, in
the same individual man or woman, the forms,
presented to the eye, vary with every change in
the fashion of dress: but nevertheless a graceful, easy, elegant, and dignified actor or actress,

---

[*] Plin. lib. xxxiv. c. viii. He says generally " pro-
prium ejusdem, ut uno crure insisterent signa, exco-
gitasse." But from figures upon coins I cannot but think
that this style of composition prevailed long before the
eighty-seventh Olympiad, the time when Polycletus
flourished.

P

will still seem so; whatever be the dress, which
the custom of the stage may oblige them to
assume.—Not, indeed, that they will appear
equally so in all: for some modes of dress show
the person to advantage and others to disad-
vantage; but still we find no difficulty in distinguishing the easy and graceful, from the stiff
and awkward, through every disguise or con-
cealment of the natural form.

84. The case is, that there are certain postures, in which the body naturally throws itself,
and certain gestures, which it naturally displays,
when under the influence of certain passions
and dispositions of mind; so that, from our own
internal feelings and sentiments, we learn to
associate the ideas or notions of certain tempers
and characters of mind, with those of certain
attitudes and modes of carriage of the body;
which are, therefore, said to express those tempers and characters; as the features of the face
do more immediately and unequivocally: for
the communication of sentiments from one
person to another by the expression of the features, as well as by the tones of the voice, is,
as before observed, by a natural and instinctive
sympathy, anterior to, and, in a great measure,
independent of the association of ideas.

85. Upon this principle, dignity of attitude
is that disposition of the limbs and person,
which, from habitual observation of ourselves

or others, we have learned to consider as expressive of a dignified and elevated mind; while
grace and elegance of form are those dispositions and combinations of it, which, upon the
same principle, seem to express refinement of
intellect, polish of manners, or pleasantness of
temper : for, though we apply the words grace
and elegance to inanimate objects, it is always
metaphorically and by analogy; as we talk of
lightness and heaviness of form, at the same
time that we know that gravitation has nothing
to do with form, but depends entirely on substance.

86. Hence it is, that while our ideas of
dignity of attitude and gesture have always
continued nearly the same, those of grace and
elegance have been in a perpetual state of
change and fluctuation: for our notions of
what is *mean*, and what is *elevated*, depend
upon the natural and permanent sentiments of
the soul; but those of what is refined or polished ; and pleasant, or the contrary, depend much
upon artificial manners, which are incessantly
varying. Not, however, that I would infer that
there are no certain and natural principles of
grace and elegance : for there are, unquestionably, certain and natural principles of good
manners, arising from natural mildness, amenity, and pleasantness of disposition, which
some particular attitudes and gestures of the

body are, by the laws of its physical constitution, more appropriate, than others, to express:
but these are liable to the influence of artificial
habits, and the arbitrary caprice of fashion; of
which we have seen very remarkable instances
in our own times. It is but a few years since,
the first principle of grace in French dancing
was, that the body should not feel the movement
of the limbs, but remain like an inflexible pillar
or barrel, unaffected by all the violent contor-
tions and distortions of the legs and arms, which
grew out of it: yet if there be any one principle
of grace more certain than another, it is that of
a general harmony of movement and gesture
through the whole body; which is, indeed,
equally necessary to all expression: for if the
same sentiment does not appear to predominate
through the whole frame, and to influence every
part of it alike, the effect must be very feeble
and imperfect. To throw the limbs into extravagant and unnatural postures, or move them
with great violence and rapidity, while the body
remains motionless and erect, may show great
skill and agility; which, if displayed with ease,
may be mistaken for grace; but, nevertheless, if
it means nothing, it is mere trick; and trick of
the most despicable kind.

87. Dancing is mentioned by Aristotle as an
imitative art, whose business was to express the
sentiments and affections of the mind, by the

10

attitudes and gestures of the body, in the most pleasing and intelligible manner *; and this character, it has lately begun to assume again, though probably in a very inferior degree: for the distortions of tumbling still continue to be mixed with the graces of pantomime; and, as they appear difficult, the mass of mankind will probably continue to be pleased with them, for the same reason that they are more pleased with an optical deception, than with a picture of Titian. Every thing that excites wonder pleases; and the pleasure, which it affords, is of a kind that every individual of the human race can relish: but just and natural expression of refined or elevated sentiments, can only excite sympathy in those who have felt them.

88. It has been observed by travellers that the attitudes and gestures of savages, particularly those of high rank among them, are extremely dignified and graceful; which arises from their being unperverted and unrestrained, and therefore expressing naturally and emphatically the sentiments of the mind; which, in men who have obtained their rank, as men always do in the early stages of civil society, by

---

* Poetic. f. iii. Several kinds of the military dramatic dances of the Greeks are described by Xenophon; as performed by those under his command, on their return from the expedition against the King of Persia. ἈναϚ. lib. vi. c. i.

their talents and courage, will of course be bold
and elevated, if not polished and refined.

89. In the fine age of the arts in Greece,
civilization had just arrived to that state, in
which the manners of men are polished, but
yet natural; and consequently their attitudes
and gestures expressive and emphatical, without ever being coarse or violent. All the more
noble and amiable sentiments of the mind were
indicated by the correspondent expressions of
the countenance and body; while those of a
degrading and unsocial east were suppressed
and concealed : their modes of dress too, having
been adapted to display to advantage the natural
motions and gestures of the body, and not to
constrain, disguise, or conceal them, like those
of modern Europe, the artists had constantly
before their eyes every possible variety of
models in which expressions of grace, elegance,
and dignity were displayed in every possible
mode and degree.   In the gymnastic festivals
too, where men of high rank and liberal education entered into contests of personal strength
and agility, they had opportunities of seeing
these models exhibited without reserve, not
only in every accidental variation of attitude
and position, but in every mode and degree of
muscular effort and exertion.

90. By studying and imitating these, and not
by applying to any abstract rules or predeter-

minate lines of grace, elegance, or beauty, the
great sculptors of Greece appear to me to have
produced those master-pieces, which have been
the admiration of all subsequent ages and generations of civilized men: for as to lines, I know
of none, that may not be graceful, elegant, and
beautiful in proper circumstances and situations, and none that are not the reverse when
employed improperly *. This just application of
them, just feeling alone can determine : for
those who have attempted to regulate it by
system, have only set up system against sentiment ; and thus co-operated with the caprices
of novelty and fashion in diffusing false taste
through the world :—zigzag walks, serpentine
canals, spiral columns, broken or scooped pediments, have all sprung from this systematic line
of beauty, and, for some periods, triumphed
over the common sense and common feelings
of mankind.

91. In architecture, indeed, this sacrifice of
feeling to system has been less prevalent, than
in other arts; which, being less immediately

* Mr. Loudon, on Landscape Gardening, has exemplified Mr. Price's distinctions of the *beautiful*, the *picturesque*, the *deformed*, the *ugly*, and the *grand*, by engraved
outlines of each respectively. My friend will scarcely
thank him for any such illustrations; which, whatever
form they assume, will be as fatal to his hypothesis as
daylight to a groupe of spectres.

appropriated to the uses of common life, were
less under the influence of common sense: for
though spiral columns, and scooped pediments,
were for a time in fashion, it was more with
painters than with architects; and painters, as
before observed, have reasons, peculiarly belonging to their own art, for preferring them.
Undulating walls and serpentine balustrades
have no where, that I know of, been in use;
nor have I seen or heard of curved roofs on this
side of China, except in imitations introduced
into this country principally by a person, who
gave equal proofs of the purity of his taste
when he censured the temples of Athens, and
designed those of Kew.

92. Architecture, indeed, has been rather
too cautious and timid, than too bold in its
exertions; having never, as my friend Mr.
Price has observed, completely emancipated
itself from the regular confined lines of the
street and the square, which its first ornamental
productions were calculated to adorn. In such
situations, common congruity required that the
whole should be bounded by parallel lines, and
that all the subordinate parts should correspond
with each other, so that the general mass might
be one and entire; and, as the points, from
which it could be seen, were limited in their
extent and distance, this uniformity could every
where be perceived at a glance: but why the

same system should be carried into the country,-
amidst forests, lawns, and mountains, it is not
easy to guess.   A certain degree of regularity,
indeed, such as that very subordinate parts, oc-
cupying the same situations, and serving the
same purposes, as columns, capitals, mouldings,
&c. should be of the same form, common
sense requires ; since, in such instances, no
reason could be given for deviation : but that
the principal parts should all be regular, and
correspond with each other, in situations, where
all the accompaniments are irregular, and none
of them corresponding with each other, seems
to me the extreme of absurdity and incongruity.

9.3. By the old system of laying out ground,
indeed, this incongruity was, in a great degree,
obviated : for the house being surrounded by
gardens, as uniform as itself, and only seen
through vistas at right angles, every visible
accompaniment was in unison with it; and the
systematic regularity of the whole discernible
from every point of sight : but when, according
to the modern fashion, all around is levelled
and thrown open ; and the poor square edifice
exposed alone, or with the accompaniment only
of its regular wings and portico, amidst spacious
lawns interspersed with irregular clumps, or
masses of wood, and sheets of water, I do not
know a more melancholy object : it neither

associates nor harmonizes with any thing; and, as the beauties of symmetry, which might appear in its regularity, are only perceived when that regularity is seen; that is, when the building is shown from a point of sight at right angles with one of the fronts, the man of taste takes care that it never shall be so shown; but that every view of it shall be oblique, from the tangent of a curve in a serpentine walk; from whence it appears neither quite regular, nor quite irregular; but with that sort of lame and defective uniformity, which we see in an animal that has lost a limb.

94. The view from one of these solitary mansions is still more dismal than that towards it: for, at the hall door, a boundless extent of open lawn presents itself in every direction, which the despairing visitant must traverse, before he can get into any change of scenery: and, to complete the congruity of the whole, the clumps, with which this monotonous tract is dotted, and the winding stream or canal, by which it is intersected, are made as neat and determinate as ever the ancient gardens were; which having been professedly a work of art, and an append-age to the house, the neatness and even formality of architecture were its proper characteristics; and when its terraces and borders were intermixed with vines and flowers (as I have seen them in Italian villas, and in some old

English gardens in the same style) the mixture of splendor, richness, and neatness, was beautiful and pleasing in the highest degree. But the modern art of landscape gardening, as it is called, takes away all natural enrichment, and adds none of its own; unless, indeed, meagre or formal clumps of trees, and still more formal patches of shrubs, may be called enrichment. Why this art has been called landscape gardening, perhaps he, who gave it the title, may explain :—I can see no reason, unless it be the efficacy, which it has shown in destroying landscapes, in which, indeed, it seems to be infallible; not one complete painter's composition being, I believe, to be found in any of the numerous, and many of them beautiful and picturesque spots, which it has visited in different parts of this island.*

* In answer to this, we are gravely told by an eminent Professor, that he alone has made three thousand such compositions, and published between two and three hundred of them, the extensive sale of which proves public opinion to be very different from mine. (Enquiry, &c. by H. Repton, Esq. p. 121.) These are not however, he admits, painters' landscapes; but things *sui generis*, certain non-descripts, named after the art because utterly incompatible with it, as *lucus a non lucendo ;* and adapted to the taste of another species of non-descript, called in true British Latin, *elegantiæ formarum spectator.* (p. 3. 122. &c.) *Elegans formarum spectator* had before been heard of in Roman Latin.

95. The practice, which was so prevalent in the beginning of this century, of placing the mansion-house between two correspondent wings, in which were contained the offices, has of late fallen into disuse; and one still more adverse to composition succeeded;

Had I read the work, which I am accused of pillaging, (p. 118.) I should candidly have acknowledged every debt, which casual coincidence of opinion might seem to have incurred: though, when an author favours the public with such profound remarks as, " *that a building should not be larger than its situation will admit;*" and " *that a house would not be habitable unless the ground sloped sufficiently to drain off the water from it;*" (both supplied by a single page, 87) he ought not surely to pronounce every such coincidence a plagiarism, nor triumph in the concession of what was never disputed.

As for my own principles and practice, I beg to assure Mr. Repton that they still continue unaltered; though many points are here introduced, which, not belonging peculiarly to landscape, were not noticed in a work on that subject. Consistently with those principles, and that practice, I choose to retain, what offends him so much, cross roads and directing posts within 200 yards of my house, rather than sacrifice, as he has done in so many instances, all the charms of retirement, intricacy, and variety, to the vanity of a splendid approach, or the ostentation of undivided property. I also continue to prefer the enrichments of my fore-grounds, composed of fragments of rock, trailing plants, flowering shrubs, and trees, to the groupes of cattle in his drawings; which, though harmless and quiet on paper, are very apt, in nature, to destroy all other enrichment, and to show themselves in every place, but where they are wanted.

namely, that of entirely hiding the offices
behind masses of plantation, and leaving the
wretched square solitary mansion-house to
exhibit its pert bald front between the dwarf
shrubberies, which seem like whiskers added to
the portico or entrance. To break its formality with large trees is impossible ; for as it has
no parts, but consists of one uniform square
mass, not an angle of it can be shown without
the stiff and bald formality of the whole being
discovered. Had the offices been shown with
it, in subordinate ranges of less elevated building, though the forms had individually been
bad, yet by dividing and grouping them with
trees, pleasing effects of composition might
have been produced ; at once to gratify the eye
with some varieties of tint and light and shadow, and to amuse the imagination with some
appearance of intricacy. Where they are only
masked by shrubberies, this may still be done ;
but unfortunately they are often concealed in
recesses, or behind mounds ; the improver
generally picking out the most retired intricate
and beautiful spot, that can be found near the
house, to bury them in.

96· When that is the case, I know of no
remedy but the hanging terraces of the Italian
gardens ; which, if the house be placed upon
an eminence, with sloping ground before it,
may be employed with very good effect ; as

they not only enrich the foreground, but serve as a basement for the house to stand upon, which at once gives it importance, and supplies it with accompaniments. Such decorations are, indeed, now rather old fashioned; but another revolution in taste, which is probably at no great distance, will make them new again.

97. Some few attempts have lately been made to adapt the exterior forms of country-houses to the various character of the surrounding scenery, by spreading them out into irregular masses: but as our ideas of irregularity, in buildings of this kind, have been habitually associated with those of the barbarous structures of the middle ages, a mistaken notion of congruity has induced us to exclude from them, every species of ornament, or scale of proportion, not authorized by the rude and unskilful monuments of those times: as if that, which is, at once, convenient and elegant, needed any authority to justify its use; or a house, that is picturesque without, must, from a principle of congruity, be heavy, clumsy, and gloomy within. It has already been observed that the architecture of the Gothic castles, as they are called, is of Grecian or Roman origin: but, if it were not, there could be no impropriety in employing the elegancies of Grecian taste and science, either in the external forms and proportions, or interior decorations of houses built in that

style: for, surely, there can be no blamable inconsistency in uniting the different improvements of different ages and countries in the same object; provided they are really improvements, and contribute to render it perfect.

98. It is now more than thirty years since the author of this inquiry ventured to build a house, ornamented with what are called Gothic towers and battlements·without, and with Grecian ceilings, columns, and entablatures within; and though his example has not been much followed, he has every reason to congratulate himself upon the success of the experiment; he having at once, the advantage of a picturesque object, and of an elegant and convenient dwelling; though less perfect in both respects than if he had executed it at a maturer age. It has, however, the advantage of being capable of receiving alterations and additions in almost any direction, without any injury to its genuine and original character.

99. In all marked deviations from the ordinary style of the age and country, in which we live, the great difficulty is to avoid the appearance of trick and affectation; which seem to be, in some degree, inseparable from buildings made in imitation of any obsolete or unusual style: for, as the execution, as well as the design of almost every age and country, has a particular character, these imitations are

scarcely ever in perfect harmony and congruity throughout; but generally proclaim
themselves, at first sight, to be mere counter-
feits; which, how beautiful soever to the eye,
necessarily excite unpleasant ideas in the mind.
A house may be adorned with towers and battlements, or pinnacles and flying buttresses;
but it should still maintain the character of a
house of the age and country in which it is
erected; and not. pretend to be a fortress or
monastery of a remote period or distant country: for such false pretensions never escape
detection; and, when detected, necessarily excite those sentiments, which exposed imposture never fails to excite.

100. Rustic lodges to parks, dressed cottages,
pastoral seats, gates, and gateways, made of
unhewn branches and stems of trees, have all
necessarily a still stronger character of affectation; the rusticity of the first being that of a
clown in a pantomime, and the simplicity of the
others, that of a shepherdess in a French opera.
The real character of every object of this kind
must necessarily conform to the use, to which
it is really appropriated; and if attempts be
made to give it any other character, it will
prove, in .fact, to be only a character of imposture: for to adapt the genuine style of a herds-
man's hut, or a ploughman's cottage, to the
dwellings of opulence and luxury, is as utterly

impossible, as it is to adapt their language, dress, and manners to the refined usages of polished society.

101. The best style of architecture for irregular and picturesque houses, which can now be adopted, is that mixed style, which characterizes the buildings of Claude and the Poussins : for as it is taken from models, which were built piece-meal, during many successive ages ; and by several different nations, it is distinguished by no particular manner of execution, or class of ornaments ; but admits of all promiscuously, from a plain wall or buttress, of the roughest masonry, to the most highly wrought Corinthian capital : and, in a style professedly miscellaneous, such contrasts may be employed to heighten the relish of beauty, without disturbing the enjoyment of it by any appearance of deceit or imposture. In a matter, however, which affords so wide a field for the licentious deviations of whim and caprice, it may be discreet always to pay some attention to authority ; especially when we have such authorities as those of the great landscape painters above mentioned ; the study of whose works may at once enrich and restrain invention.

102. In choosing a situation for a house of this kind, which is to be a principal feature in a place, more consideration ought to be had of

Q

the views towards it, than of those fromwards
it : for, consistently with comfort, which ought
to be the first object in every dwelling, it very
rarely happens that a perfect composition of
landscape scenery can be obtained from a door
or window ; nor does it appear to me particularly desirable that it should be; for few persons
ever look for such compositions, or pay much
attention to them, while within doors. It is in
walks or rides through parks, gardens, or pleasure grounds, that they are attended to and
examined, and become subjects of conversation;
wherefore the seats, or places of rest, with which
such walks and rides are accommodated, are
the points of sight, to which the compositions
of the scenery ought to be principally adapted.
To them, picturesque foregrounds may always
be made or preserved, without any loss of
comfort or violation of propriety : for that sort
of trim neatness, which both require in grounds
immediately adjoining a house, is completely
misplaced, when employed on the borders of a
ride or walk through a park or plantation. If
the house be the principal object or feature of
the scene from these points of view, the middle
ground will be the properest situation for it;
as will clearly appear from the landscapes of
the painters above cited : this is also the situation, which considerations of domestic comfort
will generally point out; as being the middle

5

degree of elevation, between the too exposed ridges of the hills, and the too secluded recesses of the vallies. In any position, however, above the point, of sight, such objects may be happily placed ; and contribute to the embellishment of the adjoining scenery: but there are scarcely any buildings, except bridges, which will bear being looked down upon ; a foreshortening from the roof to the base being necessarily awkward and ungraceful.

103. Sir John Vanbrugh is the only archi-tect, I know of, who has either planned or placed his houses according to the principle here recommended; and, in his two chief works, Blenheim and Castle Howard, it appears to have been strictly adhered to, at least in the placing of them. The views from the principal fronts of both are bad, and much inferior to what other parts of the grounds would have afforded; but the situations of both, as objects to the surrounding scenery, are the best that could have been chosen ; and both are certainly worthy of the best situations, which, not only the respective places, but the island of Great Britain could afford.

104. The direct reverse may be said of the late Mr. Brown; who, in the only place, in which he was employed both as architect and improver, with unlimited powers of design and expence in both, has built a house, which no

situation could adapt to any scenery, except that of a square or a street; and placed it where no house could have served as an embellishment to the scenery, which does surround it. Such ever has and ever will be the difference between the works of artists of genius, who consult their feelings, and those of plodding mechanics, who look only to their rules. The former will necessarily be unequal and irregular; and produce much to blame and ridicule, as well as much to applaud and admire; whereas the latter, howsoever extolled by the fashions of the day, will never rise above negative merit.

Το δε φυα, κρατιστον απαν.
Πολλοι δε διδακταις
ανθρωπων αρεταις κλεος
ωρυσαν ελεσθαι.
ανευ δε θευ, σεσιγα-
-μενον γυ σκαιοτερον χρη-
-μ' εκαστον.

PINDAR. Olym. θ. 152.

105. Among the accompaniments of a house, considered as an object in a landscape, water is one of the most important; and one, which, in this humid climate, may almost every where be obtained, if the situation be chosen with tolerable skill and judgment: but in most of the artificial pieces of water that I have seen, an ill-judged affectation of copying simple

nature has destroyed all appearance of nature
or simplicity; together with all beauty or picturesque effect. An artificial pool or lake may
be made exactly to imitate a natural or accidental one; and, if it be diversified with
broken and uneven banks, bays, promontories
and islands, according to the directions given
by Mr. Price in his excellent essay on the subject, it may form one of the most beautiful
features in the composition of a landscape.
But this has never satisfied improvers : their
ambition has always been to make artificial
rivers; and thus to imitate that which is, in
reality, inimitable : for, without running water,
the river can be but a mere canal. Even, if
the curling, rippling, and foaming of the water,
which constitute the principal beauties of natural rivers, could be dispensed with, no con-
trivance of art, nor exertion of labour, can
ever mould the banks into that endless variety
of picturesque forms, into which they are hol-
lowed and broken by the various eddies and
falls of a running stream. An artificial river,
therefore, even if it could be made beautiful
to the eye, will always be an impostor, whose
false pretensions will offend the mind. A
natural brook, on the contrary, be it ever so
small, may be extremely beautiful in a confined situation; and where the ground admits
of its expansion, it may be made to issue from,

or terminate in a lake or pool, with extremely
happy effect: but if ever an attempt is made
to turn it into a river by widening it and dam-
ming it up, it is utterly ruined.

106. In every other attempt of art to counterfeit the operations of nature or effects of
accident, it ought to be equally cautious in
proceeding no further than it is certain of
success, as the detection of imposture always
renders it odious and disgusting. If a comfortable and convenient walk or ride can be so,
conducted through wood, or forest scenery, as
to appear a mere sheep-track, or accidental
opening, it will be the more pleasing to the
imagination: but if it is to go along the sides
of banks, or other grounds, so formed, that a
convenient road must necessarily be a work
of labour and art, it had better avow its character boldly; and stand forth as an artificial
terrace or shelf, than bunglingly attempt to
hide it in the broken banks and unequal sides
of an accidental slip: for such breaks and
inequalities, if natural or accidental, would
also extend to the surface, and completely dis-
qualify it for the use, to which it is appropriated. Where the ground is rocky, indeed,
rugged and unequal banks may be obtained
by breaking instead of hewing the stone to be
removed; and this may almost always be done
with good effect: but if the terrace or walk be

to be formed out of mere earth, irregularities and inequalities will always appear either affected or slovenly.

107. It has already been shown that small‑ness of size does not contribute to make objects more beautiful; so far as beauty is a quality pleasing to the sense only; and I think it is easy to show that it contributes as little to that which addresses itself to the imagination.   It is true, as the author of the Inquiry into the Sublime and Beautiful observes, that we often speak of a *pretty little thing*, and of a *great ugly thing* *; but we also speak of a *large handsome woman*, a *large handsome horse*, and a *large handsome house*; and surely *hand‑some* means beautiful as well as *pretty*.   It is true likewise, as the same author observes, that diminutives in all languages are terms of endearment; but that is because they are the terms naturally applied by parents to their children; whence ideas of parental affection are always associated with them; which being the first and the strongest of our merely mental affections, the terms that express it are meta‑phorically applied to other objects; for which we feel any affection similar either in its mode or degree: but if we join the diminutive to a term, which precludes all such affection; or

* Part III. f. xiii,

Q 4

does not even, in some degree, express it, it immediately converts it into a term of contempt, and reproach: thus a bantling, a fondling, a darling, &c. are terms of endearment; but a witling, a changeling, a lordling, &c. are invariably terms of scorn: so in French, *mon petit enfant* is an expression of endearment; but *mon petit monsieur* is an expression of the most pointed reproach and contempt.

108. The marital affection of a man for a woman partakes of the nature of parental affection; as that of the woman for the man does of filial; whence the terms of endearment would naturally be transferred from the one to the other: that yielding delicacy too, which constitutes the principal charm of the female character, as it is nearly allied to comparative weakness, so is it, in some degree, allied to comparative littleness of person; which may therefore be considered as an ingredient of feminine attractions, though it has nothing whatever to do with abstract beauty of form; which, as Aristotle observes, is limited only within those degrees of magnitude which bound the field of vision in one extreme, and preclude distinct discrimination of the parts in the other *. Between these, all degrees of

---

* ὅτε παμμικρον αν τι γενοιτο καλον ζωον' ὅτε παμμεγεθες. ὥστε δει, καθαπερ επι των σωματων, και επι των ζωων, εχειν μεν μεγεθος, τουτο δε ευσυνοπτον ειναι.—ARISTOT. POET. f. xvi.

magnitude contribute to beauty in proportion as they show objects to be perfect in their kind. The dimensions of a beautiful horse are very different from those of a beautiful lapdog; and those of a beautiful oak, from those of a beautiful myrtle; because nature has formed these different kinds of animals and vegetables upon different scales; and that degree of magnitude in each individual, which approaches nearest to that of the mean proportion of the species or variety, to which it belongs, is the best adapted to beauty. Great things may be more ugly than small, because deformity will be prominent and conspicuous, in proportion to the scale upon which it is exhibited; and also because the scale of deviation is, in every thing, more extensive than that of coincidence or congruity; there being always many ways of going wrong, where there is but one of going right.

109. The notion of objects being rendered beautiful by being gradually diminished, or tapered, is equally unfounded; for the same object, which is *small by degrees, and beautifully less*, when seen in one direction, is *large by degrees, and beautifully bigger*, when seen in another. The stems of trees are tapered upwards; and the columns of Grecian architecture, having been taken from them, and therefore retaining a degree of

analogy with them, were tapered upwards too:
but the legs of animals are tapered downwards; and the inverted obelisks, upon which
busts were placed, having a similar analogy to
them, were tapered downwards also; whilst
pilasters, which had no analogy with either,
but were mere square posts terminating a
wall, were never tapered at all. Precise rules
and definitions, in matters of this sort, are
merely the playthings or tools of system-
builders; who might just as reasonably amuse
themselves with the philosopher of Logado,
in finding out the mean proportion between
the annual and diurnal revolutions of the sun,
and the accidental variations of the wind, in
order to fix a sun-dial upon the weathercock
of the town-house: indeed, in all matters of
taste and criticism, general rules appear to me
to be, like general theories in government and
politics, never safe but where they are useless; that is, in cases previously proved by
experience.

110. A rule implies a general negation;
and so limited and uncertain is human knowledge, in all subjects of this kind, that it never
can reach every possible case, nor make any
general assertion, which will not be liable to
many exceptions. The business of poetry, as
well as of painting, sculpture, and gardening,
is to please; and though we may analyze the

principles of mental, as well as of corporeal
pleasures, we can never discover the full extent of their operation, nor consequently establish any general rules for their limitation.
The pleasures of imagination, in particular,
have been varied and augmented in every succeeding age of civilized society; and we know
not how much further they may yet be varied
and augmented.

111. Critics have done nearly the same in
taste, as casuists have in morals; both having
attempted to direct, by rules, and limit by
definitions, matters, which depend entirely on
feeling and sentiment; and which are therefore so various and extensive ; and diversified
by such nice, and infinitely graduated shades
of difference, that they elude all the subtilties
of logic, or intricacies of calculation. Rules
can never be made so general, as to comprehend every possible case, nor definitions so
multifarious and exact, as to include every
possible circumstance or contingency. *To do
unto others as we would have others do unto
us,* is, perhaps, one of the best general axioms
of morality, that ever was uttered : but, nevertheless, it is not without exceptions ; for vicious persons may wish others to assist them
in wicked actions, and do that to them, which
would aggravate, instead of justifying, the
wickedness of their doing the same to others.

Neither is the emendation, that has been pro-posed, I think by Dr. Johnson, *of doing that justice to others, which we would have others do unto us,* much more perfect; for if a good man confine his beneficence to that justice, which his modesty might induce him to require from others, his goodness will be of a very negative kind.

112. Perhaps the safest general axiom, that can be adopted for moral improvement, is, *to cherish and indulge all the mild and benevolent passions and affections, as far as is consistent with prudence; and to control and subdue, to the utmost of our power, all those that are violent, sordid, or selfish:* for without some mixture of passion, sentiment, or affection, beneficence itself is but a cold virtue; and philosophers and divines, who have laboured to subject them all to the dominion of reason, or sink them in the more brilliant illuminations of faith, have only succeeded in suppressing the mild and seductive, together with some few of the sordid and selfish passions; while all those of a sour and sanguinary cast have acquired additional force and acrimony from that pride and confidence, which the triumph over the others naturally inspired. The censor Cato, the saint Bernard, and the reformer Calvin, were equally insensible to the blan-dishments of love, the allurements of pleasure,

and the vanity of wealth; and so, likewise,
were the monsters Marat and Robespierre:
but all equally sacrificed every generous and
finer feeling of humanity, which none are
naturally without, to an abstract principle or
opinion; which, by narrowing their understandings, hardened their hearts, and left them
under the unrestrained guidance of all the
atrocious and sanguinary passions, which party
violence could stimulate or excite.

113. This will always be the effect of such
principles or opinions, whatever they are; whether true or false; whether mild or severe*;
provided they are embraced with a degree of
eagerness and avidity sufficient to give men
confidence in their infallibility, and make them
supersede the feelings of nature. To enforce
the doctrines of a religion, which prohibits
violence and bloodshed in every case, even
that of self-defence, more violence has been
exercised, more blood shed, and more cruel
tortures inflicted, than in any other dispute
or quarrel, that ever was engendered by the
turbulent and unruly passions of men; and
whether the point at issue be a dogma of religion, an axiom of philosophy, or a maxim of

---

* " Neque enim multum interesse putamus ad hominum fortunas, quales quis opiniones abstractas de natura
et rerum principiis habeat."

VERULAM. Nov. Org. Scient. l. i. cxvi.

politics, its effects will be the same, provided it has sufficient influence to enslave the natural affections of the soul, and induce men to prefer a theorem of the head to a sentiment of the heart.

114. Had Lord Bacon seen such events, as have lately happened, he would not have said *that atheism did never perturb states* *: for if men once unite to maintain systematically that there are many Gods, one God, or no God, the moral effects will be exactly the same: the dogma instantly becomes the rallying point of a sect or faction; and all the selfish, violent, and atrocious passions are collected into its vortex. It is true, that a negative dogma is less likely, than an affirmative one, to engage such passions †; because it is less flattering to that opinionative pride and presumption, which is necessary to give them vigour and energy sufficient for any great exertions: but, nevertheless, that it may become the rallying point of a faction, and be a motive for very bloody persecution, we have had abundant proof. If men can once suppose an opinion to be infallibly certain, they will feel an inclination to propagate it; and

---

* Essays, 18.

† " Is humano intellectui error est proprius et perpetuus, ut magis moveatur et excitetur affirmativis quem negativis."—VERULAM. in Nov. Org. Scient. lib. i. xlvi.

consequently square their morality to that inclination; which will lead them to employ force, if persuasion do not prevail. Truth, they say, is the foundation of all virtue; and truth is, to every man, that which he himself thinks *.

115. Rules and systems have exactly the same influence upon taste and manners, as dogmas have upon morals. If a person be polite by rule; how just soever his rules may be, or with whatever strictness and exactitude he may observe them, his behaviour will be constrained and formal; and void of all that graceful ease, and ready adaptation to every varying shade of circumstance and situation, which constitute what is called good breeding; and which can only proceed from a just and discriminating tact, cultivated and refined by habitual exercise. Persons, who attempt to display their taste and talents in art or literature by rule, always err in exactly the same manner. Their rules and systems can never reach every possible case; and, even if they could, the very act of applying them would distract the attention from the sentiment excited; and, consequently, prevent or destroy all just feeling, by making

* " Quod enim mavult homo verum esse, id potius credit." Ibid. xlix.

them hesitate and doubt whether they ought
to feel or not, till they had tried their sentiments by the standard of their opinions: but
sentiment, that is checked or impeded, is at
the same time enfeebled; and thus, though
rules and theories may prevent those, who
have no just feeling or natural tact, from
judging totally wrong, they in an equal degree, prevent those who have, from judging
entirely right.

116. More than a century has now elapsed,
since the taste and magnificence of the principal sovereigns of Europe first formed academies in their respective kingdoms, for the
study of the arts of painting, sculpture, &c.;
in which professors of all the different sciences,
connected with those arts, were appointed,
models provided, and such of the students, as
seemed to make the greatest progress, and
possess the most promising talents, sent to
travel at the expence of the institution, that
they might profit by a comparative view of the
different styles and manners of all the different
schools, and acquire all the information, which
the remains of antiquity, and the most perfect
works of their predecessors in the respective
arts, could afford. Under the fostering influence of institutions so favourable, it might
naturally be supposed that these arts must have
been ever since in a progressive state of im-

provement; and, considering the high degree of excellence, from which that of painting started, that it must now be little short of abstract perfection. This is, however, so far from being the case, that not one of these academies has yet produced an artist, whom public opinion has ranked among painters*. Heaven-

* The candid reader will observe that I am speaking only of the regular students of academies, and not of those who have incidentally belonged to them.

The most complete establishment of the kind, that has ever existed, is the French academy : but though France produced several great painters before its institution, it has not produced one since. Generations of academicians have arisen and passed away one after the other, each the pride and wonder of their day; but we look in vain for a Poussin, a Le Sueur, or Bourdon among them.

Happily our own academy has hitherto escaped the contagion of system; and every artist taken up a style of his own, suited to his taste or talents; so that an English exhibition displays more variety than all those on the continent together. By thus continuing to apply the principles of British liberty to British art, we may reasonably hope to reach a degree of excellence in painting, which has never yet been attained: for painting, in modern Europe, has never approached that state of abstract perfection, which we admire in the sculpture of ancient Greece; and there can be no reason in the nature of things why it should not attain it.

The system of all the foreign academies, whose productions I have seen, is not only *one*, but a very bad one; so that, as Mr. Hopner has observed, they are not only not approaching the excellence of the great painters of Italy and Flanders, but going in a road which leads directly from it.

R

born genuises have been continually announced by them; and students of the highest expecta- tion, every year, sent forth; but all went and returned through the same beaten track of mediocrity, and just acquired enough of the art ˏto make them miraculous boys, and con- temptible men.

117. This effect has been so uniform and universal, during so long a period of time, and in so many different countries, that it cannot be merely accidental, or proceed from the casual incapacity of individuals; but must be owing to some radical vice in the institutions themselves: which radical vice, I believe to be nothing more than *system*; which whether it be good or bad, true or false, equally teaches men to work by rule, instead of by feeling and observation. Those, who live and study toge- ther, naturally and imperceptibly imitate each other: whence every academy acquires a style and principle of its own; which, by degrees, limits and cramps all the exertions of those who belong to it. Whatever they look at, either in nature or art, is seen through a par- ticular medium of their own, which charac- terizes and vitiates every copy or imitation, which they make from it. Hence whatever acquisitions they make, either of theoretical knowledge or practical facility, are merely the knowledge and facility of doing wrong; so

that the figures, with which they cover canvass, become as much the result of mechanic
labour as the canvass itself.

118. That, which constitutes the great characteristic difference between liberal and mechanic art; and which gives to the former all
its superiority, is feeling or sentiment; a quality, that is always easily perceived, but inca-
pahle of being described. It is this which gives,
in different ways, those inexpressible charms
-and graces to the works of Corregio, of Rubens,
of Rembrandt, and of Claude: which, amidst
inaccuracies, that every student of every academy knows how to reprobate and avoid, still
continue to fascinate every beholder ; and will
continue to do so, as long as a trace of them
shall remain. Had these great artists been bred
. in the trammels of an academy, they also would
have avoided their inaccuracies : but the same
causes, that restrained their deviations one way,
would have restrained them another ; and, by
preventing them from transgressing rules, prevented them from soaring above them. Their
knowledge in this case might have been more
correct, and their practice more regular : but
their observation would have been less various
and extensive ; their use and application of it
less free and vigorous ; and their execution
more mannered, and less adapted to the re-

spective subjects, upon which it was occasion‑
ally employed.

119. If, however, academical science and
precision can be united with feeling and sentiment, there is no doubt that the result would
be a degree of perfection hitherto unknown to
the art ; and which perhaps the limited powers
of human nature are not capable of reaching.
Annibal Caracci has combined them in a greater
degree than any other painter : but yet how
inferior is he, in the first, not only to the great
artists of antiquity, but to Raphael ; and, in the
second, to the great Flemish painters, Rubens,
Vandyke and Rembrandt ! In the expression
of sentiment and passion, he is, indeed, superior to all the moderns, except Raphael ; but
the sentiment or feeling, of which I am now
treating, is of a different kind ; and belongs to
the execution, rather than the subject or design
of the picture. It is that felicity in catching
the little transitory effects of nature and expressing them in the imitation, so that they
may appear to be dropped, as it were, fortui-
tously from the pencil, rather than produced by
labour, study, or design : it is that, in short,
which distinguishes a work of taste and genius
from one of mere science and industry ; and
which often raises the value of an inaccurate
original above that of the most correct copy.

120. The art of sculpture is necessarily, from the process of its execution, less susceptible of this kind of excellence, than that of painting; and, as it is now generally practised, cannot admit of it in any degree whatever. Among the great artists of antiquity, however, the brass or marble statue was not a mere servile copy, set out by the rule and compass, and finished with the rasp and file, from the model of the sculptor, by the hands of ignorant mechanics: the touches of the master visited every part of it; and the last finish was by the chisel, wielded by the hand that had modelled, and directed by the mind, that had conceived the whole.

121. The Latin having been the language in which all public business was transacted throughout the Roman empire, a competent knowledge of it was necessary for all, who sought public employment either civil or military. Public schools were therefore erected for the study of it, early in the second century of Christianity; and public professors of rhetoric appointed through all the principal cities of the western provinces *; from whose appointment, we may date the complete corruption and decline of Latin eloquence. Rule and system were then substituted to tact and sentiment; the form and length of every period

* Juvenal. Sat. xv. 110.

R 3

were prescribed ; and the various figures of
speech distributed through the discourse, with
all the exact precision of mathematical proportion. Style then became mere trick of mechanism, deriving no character, either from the
mind, from which it sprang, or the subject,
upon which it was employed ; and consequently
having no means of exciting interest or commanding attention, but that unceasing and unmeaning glitter of tinsel ornament, which ever
distinguishes the productions of those, who
have become eloquent by studying words rather
than things ; and whose ideas are consequently
subservient to their expressions, instead of their
expressions being adapted to their ideas.

122. If a subject be properly felt, and properly understood, it will of itself supply the
mind with proper expressions : for the common
use of language, necessary to acquire matter
sufficiently copious to enable any person to
speak or write well, will supply words proper
and abundant, if the orator or author have
memory to retain, and judgment to select :
but, if he have not, the arts of rhetoric or criticism will never give him either ; though they
may teach him to abuse both, by substituting
fashion to feeling, artifice to nature, and affectation to simplicity. The Greek being merely
the language of polite literature and social
amusement, the study of it was left to the taste

of individuals, uncramped and unperverted by the pedantry of public teachers; whence it continued to be written with a considerable degree of spirit, ease, and elegance, when all the force and vigour of the Latin was dissolved into froth, or diluted into vapid and turgid inflation.

123. Perhaps it is fortunate for our own language, that it is not made a specific branch of study in our public schools and colleges; as it thus escapes free from the rules and restrictions, in which public professors of rhetoric would fetter and entangle it; and, of what sort these rules would be, we have many instances to show, in an elaborate work upon the subject, written by one of the most able and judicious professors, that any university could ever boast. I shall quote one out of the many; and lest I should injure his meaning by debasing his expressions, give it in his own words.

124. " Addressing the several parts of one's " body," says Dr. Blair in his sixteenth lecture, " as if they were animated, is not congruous to " the dignity of passion. For this reason, I " must condemn the following passage in a very " beautiful poem of Mr. Pope's, Eloisa to " Abelard :

" Dear fatal name ! rest ever unreveal'd,
Nor pass these lips in holy silence seal'd,

Hide it, my heart, within that close disguise,
Where, mix'd with God's, his loved idea lies :
O write it not, my hand—the name appears
Already written—wash it out my tears."

" Here are several different objects and parts
" of the body personified; and each of them is
" addressed and spoken to : let us consider with
" what propriety. *Dear fatal name*, &c. To
" this no reasonable objection can be made : for
" as the name of a person often stands for the
" person himself, and suggests the same ideas,
" it can bear this personification with sufficient
" dignity. Next Eloisa speaks to herself, and
" personifies her heart for this purpose: *hide it,*
" *my heart*, &c. As the heart is a dignified
" part of the human frame, and is often put
" for the mind or affections, this too may pass
" without blame. But when from her heart
" she passes to her hand, and tells her hand
" not to write his name, this is forced and un-
" natural; a personified hand is low, and not
" in the style of true passion ; and the figure
" becomes still worse when, in the last place,
" she exhorts her tears to wash out what her
" hand had written, *O write it not*, &c. There
" is in these two lines an air of epigrammatic
" conceit, which native passion never suggests;
" and which is altogether unsuitable to the
" tenderness, which breathes through the rest
" of that admirable poem."

125. Every common reader, I believe, from the time of the publication of the poem to the present day, has felt the lines, here censured, to be extremely affecting, and strongly expressive of the perturbed and impassioned state of mind of the person in whose name they are written.   But common readers never think of making such frigid distinctions in the comparative rank and dignity of the different parts of the body, as that which the learned professor here makes between the heart and the hand : a distinction as unfair in its statement, as it is cold and frivolous in its application ; for the hand is as often used metaphorically to signify energy or power, as the heart is to signify affection, or the head intellect.   " He had a head to contrive, a tongue to persuade, and a hand to execute any mischief," says a noble historian, of the leader of an adverse party ; by which, it is to be presumed that he did not mean to signify his manual dexterity in wielding a dagger, or pulling a trigger, but his vigor and capacity for conducting and executing, as well as designing and promoting those public measures, which the historian thought mischievous.

126. I cannot but think that, had Dr. Blair known that a passage of an ancient Greek poet, which has stood the test of ages, and been universally felt and recognized as one of the most tender and pathetic in any language, equally

violates his rule, he would have been less con-
fident of its infallibility; or at least more cautious in the application of it. The passage, I
mean, is that part of the celebrated soliloquy
of Euripides's Medea, in which she apostro-
phizes her children, when about to murder
them:

——————————————— δοτ' ω τεκνα,
Δοτ', ασπασασθαι μητρι, δεξιαν χερα.
Ω φιλτατη χειρ, φιλτατον δε μοι στομα,
Και σχημα και προσωπον ευγενες τεκνων,
Ευδαιμονοιτον· αλλ' εκει· ταδ' ευθαδε
Πατηρ αφειλετ'. ω γλυκεια προσβολη,
Ω μαλθακος χρως, πνευμα δ' ηδιστον τεκνων,
Χωρειτε, χωρειτ ———————————

That the learned professor should have overlooked so known and celebrated a passage as
this, is very remarkable, and only to be accounted for by the very limited and superficial
knowledge of the Greek writers, which his lectures display. It may be said, indeed, that
Medea does not apostrophize her own hand,
or her own features: but our critic makes no
such distinction; and if he did, there would be
an example against his general rule, quite as
strong, and as much in point, from the same
excellent tragedy; and of little less authority:
for Medea, when about to kill her children,
addresses her own hand in the following spirited
and expressive lines; in which it evidently

stands for the general energy or active power both of her body and mind :

Αγ' ω ταλαινα χειρ εμη, λαϐε ξιφος,
Λαϐ', ἑρπε προς βαλϐιδα λυπηραν βιου,
Και μη κακισθης, μηδ' αναμνησθης τεκνων,
'Ως φιλταϐ, ὡς ετικτες· αλλα τηνδε γε
Λαθου βραχειαν ημεραν παιδων σεθεν,
Καπειτα θρηνει· και γαρ ει κτενεις σφ', ὁμως
Φιλοι γ' εφυσαν, δυστυχης δ' εγω γυνη.

One of the most pathetic passages in Shak-speare is that, in which Lear not merely exhorts his own eyes not to weep over the ingratitude of his daughters, but even threatens to tear them out, if they do :

—— —— old fond eyes
Beweep this cause again, I'll pluck you out;
And cast you with the waters that you lose,
To temper clay.

The impression, which Garrick always made with these lines, can never be forgotten by those who ever felt it: yet had such canons of criti-cism, as those above, been fulminated from a professor's chair, in Shakspeare's time, he might have been intimidated from venturing so bold an apostrophé; though he appears to have had at least a proper degree of contempt for the systematic rules of criticism; which in the lat-ter period of his life, when his talents had intro-duced him to the acquaintance of learned men;

could not have been unknown to him. But, as an able defender and elegant expounder of those rules has observed, " The most ingenious " way of becoming foolish is by a system : and " the surest method to prevent good sense is to " set up something in the room of it *." He, who either writes or acts according to the impulse of natural feeling and common sense, will, unless very perversely organized, be right sometimes : but he, who does either by system, may stand a chance of being uniformly and unvariably wrong.

127. It is said that a learned and eminent Greek professor, who, by a long course of study, had made himself completely master, in theory, of the whole art of war, once delivered a very eloquent and elaborate lecture upon that art in the presence of Hannibal; who, instead of expressing any of that rapture of applause, with which the rest of the audience received it, observed coldly that he had met with many prating old fools in his time, but never with so silly a prater as this †.

* Lord Shaftesbury, Adv. to Authors, p. iii. f. 1.

† " Locutus esse dicitur homo copiosus aliquot horas de imperatoris officio, et de omni re militari. Tum, cum cæteri, qui illum audierant, vehementer essent delectati, quærebant ab Annibale, quidnam ipse de illo philosopho judicaret : hic Poenus non optime Græce, sed tamen libere respondisse fertur, multos se deliros senes sæpe vidisse, sed qui magis, quam Phormio, deliraret, vidisse neminem." Cic. de Orat. l. ii.

Probably, were the author of the Iliad to hear the learned and elaborate discourses, which the theoretical professors and teachers of his art, both ancient and modern, have delivered in their respective schools and colleges, so much to the edification of the public at large, as well as of their own pupils, he would pronounce nearly the same judgment; from which the author of the present inquiry would scarcely venture to claim an exemption. Yet, so important and indispensable does the art, which we profess, appear to us all, that for any one to *attempt to understand poetry without having diligently digested Aristotle's treatise upon the subject,* has been pronounced to be *as absurd as to pretend to a skill in geometry without having studied Euclid* *. Nevertheless Homer, Hesiod, Pindar, Sophocles, Euripedes, &c. &c. who may surely be allowed to have known something of their art, lived long before this treatise or any of the kind was written or thought of; and the whole history of literature obliges us to acknowledge that, in proportion as criticism has become systematic, and critics numerous, the powers of composition and purity of taste have, in all ages and countries gradually decayed. The case is that men's minds become cramped and fettered, so that

* Warton on Pope's Essay on Criticism, p. 645.

they look to the authority of rules and their propounders instead of to nature—" magistrum respicientes naturam ducem sequi desierunt *" —and as this authority is frequently usurped for a time by those who have no other title to it than trick of style and froth of eloquence employed to re-echo the voice of a popular or triumphant party in politics, religion, or philosophy, its decisions are as capricious as its laws are imperfect; whence public opinion is misled, taste perverted, and the general style of composition corrupted and depraved. How far this effect is produced by those societies or bands of critics, whose labours issue monthly from the press, I shall leave to others to inquire ; only observing that, whatever may be their effects upon taste, they contribute much to the diffusion of general, though of superficial knowledge ; and, if conducted with the ability and impartiality, which have, in most cases, distinguished some publications of this kind, might contribute to the improvement as much as to the extension of science. Others have assumed

---

* Quinctill. Inst. l. v. c. x.
✦ " Verum ego hanc vim intelligo esse in præceptis omnibus, non ut ea secuti oratores eloquentiæ laudem sint adepti, sed quæ sua sponte homines eloquentes facerent, ea quosdam observasse, atque id egisse : sic esse non eloquentiam ex artificio, sed artificium ex eloquentia natum."

Cic. de Orat. lib. i.

the office without any better apparent qualification than a sort óf flippant confidence, which,
while it dazzles and overawes the ignorant,
enables them to pronounce the most peremp-
tory decisions upon the most abstruse points
of learning without understanding even its first
elements.

The following instance from a publication of
this kind, the authors of which proclaim themselves to be *among the first critics and scholars of the age* ; and have, perhaps, obtained
as extensive a circulation of their work as if
they really were so, may serve as an illustration.

After reviewing and criticising with much
solemnity the different Greek translations of
Gray's Elegy, and bestowing with due delibera-
tion the palm of superiority upon the Etonian
Nestor, they produce the following specimen
of *what the splendid imagery, and genuine
grandeur of diction exhibited in his immortal
poem " The Bard" might be in the language
best adapted to do them justice.*

Οσσε κυλινδομενος δεινως ωμωξεν ὁ μανῖις,
Μακρον γενειον, και μεσαιπολιαι τριχες
'Ωσει κομητης εν ταραχθεντ᾽ αερι
Εϛιλβον᾽ οδυρομενος δ᾽ αειδεν,
Ασματι δακρυα μιξας.

British Critic, p. 244.

What degree of justice is done them here, or
whether this be any language at all, I shall now
take the liberty to examine.

οσσε κυλινδομενος, if it means any thing, means
*tumbling the eyes or rolling them out of the
sockets* ; and

μακρον γενειον is rather a *long chin* than a
long beard, which is, ϐαϑυς πωγων, or ϐαϑεια γε-
νειας.

δεινως ωμωξεν, *cried out terribly*, is quite ludicrous ; and

ὁ μαντις, with the article, and without any
explanatory adjunct, can only signify an *augur*
or *professional foreteller of events* ; a person
very different from the hero of the ode.

μεσαιπολιος signifies *a person half grey*, or
verging upon old age : but I don't believe that
the epithet can be applied to τριχες ; which is
not otherwise the proper word to express the
long flowing hair of the venerable bard. It
should have been κομαι, χαιται or εϑειραι.

κομητης in a philosophical treatise on the
subject, where the context would remove all
ambiguity, might stand alone for αστηρ κομητης,
and signify a *comet :* but as used here it signifies literally a *shaggy, hairy,* and metaphorically, *a very impudent fellow.*

The use of the verb τερασσω is so general that
it may possibly be applied to αηρ; but it is a
sort of expression that should not be employed

3

without authority; and with which the verb στιλϐω, signifying *the glitter of smoothness, polish.* or *transparency,* is as incompatible as it is with the grisly head or grisly chin of the hoary bard.

οδυρομενος is quite unsuitable to the personage, whose grief is *indignant,* not *whining* ; and

ασμα is not a word to be sounded with the Pindaric lyre. It should be αοιδη, υμνος, or μελος.

The pronoun is also wanting in the fourth line, as the conjunctive particle is in the second : but accuracy of syntax to connect words so misused and misplaced would be quite out of character; and the composition is throughout consistent, there not being one proper expression in it.

The Greek is certainly the only language through which a foreigner, not master of English, can enjoy the unparalleled splendour and energy of this ode : but the difficulty of preserving in a translation that splendour and energy, amidst all the mysterious majesty, which envelops and exalts it, would be scarcely surmountable. Perhaps the sublime image, which we have seen so bunglingly mangled and debased may be thus expressed :

Παρ κελαδοντα ρεεθρα,
ὁ μελαγχλαινος ανηρ

S

εστα προβλητι

επι σκοπελω προφανεις,

γλαυκοις δεδορκως ομμασιν

ὁ τωνδε δεινων επεων αοιδος

κρατος δε και πολιω

γενειω εσκεδασμεναι,

αστερος ἁτε κοματα,

εθειραι ερωοντο

αερ᾽ εν θολερω·

θερμα δ᾽ ὁ τεγγων δακρυα στοναχαις *

ουλον μελος φοβερα

ηειδε φωνα.

It is, however, with much doubt and diffi-
dence that I submit this attempt to the public;
being at least sensible of the danger and difficulty of it, which the *British Critic* appears to

---

* This line, which a synod of North-British Critics
have peremptorily pronounced to be nonsense, is taken
from the tenth Nemean of Pindar, v. 141 ; and until they
passed sentence upon it in No. xiv. of the Edinburgh
Review, was universally thought to express, with peculiar force and delicacy, the mixture of indignation and
tenderness so appropriate to the grief of the hero of the
modern as well as of the ancient ode.

The second line, ὁ μελαγκλαινος ανηρ, they are pleased to
say can only mean a *parson* ; so that the μελαγκλαινοι
Περιηποι at Bion's funeral must be the vicar and curate, or
perhaps the dean and chapter officiating on the occasion,
as a reverend gentleman appears officiating in the funeral
scene of Hogarth's " *Harlot's Progress.*" That such
critics should know any thing of the distinct use of the
articles in Homeric, Pindaric, and Attic composition, it
would be absurd to expect.

have been as incapable of perceiving as of sur-
mounting :—but now as heretofore—" qui
stultis videri eruditi volunt, stulti eruditis videntur."

Who this illustrious member of *a society of
the first critics and scholars of the age* is, I
am not anxious to inquire ; it being sufficient
to know *what* he is. He may, nevertheless,
hold a high station in the critical synod ; since
all pre-eminence is comparative; and compared
with the translator, who makes Herodotus
assert, that the *Indians have a vertical sun at
the hour of the morning when the Greeks
withdrew from the forum*, he is certainly
deserving of a very high one.

With this notable translation, indeed, I am
no otherwise acquainted than through Major
Rennel's quotations; who, being avowedly no
scholar, consulted, it seems, the translator,
whenever he had any doubts concerning the
meaning or accuracy of the translation. Possessing, however, a competent share of that, in
which this translator seems to be as deficient
as in the language, which he pretends to trans-
late, he is very much perplexed at finding an
ancient historian, who had no other means of
ascertaining the middle of the day but the sun's
being in its meridian altitude, assert that it was
vertical at a previous hour in the morning;
and that too in direct contradiction to an opi-

s 2

nion, which he, in common with the rest of his
countrymen and contemporaries, held, of the
regions of the earth, where the mid-day sun
is vertical, being uninhabitable through heat.
(Geography of Herodotus, p. 8.) Had the
Major, however, consulted a schoolboy instead
of this oracular critic, he might have learnt
that there is no mention of a vertical sun in
the original; the historian having merely observed *that the greatest heat of the sun was
at a certain hour of the morning, when the
business of the forum ceased, and not in the
middle of the day, as in other countries,*
Θερμοτατος δε εστι ὁ ἡλιος τατοισι τοισι ανθρωποισι
το εωθινον· ἀ καταπερ τοισι αλλοισι μεσαμβριης, αλλ᾽
ὑπερτειλας μεχρις ἀ αγορης διαλυσιος. Lib. iii. 104.
Thus rendered in the quotation—" In distinction from all other nations, the heat with
these people (the Indians) is greatest, not at
mid-day, but in the morning. They have a
vertical sun, when with us people withdraw
from the forum."

This error, as well as others of the kind,
with which most of the quotations abound,
could not have arisen from misunderstanding
the Greek; but from misunderstanding the
French. A typographical inaccuracy perhaps,
or even an accidental erasure in a particular
copy of M. Larcher's version may have turned
plus chaud into *plus haud*; of which an ob-

vious emendation would make *plus haut*; and *le soleil le plus haut,* in India, the English translator might naturally think could only mean a *vertical sun.* If, however, he choose to derive his errors from any other source, he is welcome to the benefit of it: for of M. Larcher and his version I know nothing, except that I have heard him spoken of by competent judges on the continent, as a man of sound understanding if not of profound learning; and one who was therefore not likely to transmute the clear plain sense of the clearest and plainest of all writers into utter nonsense[*].

A synod of such critics, as these translators into, and out of a language so little known to them, gravely sitting in judgment and deliberately passing sentence upon the works of persons of real talents and learning, is in itself only ridiculous; but their decisions being listened to and received by the public is a melancholy symptom of the decline of taste and literature.

[*] The error may have originally sprung from a mistake in Stephens's Thesaurus, v. ὑπερτέλλω; and been successively copied and augmented by the Latin, French, and English translators; though the real meaning of the word is as clear and obvious, as the plain sense of the context, the simplest etymology, and the authority of the best writers can make it. See Euripid. Phœniss. v. 1021. Ed. Porson. &c. A dictionary is the remembrancer of a scholar, and the oracle of a dunce.

CHAPTER III.

OF JUDGMENT.

1. JUDGMENT is more properly the result of a faculty than a faculty itself; it being the decision, which reason draws from comparison: whence the word is commonly used to signify the talent of deciding justly and accurately in matters, that do not admit of mathematical demonstration; in which sense, judgment may be properly considered as a mode of action of reason. It is the opposite of wit, as Locke, and after him, the author of the Inquiry into the Sublime and Beautiful have justly observed; wit being chiefly employed in discovering resemblances, and judgment in detecting differences.

2. Reason, in the strict sense of the word, has little or nothing to do with taste; for taste depends upon feeling and sentiment, and not upon demonstration or argument. The word beauty is, indeed, often applied to a syllogism or a problem; but then it means clearness, point, or precision; or whatever else be the characteristic excellence of that, to which it is applied. So far as reason is employed upon relations of number and quan-

tity it is certain and decisive; and thus far its results must appear the same to all mankind : but, though it is common, in the laxity of colloquial speech, to say that we feel the force of a demonstration;- yet feeling has in reality no concern in it; demonstration being purely a matter of science.

3. No reasoning, except that upon the relations of number and quantity, admits of absolute demonstration; for all reasoning from cause and effect, or from analogy or similitude, is from the habitual association of ideas; and consequently can amount to no more than this; that the thing appears so to us, because it always has appeared so, and we know of no instance to the contrary. I have seen the sun set to-night, and conclude that it will rise again to-morrow; because my own experience and the tradition received from others have taught me to associate the idea of its rising again, after a certain number of hours, with that of its setting; and habit has rendered these ideas inseparable. But, nevertheless, I can give no demonstrative reason from the nature of things why it should rise again; or why the Creator and Governor of the universe may not launch it, as a comet, to wander for ever through the boundless vacuity of space. I only know that during the short period, and within the narrow sphere, which bound my knowledge of this

universe, he, hath displayed no such irregular
exertions of power: but still that period and
that sphere shrink into nothing in the scale of
eternity and infinity; and what can man know
of the laws of God or nature, that can enable
him to prescribe rules for Omnipotence?

4. What we call the laws of nature are
merely certain rules of analogy, which we
draw from the general results both of mathematical demonstration, and habitual association; and employ, as the general, criteria of
our belief, in those particulars, of which we
have no actual experience.

5. In matters of demonstration, these rules
are fixed and certain; for we know that the
relative proportions of a triangle must still be
the same, whatever be its actual dimensions.
But, in things, that we know merely from the
habitual association of ideas, they are only
probable; and our assent or dissent to them
can amount only to belief or disbelief: I
believe it impossible for one man to drive an
army of fifty thousand before him, because
I have never known any such disparity in
individual men: but, nevertheless, I cannot
demonstrate, from any certain principles of
science, that there might not have been a
particular man endued with such a degree
of superiority over the rest of his fellow
creatures.

6. This distinction is of little or no importance in the common concerns of life: for we are no more disposed to doubt that the sun will rise to-morrow, morning, than that the three angles of a triangle are equal to two right angles : but, nevertheless, it is of the utmost importance in fixing the just bounds of poetical fiction; and that is the subject, to which the nature of my present inquiry leads me to apply it.

7. One of the boldest of the bold fictions of the Odyssey is the poet's making Ulysses swim during three days and two nights without food or rest: but, nevertheless, this does not destroy, or even lessen the interest of the story; for though, as the human frame now appears to us, we know that there is no man capable of such exertions; and may thence *believe* that no man ever was: yet this is mere *belief*, founded on no demonstration, and may therefore differ in different individuals. The Indian prince thought it impossible that water should become hard; and the inhabitant of the South Sea island, that it should become hot, for exactly the same reasons, as induce us to think it impossible that glass should become malleable, or iron become transparent; which reasons are merely habits of association arising from uninterrupted and unvaried experience and observation.

8. Had the poet, instead of making Ulysses swim for so long a time by the aid of the girdle of Leucothöe, made him appear, like Saint Anthony, in two different and remote places at the same instant of time, the case would have been altered : for difference and identity of substance, space and time, are matters of demonstration by number and quantity; and therefore must be the same in all ages, and appear the same to all mankind. Had the fiction of the poet, therefore, been thus changed, it would have been not merely wonderful, or even incredible, but utterly impossible and absurd; so that it would have destroyed, in a great measure, the interest of the subsequent events. To this objection, the fiction of the same hero's having the winds tied up in a bag is certainly liable; and would be still more so, were not he himself the narrator of it: but as he never shows any scruples in cajoling his audience; and always does it with the utmost gravity and most circumstantial precision, we may reasonably suppose that the poet meant him to be doing so in this instance.

9. Aristotle has observed *that, in poetry, that, which is credible, but impossible, is preferable to that, which is possible, but incredible* *. This great philosopher's acuteness

---

* προς τι γαρ την ποιησιν αιρετωτερον πιθανον αδυνατον, η απιθανον και δυνατον. Poet. f. xlvi.

seems, however, in this instance to have forsaken him : for, in reasoning from experience
or analogy, *possibility* is only a degree of *cre-
dibility*; and the greater degree must necessarily include the less; wherefore that, which
is thought to be *credible*, must previously be
thought to be *possible*. A negative, too, in
its nature, excludes all degrees whatever; for,
where there is *none*, there cannot be either
more or *less :* and though a negative on one
side may, in some cases, imply an affirmative,
either contingent or absolute, on the other, it
is surely most absurdly paradoxical to assert
that an absolute negative, on one side, may
include a contingent affirmative, on the same
side. Yet this is the conclusion, to which we
must come, before we can admit of a *credible
impossible :* but the nature and extent of human knowledge had not been ascertained in
the time of the Stagirite; it being to the profound investigations of our own countrymen,
particularly Locke, that we owe these most
important discoveries in philosophy. I am of
course supposing equal, or at least nearly
equal degrees of knowledge in the persons to
whom the events or circumstances are related
or exhibited ; there being no doubt that very
ignorant persons may think even probable,
what the learned know to be impossible.

10. I do not mean, however, to infer that,
in order to relish the Homeric fictions, it is

necessary to believe that Ulysses actually did swim for so long a time; or that Achilles drove a whole army before him, like so many grasshoppers... On the contrary, we only read these things as fictions; and never suppose them true, even when most interested in them: for if the events are not *demonstrably* false; but are such as the men, there described, could have produced, had such men ever existed; we never stop to inquire whether they ever existed or not; or whether they are such as now exist; but consider the descriptions as embellished pictures of human nature, with the expression of which we sympathize, according to the degrees of truth and energy, with which the passions and affections are displayed.

11. This is abundantly proved by the effects of dramatic exhibitions: for, notwithstanding all that critics have said of the probability of the plot, and the coincidence of the representation with the reality, arising out of a strict observance of the unities of time, place, and action, there never was, as Dr. Johnson has observed *, the smallest degree of this kind of probability, or coincidence, preserved in any dramatic exhibition whatsoever; no kind of deception having ever been intended; nor any being, in

---

* Preface to Shakspeare.

any case, required to excite sympathy *. At the very moment, that our tears are flowing for the sorrows of Belvidera or Callista, we know that we are in a theatre in London, and not either at Venice or Genoa; and that the person, with whose expressions of grief and tenderness we sympathize, is not the wife of Jaffier or Altamont, but of Mr. Siddons. If there were any deception, so that we did, for a moment, suppose the incidents, which excite those expressions, to be real, our feelings would be of a very different, and much less pleasant kind.

12. This is not the case with a fanatical orator or field preacher: his enthusiasm must be thought by his audience to be real and sincere, or it will have no effect: if once they suspect him to be an *actor*, there is an end of his influence; and, if he be listened to any longer, it is through mere curiosity; when his extravagant rants, being heard without sympathy, are uttered without influence. The matter and expression of his discourse are then canvassed with the same liberty and impartiality; as those of a drama on the stage;

* The Abbé du Bos had before observed that dramatic exhibitions were never meant to be deceptions in any degree; (Reflexions critiques, part i. f. xliii.) but, nevertheless, he continues to argue, in other parts of his work, as if they were.

and unless there be real sense and argument in the one, and energy and perspicuity in the other, he will soon find himself treated with scorn and derision. As long, however, as he can appear to feel the passions, which he strives to impress, he will seldom fail of impressing them upon the ignorant and credulous; and then it signifies little what he says: merely ringing the changes upon the words sin and repentance, damnation, and redemption, &c. &c. is all that is required to excite the admiration, and win the confidence of the affrighted and astonished rabble*.

13. It was by these means that the club orators in France obtained their influence: the tumultuous assemblies of the populace, which they addressed, were as little capable of understanding, as of uttering reason; but the words liberté, egalité, trahison, vengeance, &c. repeated with a loud voice, strong emphasis, and vehement gesticulation, filled their minds with mysterious hopes, fears, and suspicions; and led them to the commission of all those dreadful excesses, which have disgraced the revolution; and rendered all the wild efforts for universal liberty subservient to the cause of universal despotism.

---

* " Collidere manus, terræ pedem incutere, femur, pectus, frontem cædere, mire ad pullatum circulum facit." QUINTIL. Inst. l. ii. c. xii.

3

14. Shakspeare has represented the Roman rabble to be just as fickle, as rash, and as sanguinary, as the Parisian: but had he made Mark Antony speak no better than Robespierre, Danton, or Hebert, the London audience would have hooted him from the stage, though the Roman might have applauded him in the rostrum*: for the spectators in the theatre sympathize with none of the passions, which agitated those in the forum. They know that the person representing Mark Antony is an actor dressed out for the purpose; and that the events exhibited are entirely fictitious, merely meant to give an appropriate meaning to the speeches uttered; with the energies of sentiment and expression of which they only sympathize †.

15. It is from knowing and feeling that the persons, whom we see on the stage, are mere

* From the mountebank tricks which Mark Antony played over the body of Cæsar with so much effect, it is probable that his real style of eloquence was not much better. See Appian. de Bello civili.—Augustus observed that he wrote to be admired rather than understood— " quasi ea scribentem quæ mirentur potius homines quam intelligant." Sueton. in Aug. f. lxxxvi. He has left a numerous tribe of disciples.

† Demosthenes being asked what was the first qualification of an orator? answered, Action. What the second? Action. What the third? Action.

He had learned, from long and humiliating experience, that the strong sound sense, which distinguishes his ora-

actors and actresses; and not the personages, whose names and characters they assume, that we cannot suffer the same licence of 'fiction in dramatic, as in epic poetry. As we see no representation of Ajax or Achilles, while reading or hearing the Iliad, we have no predetermined ideas of what their size and strength might have been; and the mind consequently draws imaginary portraits of them, proportioned to the actions, which it finds attributed to them *: but when these heroes are brought upon the stage, they are instantly reduced to the dimensions of the actors, who personate them; and if they even talk of driving whole armies before them, or sacking cities by the strength of their single arm, we immediately feel the absurdity of it; and the whole becomes farcical and ridiculous; of which we have a memorable instance in Dryden's Almanzor.

tions, though it constitute their principal merit in the closet, contributed but little to their effect in the forum.

" Actio, inquam, in dicendo una dominatur: sine hac summus orator esse in numero nullo potest ; mediocris hac instructus summos sæpe superare. Huic primas dedisse Demosthenes dicitur, cum rogaretur quid in dicendo esset primum; huic secundas; huic tertias . . . . . sententiæ sæpe acutæ non acutorum hominum sensus prætervolant: actio, quæ præ se motum animi fert, omnes movet." Cic. de Orat. lib. iii. ad fin.

* μαλλον δ'ενδεχεται εν τη εποποιια το αλογον, δι' ο συμβαινει μαλιστα το θαυμαστον, δια το μη ορᾳ εις τον πραττοντα.

ARISTOT. Poetic. f. xliii.

16. Upon this principle, that sort of semblance' to truth, which, for distinction's sake,
we will call *poetical probability,* does not arise
so much from the resemblance of the fictions
to real events, as from the consistence of the
language with the sentiments, of the sentiments and actions with the characters, and of
the different parts of the fable, with each
other: for, if the mind be deeply interested;
as it always will be by glowing sentiments and
fervid passions happily expressed, and naturally arising out of the circumstances and incidents of a consistent fable, it will never turn
aside to any extraneous matter for rules of
comparison; but judge of the probability of
the events merely by their connection with,
and dependence upon each other.

17. All change of place; and all progression
of time in a drama, beyond that actually employed in the representation of the piece, must
be *equally* violations of truth and probability,
if they be any violations of it at all: for whether the change of scene be from one street to
another, or from one kingdom to another,
there is equally, in the representation, a supposition of that which is not; and in that
which is not, there can be neither mode nor
degree. In the Electra of Sophocles, the most
perfect piece, perhaps, extant of the Greek
theatre, a conspiracy of the most secret and

dangerous nature is carried on against a bloody
and suspicious usurper, at the door of his own
palace, in the public street, and in the presence
of a multitude of persons; all which incongruities are heaped together to preserve the
unity of the place; the sacrifice of which would,
surely, have been a much less important sacrifice of probability. Had Aristotle known no
other great epic poem than the Iliad, his sagacity would have discovered, and his ingenuity
proved that unity of place was as necessary to
epic as to dramatic poetry; and all succeeding
critics would have repeated, exemplified, and
explained the dictates of their oracle : but the
Odyssey luckily saved epic poetry from any
such limitation; and allowed the taste and
genius of Virgil to display itself in those various
changes of scenery, which he was so eminently
qualified to describe and embellish; but which,
nevertheless, the natural cautiousness and modesty of his disposition would not have allowed
him to introduce, contrary to the established
rules of criticism; though those rules were
nothing more than general deductions from the
particular, and, in many instances, accidental
practice of such poets as himself. The authors
of the Iliad and Odyssey (for I have no doubt
that they were two) would probably have
laughed at the restrictions, which their modes
of treating their respective fables, had imposed

upon all succeeding epic poets; and have been as much amazed, as the most ignorant of their audience, at hearing of the systematic principles of profound philosophy, in which critics, after the lapse of many ages, discovered their practice to be founded.

18. Unity of action has been held to be a still more essential requisite both of epic and dramatic poetry, than either unity of time or identity of place; and here it is asserted, the venerable authority of the father of poetry, is decisive and unquestionable; the action, in each of the two poems of the Iliad and the Odyssey, being simply one; namely, the *anger of Achilles,* and the *restoration of Ulysses.*

19. But is it quite certain that any precise and determinate idea is here attached to the word action; or whether it be not used, sometimes to signify the *subject* of the poem, which is the cause of the *actions* described in it, and sometimes the *actions* themselves, which are the effects of that cause?

20. Questions of this kind are always best answered by examples; which at once explain the matter, and solve the doubts if they admit of solution. I shall therefore briefly compare the action of the Iliad with that of the tragedy of Macbeth; not because these two poems are justly esteemed to be the highest efforts of human genius; but because, in the one, unity

of action is supposed to be most strictly pre-served; and in the other, most openly violated.

21. In the tragedy of Macbeth, there are evidently two distinct principal actions, the usurpation of Macbeth by the murder of Dun-can, and the destruction of the usurper by the restoration of Malcolm; besides many subor-dinate or episodical actions; such as the mur-der of Banquo, of Macduff's family, &c. &c.

22. But are the actions of the Iliad at all less distinct, or less numerous? Is not the quarrel of Agamemnon and Achilles one, the defeat and blockade of the Greeks another, the return of the Myrmidons and death of Hector another, besides innumerable subor-dinate actions, which result from these? Had the anger of Achilles with Agamemnon been the action of the poem, it must have ceased with their reconciliation; and then how lame and defective would have been the conclusion! The mighty and all-accomplished hero would have been introduced, with so much pomp of poetry, merely to wrangle with his prince, weep for his mistress, and carve a supper for three of his friends. Yet a German critic of more sense and learning, than feeling or sentiment, thinks that the original poem must have ended thus, since the unity of action requires it *.

* Wolfii Prolegom. in Homer. Among Milton's hints for tragedies, it is proposed to render the action of Mac-

23. Strict unity of action, indeed, requires
that the whole poem should be confined to the
quarrel and reconciliation : for the defeat and
blockade of the Greeks are as much distinct
actions, as the death and funeral of Hector,
and are not at all more connected with the
principal subject. It is true that all the distinct
actions, both principal and subordinate, are
connected with each other; and arise, in the
most natural gradation, from the anger of
Achilles, which is the subject of the poem, and
the cause of them all. But are not they equally
connected in the tragedy ? and do not all arise,
in a gradation equally just and natural, from
the *ambition of Lady Macbeth*, which is the
subject of the one, as *the anger of Achilles* is
of the other ? It is this ambition, instigated by
the prophecies of the witches, that rouses the
aspiring temper of her husband, and urges him
to the commission of a crime, the consciousness
of which embitters the remainder of his life;
and makes him suspicious, ferocious, and cruel ;
whence new crimes excite new enemies, and
his destruction naturally follows.

24. This unity of subject, and consequent
connection of events, is the leading principle of

beth one, by throwing all that relates to the murder and
usurpation into narrative. Not only in his hands, but
even in those of Shakspeare, it would thus have become
a very cold and tedious piece.

all epic and dramatic fiction; and that, by
which it is chiefly enabled to fix and rivet the
attention to transactions avowedly fabulous
and unreal: for, where the events described
or represented, spring, in their natural order
of succession, from one source, the sentiments
of sympathy, which they excite, will all verge
to one centre, and be connected by one chain.
But if new sources be introduced, new and
distinct trains of ideas will, of course, arise;
which will distract the attention, and divide
the interest; which happens in most of the
French tragedies (as well as in the Cato of
Addison, written upon the French model) where
one plot of love and another of ambition are
carried on at the same time, and often in alter-
nate scenes *.

25. This mixture is more certainly fatal to
the general interest of the piece, than that of
comic with tragic scenes; which has been so
much, and in many instances, so justly blamed,
on the English stage: for where the comic
scenes belong to the general plot, as in Othello,
they serve to bring down occasionally the high
tone of tragedy to the level of common life,
which is certainly better adapted to the stage;

---

* Χρη . . . . τα μερη συνεσταναι των
πραγματων ὕτως, ὡστε μετατιθεμενε τινος μερας, η αφαιρημενα,
διαφερεσθαι και κινεισθαι το ὁλον, ὁ γαρ προσον η μη προσον, μηδεν
ποιει επιδηλον, ὀδε μοριον τυτο ιστι.—ARISTOT. Poet. f. xvii.

where the persons that speak are known to be
mere men and women of the common class,
under whatever titles they may appear. In
expressing the glowing sentiments of heroic
passions and affections, this high tone ought,
indeed, to be kept up : for the violent agita-
tions of passion or affection always raise and
expand vigorous minds ; and give them a character of enthusiasm : wherefore their expressions,
when under the influence of them, ought to be
bold, elevated, and poetical ; the language of
poetry being, in fact, no other than that of
enthusiasm. But why this exalted style is to
be kept up in the common situations of familiar intercourse, to which tragedy must sometimes descend, I can see no reason whatever ;
and therefore decidedly prefer the mixture of
prose and blank verse, which our old dramatic
writers took from nature, to that monotonous
pomp of diction, which their successors borrowed from the French : nor do I see any impropriety in mixing sallies of pleasantry in
these familiar parts of the dialogue.

26. To draw any inference to the contrary
from the uniform style of epic poetry, is to reason upon an analogy, which does not exist :
for, as the personages of the epic are not subjected to the evidence of sense, like those of
the dramatic, the imagination is at liberty to
form what notions of them it pleases ; and it

belongs to the art of the poet to aggrandize and embellish those notions, in proportion as he wishes to impress his reader with grand and sublime ideas of the transactions, which he relates. For this purpose, a style uniformly elevated above that of the common vehicle of social intercourse is absolutely necessary ; and a metrical style is more appropriate than any other ; as it can sustain this elevation without being turgid or transposed ; and consequently descend without being debased, and rise without being inflated. Its ordinary tone is not that of common nature ; but of nature elevated to enthusiasm by supernatural inspiration ; and it is by speaking in this tone that the persons of the epic acquire a supernatural elevation of character, which the imagination readily yields to them, because its deceptions are never controverted by the evidence of the senses. Homer has no where told us that his heroes were of supernatural dimensions ; and, if he had, he would have destroyed the interest of his poem; but, nevertheless, no one, I believe, ever read the Iliad without conceiving in his mind ideas of men whose ordinary stature could not have been less than ten feet.

27. This expansion of the imagination, by a systematic elevation of language, is one of the most efficacious means of giving poetical probability ; or making supernatural events appear

credible: for, when once we have conceived supernatural ideas of the characters, we expect them to perform supernatural actions.   The fictions of the Iliad are as extravagant as those of any common romance or book of knight-errantry; and if we read them in prose, we immediately perceive them to be so; but the enthusiasm of the poet's numbers so expands the imaginations of his readers, that they spontaneously conceive ideas of his characters adequate to the actions which he makes them perform.

28. But even with this magical enthusiasm of verse, had Achilles been brought into action at once; and, without our having any previous acquaintance with him, defeated a whole Trojan army of fifty thousand men by the force of his single arm, we should have turned away with coldness and disgust from so absurd a tale: but the poet has opened his character to us by degrees; and raised it by artful contrasts, and allusions seemingly accidental, scattered through all the preceding parts of the poem:—every faculty of his mind, too, is upon the same scale as the strength and agility of his body; all that he says being distinguished by a glow of imagination, a fervor of passion, and energy of reasoning peculiar to himself:—even the tender affections of his mind partake of its greatness and its pride: his piety is reverence and not

fear; his friendship gives, but never seeks protection; his love imparts favour, which it scorns
to ask; and his grief assumes the character of
rage, and expends itself in menaces and vows
of vengeance against those who have caused it.
By an artful concatenation of circumstances,
seemingly accidental, he is shown to the reader
under the influence of every passion by turns,
all of which operate to the same end, and con-
spire to swell his rage, rendered doubly dreadful by despair and impending death.   In this
temper of mind, endowed with more than mortal strength, and clad in celestial armour, he is
shown advancing to the fight, like the autumnal
star, whose approach taints the air, and diffuses
disease, pestilence, and death.   Such an image
prepares the mind for the events that follow,
which thence seem natural consequences, instead of extravagant fictions *.

29. To describe such a character as this, or
indeed any other, requires neither feeling nor
talents : but to delineate or represent it—to
exhibit it speaking and acting under the influence of all the variety of passions, to which it
is liable—requires the utmost perfection of
both; and the more highly the picture is finished, the greater is the difficulty and the greater
the merit : for it is in the little expressions of

* αρισται των υπερβολων αι αυτο τυτο διαλανθανυσαι, οτι ιισιν
υπερβολαι.—LONGIN. f. xxxviii.

nature, and circumstances of truth, that the
mind discovers and feels the resemblance between fiction and reality; and thence gives
credit to the former, when it embellishes and
exaggerates. Truth is naturally circumstantial,
especially in matters that interest the feelings ;
for that, which has been strongly impressed
upon the mind, naturally leaves precise and
determinate ideas : whence a narration is always
rendered more credible by being minutely detailed ; provided the minute particulars are such
as really do happen in similar transactions,
with which we are acquainted.   That which is
demonstrably false can never, by any means,
acquire even the semblance of truth ; but that,
which we judge to be false only by analogy
and general experience, may acquire such semblance, by being connected with circumstances,
which, demonstration or experience tell us, are
true ; or by arising out of events, which analogy
tells us, may be true ; and the more of these real
circumstances, and probable events are connected with it, the more credible will it seem.

30. Hence we may account for the extreme
exactitude, with which, that supreme master of
fiction, the author of the Iliad, has described
every thing, in which error or inaccuracy might
be detected, either by experience, or demonstration.   The structure of the human body ;
the effects of wounds ; the symptoms of death ;

the actions and manners of wild beasts; the relative situations of cities and countries; and the influence of winds and tempests upon the waters of the sea, are all described with a precision, which, not only no other poet, but scarcely any technical writer upon the respective subjects of anatomy, hunting, geography and navigation has ever attained. The hyperboles are all in the actions of his gods and heroes; in which, exaggeration could not be detected: but in every object and every circumstance, which it was possible for his audience practically to know, the most scrupulous exactness, in every minute particular, is religiously observed. There are near twenty descriptions of the various effects of wind upon water—all different, and all without one fictitious or exaggerated circumstance—no *fluctus ad sidera tollit*; or *imo consurgit ad æthera fundo*, which even Virgil, the most modest of his imitators, has not avoided, but the common occurrences of nature, raised into sublimity by being selected with taste, and expressed with energy.

31. The untutored, but uncorrupted feelings of all unpolished nations have regulated their fictions upon the same principles, even when most rudely exhibited. In relating the actions of their gods and deceased heroes, they are licentiously extravagant: for there falsehood

could amuse, because it could not be detected :
but in describing the common appearances of
nature ; and all those objects and effects, which
are exposed to habitual observation, their bards
are scrupulously exact; so that an extravagant
hyperbole, in a matter of this kind, is sufficient
to mark as counterfeit any composition attributed to them. In the early stages of society,
men are as acute and accurate in practical
observation, as they are limited and deficient
in speculative science ; and in proportion as
they are ready to give up their imaginations to
delusion, they are jealously tenacious of the
evidence of their senses. James Macpherson,
in the person of his blind bard, could say with
applause, in the eighteenth century, " Thus
" have I seen in Cona; but Cona I behold no
" more—thus have I seen two dark hills re-
" moved from their place by the strength of the
" mountain stream. They turn from side to
" side, and their tall oaks meet one another
" on high. Then they fall together with all
" their rocks and trees." But had a blind bard,
or any other bard, presumed to utter such a
rhapsody of bombast in the hall of shells, amid
the savage warriors, to whom Ossian is supposed to have sung, he would have needed all
the influence of royal birth, attributed to that
fabulous personage, to restrain the audience
from throwing their shells at his head, and

hooting him out of their company as an impudent liar. · They must have been sufficiently
acquainted with the rivulets of Cona or Glen-
Coe to know that he had seen nothing of the
kind, and, have known enough of mountain
torrents in general to know that no such effects
are ever produced by them ; and would, therefore, have indignantly rejected such a barefaced
attempt to impose on their credulity.   In all
the numerous descriptions of the kind, which
abound as illustrations in the Iliad, the fire of
the poet never leads him to transgress the most
rigid bounds of truth ; nor is a single circumstance ever introduced, which the most scrupulous naturalist would not allow to be probable
and consistent : for, in these objects of common
observation, his audience were the most scrupulous of all naturalists ; who were only to be
satisfied, in poetry, with the same fidelity of
imitation, as the Turkish. emperor required in
painting upon exactly the same principle.

32. In the Odyssey there is generally less
detail, as well as less variety and brilliancy of
imagery ; but the attention to truth, in all circumstances of common observation, is so far
the same, that we might securely pronounce the
passage, in which the notes of the nightingale
are treated as notes of sorrow *, to be the pro-

* τ. 518—23.

.duction of a later age, even if the judgment of
the ancient grammarians, and the less question-
able authority of modernisms in the language,
had not marked the whole episode, in which it
is introduced, to be spurious * : for the habits
of life both of the poet and his audience, in that
early stage of society, must have forced them
to observe that the notes of singing birds are
notes of amorous joy and exultation ; and that
they are all mute in grief or calamity. Accordingly we find that, when be docs take an image
of distress from the lamentations of birds for
the loss of their young, he takes it from birds
of prey, which do scream and make loud moan
when their nests are plundered †. Virgil nevertheless, in his blended imitation of both passages, has, in defiance of truth and nature,
retained the more delicate and interesting
image, and attributed the thrilling note of sorrow, expressed in the scream of the eagle or
the vulture, to the song of the nightingale ‡ ;
and there can be no doubt that the courtly critics, for whom he wrote, thought this a most
judicious and elegant amendment ; nor do the
courtly or even scholastic critics of the present
day probably entertain very different sentiments : but nevertheless had the old Greek
bard obtruded such a palpable misrepresenta-

* τ. 343—587.   † π. 217.   ‡ Georgic. iv.

tion of what every one knew upon the rude
but observant assemblage of warriors, ploughmen, and herdsmen, for whom he sang, not all
the melody of either the Homeric or Virgilian
verse would have kept them together for many
minutes; at the same time that they would
have listened for hours, with all the mute and
greedy attention of implicit faith, to the extravagant tales of Cyclops, Læstrygons, Scylla,
Æolus, &c. : for of those they knew nothing,
and had therefore no grounds for disbelief;
which, among persons not used to speculative
or analogical reasoning, is generally a sufficient
motive for belief.

We have a work, in our own language, in
which the most extravagant and improbable
fictions are rendered, by the same means, sufficiently plausible to interest, in a high degree,
those readers, who do not perceive the moral
or meaning of the stories. I mean the Travels
of Gulliver; with which, I have known ignorant
and very young persons, who read them without even suspecting the satire, more really
entertained and delighted, than any learned or
scientific readers, who perceived the intent
from the beginning, have ever been.

33. The author of the novel of Clarissa Harlowe attempted to make his fictions interesting
by the same sort of minute precision and exactitude in the detailed relations of all common

circumstances; and, in some scenes, he has
succeeded admirably: but, in general, he has
failed through want of talent to fill up properly
and consistently those bold outlines of character, which first introduce his fictitious personages to the knowledge of his reader. The all-
accomplished and profligate Lovelace is ushered
into the novel with so many extraordinary qualities both of mind and person ;—such a variety
of talents both natural and acquired ; that we
eagerly look forward to the display of them in
his letters; and expect to meet with effusions of
genius and flashes of eloquence, equal, in the
familiar style, to those which the speeches of
Achilles display in the heroic.   But our disappointment is equal to our expectation : for we
find neither depth, nor elevation of thought;
neither energy, nor brilliancy of expression;
nor even the easy unaffected fluency of a well-
bred gentleman : but, instead of it the verbose
and empty redundancy of the vulgar tavern
buck, who apes the more elegant and refined
loquacity of the polished rake of fashion.

34. It may be said, perhaps, that the language and manners, as well as the dress of a
well-bred gentleman, may vary with the capricious changes of fashion; and that, therefore,
the style of writing suited to a well-bred person
of the middle of the last century might have
been very different from that suited to one of

U

the present day.—But this I deny: for the principles of good-breeding or politeness are the same in all ages and all countries; how much soever the modes of showing them may vary; and it is upon the permanent principles, and not upon the fluctuating modes, that the right use of language, in forming what is called style, depends. It matters not whether a letter be begun with *Citizen,* or Sir; or ended with *farewell,* or *your humble servant:* for these are fluctuating modes of politeness, which may vary every year: but a correct adherence to the established idiom of the language, with proper words in proper places; free from cant expressions, pedantic phrases, redundant circumlocutions, affected figures, or superfluous embellishments, have at all times constituted the style of a well-bred man of rank and talents, and will always continue to do so.

35. Neither do the principles of good breeding vary more in manners and dress, than they do in language; they having been the same in the court of Alcinous, as in that of Augustus; and the same in that of Augustus, as in that of Louis XIV: for though a well-bred gentleman, in the former, wore a plain woollen robe, and his hair cropped above his ears; and in the latter, an embroidered velvet coat, and a full-bottomed wig flowing over his shoulders; nevertheless to be neat and clean, but not finical or

affected; and easy and negligent, but not coarse or slovenly, was equally the characteristic of manly propriety in both *. When the Princess Nausicaa and her maids are washing their garments in the river, and the naked shipwrecked mariner appears as a suppliant before them, they act precisely as a high bred princess and her half bred maids would now. The one, with real dignity, and real delicacy, listens to his supplications and relieves his necessities; while the others, mistaking, as usual, affectation for dignity, and timidity for delicacy, run screaming away †.

36. In short, good breeding, whether it be shown in language, manners, or dress, is no-

---

* Forma viros neglecta decet . . .
. . . .
. . . .
. . . .
Munditiæ placeant: fuscentur corpora campo:
   Sit bene conveniens et sine labe toga.
Linguaque ne rigeat: careant rubigine dentes:
   Nec vagus in laxa pes tibi pelle natet.
Nec male deformet rigidos tonsura capillos:
   Sit coma, sit docta barba resecta manu.
Et nihil emineant, et sint sine sordibus ungues:
   Inque cava nullus stet tibi nare pilus.
Nec male odorati sit tristis anhelitus oris:
   Nec lædant nares virque paterque gregis.
Cetera lascivæ faciant, concede, puellæ:
   Et siquis male vir quærit habere virum.
           OVID. de Ar. Am. lib. i. v. 509.

† Odys. vi. 8. f. 138.

thing more than that dignity, elegance, and amenity of mind, whether natural or acquired, which I have before stated to be the genuine principle of all exterior grace of person, and of all elegance and dignity of attitude and gesture. It is, therefore, the same good taste, displayed in the ordinary intercourse and business of society, as is otherwise employed in the productions of imitative art, or the embellishments of improved nature.

S7. In all serious compositions—in every representation of character, where strong passions and affections are to be expressed, the poet, the painter, and the sculptor should alike adhere to permanent principles, and avoid all fluctuating modes and fashions: for, not only the passions and affections of the human mind, but the natural modes of expressing them, are the same in all ages, and all countries; and the less these natural modes are connected with those of local and temporary habit, the more strong and general will be the sympathies excited by them. It has been justly observed that tragedy is an exhibition of general nature, and comedy of the exceptions from it: for all personal peculiarities are more or less ridiculous; and local and temporary habits are merely personal peculiarities, extended to whole classes of individuals; which, consequently, become ridiculous as soon as the use of them has ceased:

Lovelace's tye-wig, and Clarissa's wide hoop and long ruffles are now extremely injurious to the pathos of that novel: for we can conceive nothing more ludicrously preposterous,· than a gay rake, and a young girl in the country, so dressed. Tom Jones must have equally worn a tye-wig when he came to London, and was dressed after the fashion of the day: but the author, with his usual superiority of judgment, has merely told us that he was fashionably and well dressed; and omitted all particulars, which would now cast an air of ridicule upon the person of his hero.

38. Upon the same principle, all real history, of a date sufficiently recent for such particulars to be generally known, cannot afford proper subjects for serious dramatic, and still less for epic fiction: since, even if the fashions of dress have nothing of the preposterous and ridiculous extravagance of tye-wigs, wide hoops, and long ruffles; yet, in the mind of the reader, individual is necessarily substituted to general nature; and, consequently, the imagination is cramped and restricted; so that it can no longer expand itself sufficiently to receive the exaggerated images of poetry. What exertions of personal prowess, Achilles, Ulysses, or Æneas might have been capable of, we have no means of knowing; and, therefore, listen attentively to,

and feel ourselves interested in all the extravagant feats, which the poets attribute to them :
but we all know, from unquestionable authority,
that neither Julius Cæsar, nor Henry IV. of
France, were men of remarkable bodily strength;
but that they gained victories and subdued nations by very different means : wherefore, when
poetry presumes to attribute such feats to them,
the fictions appear at once to be puerile and
absurd. Antiquaries, I believe, are generally
agreed that Æneas never was in Italy; since
the testimony of Homer clearly proves that his
posterity were reigning in Troy, when the Iliad
was composed * : but, nevertheless, the events
of that remote period were so little known;
and the accounts of them so various, uncertain,
and obscure, that Virgil was perfectly at liberty
to avail himself of a doubtful tradition for the
subject of his poem; which loses nothing of its
interest by being founded in fiction. This is
not, however, the case with the principal episode in the Henriade : for every person of
liberal education knows that Henry IV. never
was in England, nor had any personal interview
with Queen Elizabeth : wherefore the artifice
of the fiction is at once detected ; and the whole
appears to be merely a bald and common-place

* See Il. xx. v. 306.

trick to give the poet an opportunity of relating, in the person of the king, the preceding events of the war.

39. Similar objections may be made to the bringing any allegorical personages distinctly into action; not only because the artifice of the fiction is too obvious to admit of their actions becoming interesting; but also because the ideas, which we conceive of their personal existence, are never sufficiently clear and determinate to induce us to consider them as real agents: for, as all our ideas are received through the senses, we cannot, in reality, form any distinct notions of any higher order of beings than that of men, the highest that has come within the reach of our organic perceptions. The mind has, indeed, a power, in itself, of multiplying and dividing, as well as of combining and separating without end; and it is the exertion of this faculty in multiplying number, quantity, time, space, and power, that we call infinity, eternity, and omnipotence: for of these incomprehensible subjects we have no ideas whatsoever; nor can we form any ideas of beings superior to ourselves, but by employing this faculty in exaggerating our own powers of body or mind, or in combining them with those of other animals that are equally objects of sense. The gods of Homer and the angels of Milton are alike exaggerated men; and if

other poets choose to make new forms for these celestial and supernatural beings, they can only do it by combining those of different terrestrial creatures, and thus producing monsters. . In giving wings to angels, and horns, tails, and cloven feet to devils, we only make the. one partake of the nature of birds; and the other of that of. quadrupeds or reptiles. ,

40. In epic poetry, indeed, the forms of intellectual or supernatural agents never need be so particularized, as to be presented distinctly to the mind of the reader: but, in dramatic representations, there can be nothing left indeterminate for the imagination to work upon; whence, I believe, every person, who, after having been a reader, has become a spectator of the witches in Macbeth, has felt how totally they lose their grandeur by being exhibited on the stage in distinct forms. It is not, however, as a great author has supposed *, that obscurity is any efficient cause of the sublime; for obscurity is mere privation: but the ideas excited in the imagination are narrowed and debased by being thus confined to particular impressions, upon the organs of sense; and those, too, of mean and ridiculous objects; such as men, whom we know, fantastically disguised to imitate old women.

* Inquiry into the Sublime and Beautiful.

41. Such subjects are, for the same reasons, little less improper for painting, and even more so for sculpture: for though painting may show indistinct and half-concealed forms, they will still be forms endowed with shape and colour of some sort; and consequently the powers of the imagination in augmenting and expanding will be limited in their exertions. In sculpture every thing is determinate and distinct; and, consequently, every objection acquires double force.

42. Symbolical figures may, however, be very proper subjects for either art: since, in pictures and statues, we do not consider them as real intelligent agents, but as elegant signs of convention meant to convey, under visible forms, certain abstract or generalized ideas to the understanding. In this sense they are like the personifications of poetry, although they cannot be used with the same licence, or to the same extent: for passions and appetites, and even privations, are often personified with the happiest effect in poetry, of which an instance has been already cited * ; but, if a painter or sculptor would represent anger or grief, he can only do it by making an angry or weeping individual; and, if he would represent hunger or thirst, he must necessarily employ the disgust-

* Part I. c. v. f. 31.

ing image of a starved or wasted object. But to exhibit the abstract virtues, energies, or perfections either of mind or body, he has only to copy such countenances and forms as are observed in nature to be most frequently joined to them, and best adapted to express them; and then to improve and embellish those countenances and forms from his own general knowledge of the human body, so as to render them no longer portraits of individuals, but general abstract imitations of the species, appropriated, by some peculiarities of conformation and expression, to represent certain characteristic attributes more strongly and distinctly, than ever they are found to exist in any particular person.

43. Such were the figures under which the artists of Greece represented their deities. They were exact representations of men and women; every limb, feature, and muscle being strictly natural; but still of such men and women, as the general laws of our structure only prove to exist; but of which no one ever saw a complete model in any single individual. Thus every physical and moral perfection had its appropriate figure; the attributes of power, wisdom, strength, agility, fruitfulness, &c. &c. being severally represented by different variations of the human shape and countenance; and, as the artists laboured through successive

ages to express given ideas by given forms, all
the redundancies of individual caprice were
restrained; and all the powers of ingenuity and
industry united to improve and embellish those
forms only; which were therefore carried to
a degree of perfection beyond that of Nature
herself.

44. It is, however, to the genius of poetry,
particularly to that of the author of the Iliad,
whoever he was, that imitative art principally
owes this high style of excellence: for it was
by perpetually grasping at his sublime ideas,
and labouring to express them in visible forms,
that they were principally enabled to reach it.
From this inexhaustible source, Phidias drew
the sublime character of his Jupiter, which
served as a model to all succeeding artists; and
from this also was derived that elevated and
yet chaste style of heroic or general nature,
which always distinguishes the works of the
great artists of Greece, even where the exertions of their talents were free and unrestrained;
and the forms and characters prescribed by no
rules but those of their own taste.   In these
there is one systematic principle of elegance
and beauty, descending from the highest to the
lowest of their efforts—from the furniture of
the temple to that of the kitchen—not consisting in any lines of grace or beauty mechanically
applied; but in a general congruity and pro-

CHAP.
III.
Of Judg-
ment.

priety. of arrangement in the parts, resulting from accurate intelligence guided by just feeling. By having their attention at once directed to common or individual nature, and to nature elevated and improved by the genius of poetry, they raised the style of imitation above that of its archetypes, without any of that deviation into manner, which has been so fatal to taste in modern times: for, though the revivers of the art in Italy, particularly Michel Angelo and his followers, have abundantly succeeded in departing from the individual peculiarities of their models, they have not been so successful in keeping clear of their own. Their figures, it is true, are not those of any one particular age or country, or of any one particular class of individuals; but, what is worse, they are those of one particular artist; and such as have never been seen but in his works.

45. We are naturally so much disposed to admire things, which appear difficult and surprising, that I do not wonder at the admiration, with which the works of Michel Angelo have been viewed, though I was never able to participate in it. Ease in design seems to me to be quite as requisite to the perfection of art, as ease in execution: for, whether the mind, or the hand of the artist display symptoms of constrained labour, the effect upon the imagination will be the same; the " ut sibi quivis

3

speret idem" being the infallible and indispens-
able· characteristic of high excellence in both.
" If I had seen a ghost," says Partridge on seeing Garrick in Hamlet, "I should have looked
exactly as that little man did * ;" and this simple
observation contains the justest and most exalted praise, that can be bestowed. But it is of
a kind, which no one, even of his most enthusiastic admirers, ever thought of bestowing
upon any composition of Michel Angelo. We
sympathize with the struggles of Laocoon and
his sons entangled in the folds of the serpents,
because we feel that they are such as we ourselves should make in a similar situation: but
the postures, into which the figures are thrown,
in Michel Angelo's picture of the Plague of
Serpents, are such as no human figures ever
did put themselves into, except in a drawing
academy, or painter's study.

46. It is not only with relation to themselves,
but with relation to others, that *the evil which
men do, lives after them, while the good is
often buried in their graves.* The good, which
this great artist did to imitative art, by co-ope-
rating with Lionardo da Vinci, and Fra. Bar-
tolomeo di San Marco in breaking through the
dry meagre style derived from the Byzantine
painters, ended with that style; and, of course,
ceased with his first great exertions: but the

* See Fielding's History of a Foundling.

evil which he did, in making extravagance and distortion pass for grandeur and vigour of character and expression, still spreads with increasing virulence of contagion; and, while it is supported by such brilliant theories as those of the Inquiry into the Sublime and Beautiful, there can be but faint hopes of its ceasing or subsiding. If the power of exciting surprise and astonishment be the genuine principle of sublimity, the compositions of the Sistine chapel and the tombs of the Medici are certainly the most sublime works in art; except, perhaps, some later productions of this school; for this is a style, in which imitators generally surpass their archetypes.

47. Invention, in every art, becomes more easy, the further it departs from the modesty and simplicity of nature: whence this style is flattering both to vanity and indolence; men being naturally pleased to find that they can produce, without much exertion of thought or science, works, which are more original and surprising, and therefore, according to this new system, more sublime than those, which are the slow result of deep research, long study, and accurate observation. The peculiarities of trick and eccentricities of manner are thus exalted into the characteristics of heaven-born genius and native talent; and if the public do not receive these gigantic efforts with the favour

which the artist expects, he comforts himself
that his works are above vulgar capacities; the
taste for the true sublime having been always
confined to the chosen few.

48. The great artists of antiquity, though
they exalt the characters of their gods and
heroes above those of ordinary nature; yet,
when exhibited in action, they put their limbs
and bodies into such postures, as such actions
would spontaneously produce in common life.
Jupiter wields his thunderbolt, Neptune his
trident, and Minerva her spear, exactly as we
should : but, in the figures of Michel Angelo,
all is directly reversed. The characters, though
remote from ordinary or individual nature, are
oftener below than above it, in dignity of expression; but then their attitudes and gestures
are such, as ordinary nature never does display,
under any circumstances; except such as influence it in a painter's or sculptor's study, or
academy. Even in representing sleep, he could
not employ a natural or easy posture; but has
put Adam into one, in which, all the narcotic
powers of opium could scarcely have enabled
him to rest.

49. It was not however to conceal any want
of industry or science that Michel Angelo ran
into this error; but from an eager and injudi-
cious desire to display knowledge, where he
should have consulted feeling, and expressed

sentiment. Though not to be compared even
with a third rate artist of ancient Greece in
knowledge of the structure and pathology of
the human body, he appears to have known
more than any of his contemporaries; and
when he made his knowledge subservient to his
art, and not his art to his knowledge, he produced some compositions of real excellence.
Such are almost all those, which he designed
for others to execute; such as the Raising of
Lazarus, the Descent from the Cross, and the
Entombing of Christ; in which he lowered the
tone of his invention to meet the capacities of
the colourists, Sebastian del Piombo, and Daniel di Volterra; and thus, through mere con-
descension, became natural, easy, and truly
sublime. Where he puts forth all his might,
and sacrifices just expression to what is called
grandeur of form and outline, he seems to me
to counteract his own ends: for form, considered in the abstract, is neither grand nor
mean; but owes all its power of exciting sentiments, either of the one kind, or the other, to
the association of ideas. We have learned, by
habitual observation, that certain forms of the
limbs and body are adapted to great exertions;
and certain forms of the features, to great expression, or the expression of great character,
and lofty sentiment; whence such forms excite
grand and elevated ideas of the objects, in

which they appear. In the abstract forms
themselves, there is, however, no more of
grandeur, than there is in so many mathematical lines of similar figure and dimension :
for, though we extend our ideas of grandeur
of character to the forms of inanimate objects,
it is still upon the principle of association and
sympathy ; as will be more fully explained in
the ensuing Chapter *.

50. All the effect of forms, in imitative art,
being thus owing to that which they signify or
express, truth is the principle and foundation
of all their power in affecting the mind : for, in
these cases, expression, that is not true, ceases
to be expression. If large muscles, limbs, and
features, and a vast outline of body do not
imply a capacity for great exertions, but appear heavy, torpid, unwieldy, or disjointed,

* Mr. Alison has observed that grandeur and sublimity
of form is entirely owing to association and expression:
but by endeavouring to reduce every thing to one principle, he makes that principle so completely the criterion
both of his judgment, and his perceptions, as to discover
sublimity in the forms of pieces of artillery, mortars,
spears, swords, and even daggers, because they are associated with ideas of danger, terror, &c. Essays on
Taste, p. 226.

His senses are little less complaisant to his theories in
the article of beauty ; which he also deduces entirely
from association; but seems to forget, though he abundantly exemplifies, the influence, which the association of
a favorite system may acquire in every thing.

X

they are only great in size; but void of all
grandeur of character. Even if they be drawn
with so much skill and science, as to express
fully and correctly this capacity; but are put
into action, in constrained or studied modes
and postures; or such, as the natural impulse
of the occasion would not spontaneously excite,
the expression becomes necessarily false and
affected; and, consequently, awakens no sympathy. We may, indeed, admire the skill and
ingenuity of the artist; and feel surprise at the
novelty and singularity of his inventions; but
both our admiration and surprise will be of
that kind, which is caused by the distortions
of a tumbler, or the tricks of a mountebank.

51. Upon this principle, there has always
appeared to me more of real grandeur and
sublimity in Raphael's small picture of the
Descent of God, or Vision of Ezekiel; and
in Salvator Rosa's of Saul and the Witch of
Endor, than in all the vast and turgid compositions of the Sistine chapel. Salvator, indeed,
scarcely ever attempts grandeur of form, in
the outlines of his figures; but he as seldom
misses, what is of much more importance in his
art, grandeur of effect in the general composition of his pictures. In the wildest flights of his
wild imagination, he always exhibits just and
natural action and expression; of which the

11

picture above cited is a remarkable instance.
The visionary spectres in the back ground are
wild and fantastic in their forms, as such fictitious beings might naturally be supposed to
appear ; but the mixture of horror and frenzy
in the witch, of awe and anxiety in the monarch,
and of terror and astonishment in the soldiers,
are expressed, both in their countenances and
gestures, with all the truth and nice discrimination of nature ; and with all the dignity and
elevation of poetry.   The general effect of the
whole, too, is extremely grand and imposing ;
and it is this general effect that pre-engages
the attention, and thus disposes the mind to
sympathize with the parts.   Those painters,
who, in their zeal for the grand style, affect to
despise what they are pleased to call tricks of
light and shade, do, in reality, despise the most
powerful means, which their art affords, of
producing the effect, which they profess to aim
at ; as will abundantly appear by the works of
Titian, Rubens, and Rembrandt ; who, without
any pretensions to grandeur of form, or dignity
or elevation of character or expression, have
produced grander, and more imposing pictures *, than any of those, who have sought for

, * See the Peter Martyr of Titian, the Daniel in the
Lions' Den of Rubens, the Raising of Lazarus and Cruci-
fixion of Rembrandt, &c.

x 2

grandeur in vast outlines and unusual postures.

52. Titian's expression of character is always
feeble ; Rubens's generally coarse ; and Rembrandt's ridiculously low and mean, though
admirably just and natural : conscious of his
deficiency in anatomical science, and precision
of outline, he cautiously avoided all objects
that might lead him to attempt elegance of
form, or grace and-dignity of character ; at
the same time that his sound judgment and
accurate observation pointed out the true expression of the temper and affections of the
mind, both in the countenances and gestures
of such figures, as were within his reach ; and
his unrivalled skill in the use of colours enabled him to exhibit it with a degree of exactitude and energy, which scarcely any other
painter has ever attained.

53. The principles of excellence in painting
are so distinct from those of sculpture, that
the highly elevated character of general or
ideal nature, so appropriate to the perfection
of the latter, is, perhaps, scarcely compatible
with that of the former ; which, being a more
complete imitation of its objects, requires a
stricter adherence to their individual peculiarities. In sculpture, we have only the forms
and lines of expression ; so that a statue is, in
itself, but an abstract imitation ; and, conse-

quently, [is employed to the greatest advantage
in exhibiting abstract nature : but, in painting, we have also the glow of animation ; and
the hues, as well as lines, of passion and affection; wherefore, as less is left to the imagination, the tone of imitation must be brought
down nearer to a level with the individual ob-

which it will consequently be judged.

54. In this respect, the difference between

has been already remarked, between epic and

the stage, the imitation being immediately addressed to the organ of sense, and entirely
dependent on its evidence, requires in many
cases, and admits in all, a stricter and more
detailed adherence to the peculiarities of common individual nature, than either of the sister
arts will ever allow.   Many of our most affecting tragedies are taken from the events of
common life ; and, in them, the personages
appear upon the stage in the common dresses
of the times—in laced coats, cocked hats, &c. ;
but no beauty of verse nor felicity of description could make us endure such things in epic
narration.   In the same manner, some of the
most interesting and affecting pictures, that the
art has ever produced, are taken from similar
events, and treated in a similar style ; such as

x 3

Mr. West's General Wolfe, Mr. Westall's Storm in Harvest, and Mr. Wright's Soldier's Tent; in all of which the pathos is much improved, without the picturesque effect being at all injured, by the characters and dresses being taken from common familiar life. But; in sculpture, this could not be borne; that art never having made any impression, or excited any sympathy by exhibiting common individual nature. Even in their portraits, the sculptors of the fine ages of Greece always took the liberty of enlarging the features, and invigorating the expression, of whatever kind it happened to be; and if they employed drapery, it was always of that particular sort, which is peculiarly appropriated to the art, and which may therefore be properly called sculpturesque drapery.

55. Horace's advice of preferring the characters and fictions of the Iliad to those of common nature or history, as the materials of tragedy, seems to me very ill adapted to the principle of modern drama; how well soever it may have suited the splendid musical exhibitions of the Greek theatre. The vast and exalted images, which are raised in the mind, by the pomp of heroic verse, and the amplification of heroic fiction, shrink into a degree of meanness, that becomes quite ridiculous, when

reduced to the standard of ordinary nature, and exhibited in the person of a modern actor. The impression, which the sight of Achilles, on the French stage, first made upon me will never be effaced: a more farcical and ludicrous figure could scarcely present itself to my imagination, than a pert smart Frenchman, well rouged, laced, curled, and powdered; with the gait of a dancing master, and the accent of a milliner, attempting to personate that tremendous warrior, the nodding of whose crest dismayed armies ; and the sound of whose voice made even the war horse shudder. The generality of the audience, indeed, never having viewed the original through the dazzling and expansive medium of Homer's verses, thought only of the lover of Iphigenia ; and were, of course, as well satisfied with Mons. Achille, as with any other amorous hero, *that struts and frets his hour upon the stage.* In this, as in other instances, the habitual association of ideas makes the same object contemptibly ridiculous to one, and affectingly serious to another. In this country, however, the characters of the Iliad and Odyssey have been so generally known since Pope's splendid translation, that no tragedy has been popular, in which they have been introduced; and, I believe, Thomson's Agamemnon is the only instance of their being brought upon the stage.

X 4

56. Horace 'drew his 'rules and instructions
from the practice of the 'Greek theatre; where
the actors were so disguised by masks and co-
thurni; and the whole 'performance so much
more remote from ordinary nature, than the
modern drama, that incongruities of this kind
were less prominent and offensive. The most
eminent,.too, of the Greek tragedians changed
and perverted the characters of the Iliad and
Odyssey, when they brought them upon the
stage; 'as appears from the Ulysses and Menelaus in the plays of Sophocles and Euripides,
still extant; which are gross caricatures of the
same.characters in the Homeric poems. It
was probably, from some caricature of this
kind, that Horace took the portrait of Achilles,
which he recommends to dramatic writers * :
for it is extremely unlike the hero of the Iliad;
who is, indeed, *impiger, iracundus, acer*;
active, irascible, and eager : but so far from
renouncing or denying any of the established
rights and institutions of law, morality, or religion, that he is a steady and zealous observer
of all:—pious to his gods, dutiful to his parents, hospitable and polite to his guests, kind
and generous to his subjects, faithful and affec-

* ———— " Si forte reponis Achillem:
Jmpiger, iracundus, inexorabilis, acer,
Jura neget sibi nata, nihil non arroget armis."
Ar. Poet. 120,

tionate to his friends, and open, honourable, and sincere towards all. ⸱ Neither ʹis he an inexorable enemy, till exasperated by the loss of the 'man most dear to him, and soured by despair and impending death. ʹ Despising his own life, as a frail and transitory possession of little value, while the pride of conscious superiority taught him to consider that of others, as of still less value, he becomes sanguinary through magnanimity, and gives an unbounded scope to his resentment from not thinking the objects of it worth sparing *. Considered in this point of view, the seeming incongruities in the characters of several of the mighty heroes and conquerors of real history become consistent and united. In their private and individual transactions, where their particular sympathies have been called forth, they have been mild, generous, and compassionate; but, in dealing with mankind in the mass, they have considered human life in the abstract, as a delusive mockery of vain hopes and fears, which it was almost a matter of indifference, either to preserve or destroy.

57. Had the Achilles of the Iliad, or the Ulysses of the Odyssey been such as Horace has described the one, or Euripides exhibited

* See his reply to the supplications of Lycaon, Il. xxi. v. 99.

the other *, they would not have interested the untutored, but uncorrupted feelings of an Homeric audience, how well soever they might have succeeded in the Attic theatre : for men, in the early stages of society, when manners are the general substitutes for laws, are scrupulously observant of whatever custom or public opinion has established as a criterion of politeness or good breeding ; the principles of which, as before observed, are the same in all ages and all countries, howsoever the modes of showing them may vary. Hence neither the violent and atrocious passions of the first of these heroes, nor the wily artifice and versatility of the second, ever make either of them deviate from the character of a gentleman, even according to our present notions of that character, allowing always for the change of exterior forms or ceremonies of fashion. Though the one is impetuous, and the other temperate in his expressions of resentment ; both equally preserve the dignity of high pride and conscious superiority ; and both are invariably kind, civil, and attentive to all, whom the weakness of sex or age entitled to their protection or compassion. Any of that unfeeling rudeness, with which the Ulysses of Euripides rejects the supplications of the captive Hecuba for the life

* In the Hecuba.

of her last remaining child ; or any of that
selfish coldness, with which the Æneas of
Virgil treats the unfortunate princess, whose
affections he had seduced, would have so degraded either of the Homeric heroes in the
estimation of the simple but gallant warriors,
to whom the poet sang, that all their subsequent actions would have become uninteresting, as flowing from the polluted source of
vulgar insolence or selfish meanness.   Though
we are now, perhaps, less fastidious than they
were upon such points of morality, we still
appear to be much more so than either the
Athenians or Romans were at the respective
periods of their highest degrees of civilization
and refinement : for such a scene as that of
Euripides, above alluded to, would not now
be borne on any stage ; and every modern
reader of the Æneid finds that the episode of
Dido, though in itself the most exquisite piece
of composition existing, weakens extremely the
subsequent interest of the poem ; it being impossible to sympathize either cordially or kindly
with the fortunes or exertions of a hero who
sneaks away from his high-minded and much
injured benefactress in a manner so base and
unmanly.   When, too, we find him soon after
imitating all the atrocities *, and surpassing

---

* Æneid. x. 520. 590, &c.

the utmost arrogance of the furious and vindictive Achilles*, without displaying any of his
generosity, pride, or energy, he becomes at
once mean and odious, and only excites scorn
and indignation; especially when, at the conclusion, he presents to the unfortunate Lavinia
a hand stained with the blood of her favoured
lover, whom he had stabbed while begging for
quarter; and after being rendered incapable of
resistance †.

§ 58. Indeed, I cannot but think, in spite of
all that critics have said of the *judgment* of
Virgil, as opposed to the invention of Homer,
that, if there be any quality, in which the
author of the Iliad stands pre-eminently superior to all his followers or imitators, it is in
that of judgment; or a just sense of propriety
in adapting actions to persons, and circumstances to characters; and modifying his fictions to the understandings and degrees of
information of his audience; so that they
might appear wonderful, but not incredible.
Virgil's great distinctive excellence is delicacy
of sentiment and expression, joined to the most
consummate technical skill and just feeling in
dressing out and embellishing every circumstance or incident, that he employs: but in
the appropriation of those circumstances and

* Æneid. x. 830.   † Æneid. xii. 930, et seq.

incidents, to persons and characters, he is
generally less happy than Tasso, and in no
degree whatever to be compared with him—
" cui nec viget quidquam simile aut secundum."

CHAP.
III.
Of Judg-
ment.

PART III.

OF THE PASSIONS.

CHAPTER I.

OF THE SUBLIME AND PATHETIC.

1. THE passions, considered either physically, as belonging to the constitution of the individual, or morally, as operating upon that of society, do not come within the scope of my present inquiry; it being only by sympathy, that they are connected with subjects of taste; or that they produce, in the mind, any of those tender feelings, which are called pathetic, or those exalted or enthusiastic sentiments, which are called sublime. When we see others suffer, we naturally suffer with them, though not in the same degrees; nor even in the same modes: for those sufferings, which we should most dread personally to endure, we delight to see exhibited or represented, though not actually endured by others; and, nevertheless, this delight certainly arises from sympathy.

2. Of this kind is that, which we receive from tragedy, and from all pathetic or impassioned narratives; the intrinsic truth or false-

hood of which, as before observed, does not
matter, provided they have the semblance of
truth; that is, provided the characters be consistent with themselves; the incidents with the
characters, and with each other; and the expressions of sentiment and passion such, as
such incidents would naturally excite in such
characters.

3. The great author, indeed, already so often
cited, asserts that *the nearer tragedy approaches the reality, and the further it
removes us from all idea of fiction, the more
perfect is its power*; and he has illustrated
this position by an example stated with his
usual brilliancy and eloquence: " Choose,"
says he, " a day to represent the most sublime
and affecting tragedy we have; appoint the
most favourite actors; spare no cost upon the
scenes and decorations; unite the greatest
efforts of poetry, painting, and music; and
when you have collected your audience, just
at the moment, when their minds are erect
with expectation, let it be reported that a state
criminal of high rank is on the point of being
executed in an adjoining square, in a moment
the emptiness of the theatre would demonstrate the comparative weakness of the imitative arts, and proclaim the triumph of real
sympathy *."

* Sublime and Beautiful, P. I. f. xv.

4. This is unquestionably true: but is not the triumph as much of curiosity, as of sympathy ; and would not the sudden appearance of any very renowned foreign chief or potentate, in the adjoining square, equally empty the benches of the theatre ? I apprehend that it would ; and cannot but suspect that even a bottle conjuror, a flying witch, or any other miraculous phænomenon of the kind, being announced with sufficient confidence to obtain belief, would have the same effect : wherefore, to make the comparison between the exhibitions on the scaffold, and those on the stage, fairly, we must suppose them both to be equally frequent and common ; in which case, I cannot but hope, for the honour of human nature, that scenes of mimic distress would be more attractive, than those of real suffering. Happily, in this country, the execution of a state criminal of high rank, or indeed of any rank, has of late years been a rare event ; and one, which very few persons now living have ever witnessed. At the time too, when the above statement was made, such a spectacle would have been almost equally novel in any part of Europe : but we have since had abundant and lamentable proof, in the neighbouring country, of how much its interest declines with its becoming common : for during the latter days of the tyranny of Robespierre, the

èxècutions of pretended state criminals of every rank, age, sex; and condition were scarcely noticed, or attended by any but a hired rabble; and that atrocious and despicable monster is said to have procured the condemnation and execution of the nine young and beautiful girls, who presented a chaplet to the Prussian commander at Verdun, merely to rouse the wearied attention of the populace by a more affecting exhibition *.

5. Let us suppose that, during this period of juridical slaughter and methodical murder, all the theatres of Paris had been shut; and all dramatic exhibitions suppressed for an indefinite time; and that, at the latter end of it, when men had *supped full with horrors*, and grown familiar with scenes of real distress, such a theatrical spectacle, as that above described, had been announced for one night only: then, I think that even the scaffold of Citizen Egalité himself would have been forsaken for the mimic sufferings of Andromaque or Zayre.

6. Much must, however, in all cases, depend upon the different degrees of sensibility of different individuals. The feelings of some men are so tremblingly alive, that almost every degree of mimic distress interests them; and

---

* Memoires d'un detenu.

those of others so immoveably torpid, that scarcely any real sufferings, but their own, can affect them. Large masses of people taken collectively are, indeed, naturally composed of nearly the same materials: but, nevertheless, their natural feelings are greatly altered by education, government, and habit of life. The Romans, a nation of soldiers, hardened by the trade of war, delighted in seeing trained slaves contend for their lives with each other, and with wild beasts: but when the Asiatic monarch, who, by living among them, had acquired their taste, treated his subjects with such a spectacle, they, at first, turned away from it with expressions of horror and affright; but, nevertheless, soon became reconciled to such diversions*; as we also should, if they were once introduced amongst us: for the passions, as well as the senses, easily become vitiated; and acquire a relish for higher stimulants. Cockfighting is only a humbler species of the same diversion, as hunting is only a humbler species of war; and a taste for the one would soon rise into a taste for the other.

7. Not that I mean to infer that men ever feel delight in seeing pain and agony, either suffered or inflicted: for, in these cases, it is not with the sufferings, but with the exertions

---

* Liv. Hist. lib. xli. c. 20.

of the combatants, that they sympathize:— with the exhibitions of courage, dexterity, vigour, and address, which shone forth, in these combats of life and death, more conspicuously and energetically than they would have done, had the object of contention been less important. As far as the sufferings of the wounded and dying combatants were felt by the spectators, their feelings were painful; and, in the enervated minds of the Asiatics, these painful sympathies overpowered the others; while, in the obdurate breasts of the Romans, they scarcely made any impression at all. They only heard with indignation and contempt the shrieks of agony or groans of anguish; but exulted in every triumph of skilful valour, and glowed with every display of unshaken fortitude. The one sympathized only with the weaknesses, and the other only with the energies of human nature displayed in these dreadful trials; and consequently the sympathies of the one produced only humiliation and disgust; and those of the others only exultation and delight.

8. The Romans had a mime or dramatic dance, composed by Nævius, in which the principal character, named Laureolus, after displaying his courage and address in various enormities, was crucified upon the stage; and, as this horrible catastrophé afforded the actor

opportunities of displaying great professional skill in exhibiting the pangs and agonies of so cruel a death, supported by the desperate firmness of an obdurate criminal, it seems to have been a favourite entertainment among that ferocious and sanguinary people *. One of their tyrants, however, probably Domitian, conceiving, like the elegant author above cited, that what was so interesting and impressive in the imitation, must be so much more so in the reality, exhibited a real criminal actually nailed to a cross, in the last act; and, to show that there was no trick or counterfeit in it, had him, in that state, torn to pieces by wild beasts †. What was the effect of this high sea-soned specimen of the Sublime and Pathetic, we are not informed; but we may reasonably infer that it was not such as the grand ballet-master expected; or we should have heard of its being repeated; since many of his successors had a similar taste, and were equally free from all *compunctious visitings of nature*, that might obstruct the gratification of it. The populace, however, though they had no dislike to see men worried and torn to pieces by wild beasts, preferred seeing it in equal combat, where the man and the beast were fairly op-

* Sueton. in Calig. c.lvii.—Juvenal. Sat. viii. v. 187.
† Martial. Epigr. lib. i. epigr. vii.

posed to each other; and created an interest, not only by their dangers and sufferings, but by the feats of strength, courage, and dexterity, which they displayed in avoiding or inflicting them.

9. In the decline of the empire, when all the honourable pride of the republicans was extinct, and all the sanguinary ferocity of their manners preserved, men of the highest rank, and even women, descended into the Arena, and personally entered the lists of these savage combats. By sympathizing with the triumphs of gladiators, and admiring their prowess, they naturally conceived a wish to participate in their glory: whence the same restlessness of vanity, which induced one man to stake his fortune at a gaming table, induced another to stake his life in the amphitheatre. Distinction was the reward of success, equally looked to by both; (for even avarice is but a modification of vanity) and the value of this reward is not estimated so much according to its real or imaginary importance, as in proportion to the risk to be encountered, and the agitation and anxiety to be endured in the acquisition of it: whence we perpetually see men, who are infected with the rage of gaming, risk all, that makes their lives comfortable and happy, to gain that, which, if acquired, could not make them, in the smallest degree, more com-

fortable or more happy. Such was human nature in the forests of Germany, as well as in the palaces of Rome; and such it continues to be still, in the wilds of America, as well as in the clubs and taverns of London and Paris.

10. It has been ingeniously supposed by a very excellent critic, and still more excellent dramatic writer, that the horrible rites, with which the North American savages sacrifice their captives, do not proceed so much from a spirit of cruelty or vengeance, as from a spirit of gaming: war being, with them, not merely a contest of active strength and courage, for national honour and superiority; but, like-wise, of passive fortitude and endurance, for the palm of individual firmness and energy of mind; the dreadful trials of which, by enhanc-ing the risks, animate the zeal, and stimulate the anxiety of contention, in the mighty game, which is played between the hostile tribes[*]. The vengeance of savages, however, is always extremely atrocious and violent: for, as their social relations, and, consequently, the objects of their passions, are few, the whole force of the mind goes collectively with them to the points, to which they are directed. There is no doubt, too, that, in minds, sufficiently ob-durate to behold, without any painful emo-

---

[*] See Preface to a Series of Plays on the Passions.

tions, all the lingering agonies, to which. the unhappy victims are subjected, the exertions of energy and fortitude, which are thus called forth, excite interesting, and, consequently, pleasing sympathies; and afford a spectacle of entertaining, and even grateful horror, to the savage tormentors.

11. Even in civilized societies, a sort of prurient fondness for attending the executions of criminals is often observable, which arises from the same principle: for men are not so perversely constituted by nature, as ever to feel delight in beholding the sufferings of those, who never injured them: but, nevertheless, they all feel delight in beholding exertions of energy; and all feel curiosity to know in what modes or degrees, those exertions can be displayed, under the awful circumstances of impending death. With those exertions they sympathize; and, therefore, feel an interest not in proportion to the sufferings, but to the heroism and gallantry of the person executed; unless in particular instances, where indignation at the atrocity of the crime stifles every other sentiment.

12. When the stoic philosopher says that a great and virtuous man struggling with adversity is a spectacle, upon which the gods might look down with pleasure; it is not that he supposes the nature of the deity to be cruel,

or to delight in scenes of anguish and distress; but ,because adversity and distress call forth those energies of the human mind, in which its, superiority over all other terrestrial beings seemed principally to consist; and of which the full exertion might render it an object worthy of the attention, and even of the admiration of higher orders of intelligences.

13. But, how much soever the calm energies of virtue, called forth by exertions of passive fortitude, may interest the philosophical and contemplative mind, its more active and violent efforts, displayed in feats of strength, courage, and dexterity; in the tumultuous battle, or deadly combat; are always far more interesting to the vulgar. When the Abbé du Bos, therefore, asserts that the Romans, by prohibiting human sacrifices, indirectly condemned their taste for the fights of gladiators, he confounds two things, which are extremely different; and thence attributes to those sanguinary destroyers of mankind, an inconsistency, which only existed in his own ideas. A lover of cock-fighting would think it very strange to be told that he condemned his own taste for so heroic a diversion, by expressing a dislike to see cocks killed in a poulterer's yard; and the frequenters of bull-baiting in England, or of bull-feasts in Spain, would by no means allow that a butcher's slaughter-

house could afford them equal, or similar
amusement. To render such spectacles interesting, there must be a display of courage,
vigour, and address: for it is by sympathizing
with the energetic passions, that the spectators
are amused or delighted: and though the
energies of passive fortitude might have been
displayed by the victims of superstition, as
well as by those of justice, or injustice; they
must, nevertheless, have been very flat and
insipid, compared with those, which shone
forth in the varied and animated contests of
the amphitheatre; where the contention was
equal, and life and honour the prize contended
for. Our boxing matches are contests of the
same kind upon a lower scale; and the frequenters of them would probably feel as much
horror and disgust as any other persons, were
they to see men deprived of the power of resistance, or, opposed to very unequal force,
beaten as the several combatants beat each
other: but the display of manly intrepidity,
firmness, gallantry, activity, strength, and presence of mind, which these contests call forth,
is an honour to the English nation, and such
as no man needs be ashamed of viewing with
interest, pride and delight: and we may safely
predict, that if the magistrates, through a mistaken notion of preserving the public peace,
succeed in suppressing them, there will be an

end of that sense of honour and spirit of gallantry, which distinguishes the common people
of this country from that of all others; and
which is not only the best guardian of their
morals, but perhaps the only security now left
either for our civil liberty or political inde-
pendence. If men are restrained from fighting occasionally for prizes and honorary distinctions, they will soon cease to fight at all;
and decide their private quarrels with daggers
instead of fists; in which case, the lower order
will become a base rabble of cowards and
assassins, ready at any time to sacrifice the
higher to the avarice and ambition of a foreign
tyrant.

14. It is observed, by the great father of
philosophical criticism, that the radical difference between tragedy and comedy is that
the one exhibits the characters of men superior, and the other, inferior to those of ordinary nature *; that is, tragedy displays the
energies, and comedy, the weaknesses of humanity: for, in tragedy, it is not the actual distress; but the motives, for which it is endured;
the exertions, which it calls forth; and the
sentiments of heroism, fortitude, constancy, or
tenderness, which it, in consequence, displays,
that produce the interest; and awaken all the

---

* Aristot. Poet. f. iv.

PART III. OF THE PASSIONS.

331

CHAP.
I.
Of the Su-
blime and
Pathetic.

exquisite and delightful thrills of sympathy.
The distress of a miser, for the loss of his money, is as real, and as great, as that of a lover
for the loss of his mistress; or of a hero for
the loss of his honour: but, nevertheless, as it
is purely selfish, it awakens no sympathy; nor
is it ever employed except to excite ridicule or
aversion. The pains of natural, or accidental
disease, are as distressing to the sufferer, as
the punishments inflicted by a tyrant, and are
equally subjects of sympathy to his friends:
but, as they appertain solely to himself; and
are the result of accident, intemperance, or
physical necessity, they neither display any
voluntary exertions of disinterested fortitude;
nor call forth any enthusiastic effusions of
generosity, or tenderness: wherefore no writer
has ever thought of heightening the distress of
his tragedy, by giving his hero a fit of the
gout, the stone, or the colic; though these,
perhaps, may be more real and serious evils,
than any, which he makes him endure.

15. All the distress of dramatic fiction is
known and felt, at the time of its exhibition,
to be merely fiction: but the sentiments, excited by it, are really expressed; and expressed,
too, with all the truth and energy, which real
feelings could inspire; accompanied with all
the graces of emphasis, tone, and gesture;
which can convey those feelings to the soul of

the spectator, with the full force, and vivid
freshness of real nature. The sympathies,
therefore, which they excite, are real and complete; and much more strong and effective,
than if they were produced by scenes of real
distress; for in that case, the sufferings, which
we beheld, would excite such a painful degree
of sympathy, as would overpower and suppress
the pleasant feelings, excited by the noble,
tender, or generous sentiments, which we heard
uttered. The natural feeling of every sensible
and benevolent mind, on beholding real calamity or distress, is a wish to relieve it; and
only the obdurate heart of the savage can at-
tend sufficiently to the exertions of heroism,
patience, or, fortitude, which it may excite, to
sympathize with them: but in fictitious distress,
our attention is not turned aside, or interrupted by any calls of humanity; so that our
sympathies are indulged freely, without hin-
drance or obstruction. In some persons, indeed, the degree of nervous sensibility is so
excessive, that the expressions of distress,
which they know to be fictitious, excite painful emotions: but this is a sort of morbid
sensibility; or else it arises from a morbid
imagination; which, like that of the Knight
of La Mancha, confounds, in some degree,
the representation with the reality*.

* Don Quixote, P. ii. b. ii. c. ix.

16. From the days of Aristotle, to the present time, critics have repeated, one after the other, that terror and pity το φοβερον, και ελεεινον, are the fundamental principles of tragedy: but how any man, in his senses, can feel either fear from dangers, which he knows to be unreal; or commiseration for distress, which he knows to be fictitious, I am at a loss to discover; never having found any such pliability in my own feelings; by which alone, I can judge of those of others. I sympathize, indeed, with the expressions of passion, and mental energy, which those fictitious events excite; because the expressions are real; and this is what, I believe, all other persons of just feeling do: but the acute Stagirite appears to have been led into an error, on this point, by imagining that stage exhibitions were really meant to be deceptions; which they were still less in the Greek theatres, than in ours. The most able and acute of his followers seems to have been equally misled by the same ill-founded notion*; which was, I believe, first exploded by Doctor Johnson†; though the Abbé du Bos had before ventured to dissent from it; at the same time that he tacitly admitted it in his subsequent arguments ‡.

---

* Horat. Ep. ii. 1. v. 210·   † Preface to Shakspeare.
‡ Reflexions Critiques.

17. Longinus observes that the effect of the sublime is *to lift up the soul; to exalt it into ecstasy; so that, participating, as it were, of the splendors of the divinity, it becomes filled with joy and exultation; as if it had itself conceived the lofty sentiments which it has heard* * : *wherefore, the passions of grief, sorrow, fear, &c. are incapable of any sublime expression; or of producing any sublime effect* † : these passions being selfish; and arising out of actual suffering, or the apprehension of suffering; neither of which are proper subjects for great or elevated expression of sentiment: for unless the sentiment be elevated above all selfish considerations, it can neither be pathetic nor sublime; qualities, which in all expression of passion or mental feeling, are in some degree inseparably connected ‡.

18. Hence Aristotle justly blames those tragic writers, who put, into the mouths of the personages of the drama, whining complaints

---

* ἀ γαρ εἰς πειθω τὰς ακροωμενὰς, ἀλλ᾽ εἰς ἰκστασιν αγει τα ὑπερφυα.—S. i.

Φυσει γαρ πως ὑπο τ᾽αληθὰς ὑψους ἐπαιρεται τε ἡμων ἡ ψυχη, και, γαυρον τι αναθημα λαμβανουσα, πληρουται χαρας και μεγαλαυχιας, ὡς αυτη γεννησασα ὁπερ ηκὰσεν.—S. vii.

† και γαρ παθη τινα διιστωτα ὑλὰς και ταπεινα εὑρισκεται, καθαπερ οικτοι, λυπαι, φοβοι.—S. viii.

‡ παθος δε ὑψὰς μετεχει τοσὰτον, ὁποσον ηθος ηδονης.

LONGIN. ſ. xxix.

of their own sufferings; of which he quotes two instances *; and of which, we have another now extant, in the Philoctetes of Sophocles; whose ulcerated foot and lamentations over it, howsoever just, expressive, and appropriate, would not be endured on any modern stage; not only, because the fiction is, in itself, offensive and disgusting, but because every expression or complaint of distress, that such a calamity can excite, must necessarily display some degree of this kind of selfish weakness; and consequently be unfit for tragedy; which can properly exhibit only the energies of human nature. It matters not, indeed, whether these energies be displayed in passive, or active fortitude; in suffering or acting; in the mild and gentle, or the furious and impetuous passions and affections: but it is absolutely necessary that those passions and affections should be decisive and energetic; nor is any degree of coldness, weakness, or moderation at all more allowable in the tender loves of Romeo and Juliet, than in the atrocious ambition of Lady Macbeth. The instant the tone of expression is relaxed, the characters become comic, or at least cease to be tragic.

19. All sympathies, excited by just and appropriate expression of energetic passion;

---

* Poetic. f. xxviii.

whether they be of the tender or violent kind, are alike sublime; as they all tend to expand and elevate the mind; and fill it with those enthusiastic raptures, which Longinus justly states to be the true feelings of sublimity. Hence that author cites instances of sublime from the tenderest odes of love, as well as from the most terrific images of war; and with equal propriety: it not being with the particular love of Sappho, that we sympathize, in reading her beautiful and impassioned ode: for we neither know its object; nor, unless in love, do we substitute any particular one in the place of it; but we all feel the general sentiments of rapturous and enthusiastic affection, which are so warmly and energetically expressed; and the feelings, thus excited, are really and properly sublime, as well as pathetic; that is, highly elevated above every thing selfishly low or sordid: for the word *sublime*, both according to its use and etymology, must signify *high* or *exalted*; and, if an individual choose that, in his writings, it should signify *terrible*, he only involves his meaning in a confusion of terms, which naturally leads to a confusion of ideas.

20. It is the rapture and enthusiasm of the expressions, and warmth and elevation of the sentiments, which makes the difference between the erotic compositions of Sappho, Theocritus,

and Otway; and those of Bafo, Lord Roches-
ter, and Aretine. In the first, the sexual
inclination is exalted into a generous heroic
passion; which, when expressed with all the
glowing energy and spirit of poetry, becomes
truly sublime: but, in the latter, it is degraded
into sordid sensuality; which, how elegantly
soever expressed, can never be exalted: for
mere appetite is, in its nature, selfish, through
all its gratifications, and cannot, therefore, be
in any case, sublime *.

21. Not only love, however, but its opposite, hatred or malignity, may be sublime in
poetry; as that of Shylock, in some scenes of
Shakspeare, unquestionably is: not that malignity is a sublime passion: but that, in strong
and powerful minds, such as that of Shylock
is feigned to be, it is an energetic one; and,
consequently, well adapted to excite sentiments and expressions of great and enthusiastic
force and vigour; with which we sympathize,
and not with the passion itself, which could

---

* I am aware that the doctrine of Longinus, upon this
subject, has lately been censured by a critic of very high
authority; (Blair, Lect. iv.) and attributed to a confusion
of ideas: but it appears to me that all the confusion is in
the critic himself; who, in this, as in many other instances, has confounded the effect of poetical description,
or expression of a passion, with the effect of the passion
itself; from which, it is widely different; as this author
acknowledges in another part of his work.

Z

only excite odious and disgusting feelings ; such as every person would be disposed to shun, rather than to seek.

22. In like manner, it is not with the agonies of a man writhing in the pangs of death, that we sympathize, on beholding the celebrated group of Laocoon and his sons; for such sympathies can only be painful and disgust-ing; but it is with the energy and fortitude of mind, which those agonies call into action and display: for, though every feature and every muscle is convulsed, and every nerve contracted, yet the breast is expanded and the throat compressed to show that he suffers in silence. I therefore still maintain, in spite of the blind and indiscriminate admiration, which pedantry always shows for every thing, which bears the stamp of high authority, that Virgil has debased the character, and robbed it of all its sublimity and grandeur of expression, by making Laocoon *roar like a bull* * ; and, I think, that I may safely affirm that, if any writer of tragedy were to make any one personage of his drama roar out in the same manner, on being mortally wounded, the whole audience would burst into laughter ; how pathetic soever the incidents might be, that

* " Clamores simul horrendos ad sidera tollit ;
    Quales mugitus, fugit quum saucius aram   .
    Taurus, et incertam excussit cervice securim."

accompanied it.   Homer has been so sensible
of this, that in the vast number and variety of
deaths, which he has described, he has never
made a single Greek cry out on receiving a
mortal wound.   Even in the female character,,
no such display of weakness would be endured
on the stage; nor could all the gentle inno-
cence and amiable simplicity of Desdemona,
have preserved the interest of the last scene,
if, instead of supplicating for mercy, with the
collected calmness of a strong, as well as with
the tranquil meekness of a delicate mind, she
had screamed out *Murder!* or fallen into
hysterics.

23. The means, however, which sculpture
and painting have of expressing the energies
and affections of the mind are so much more
limited, than those of poetry, that their comparative influence upon the passions is very
small; few persons looking for any thing more
in a picture or a statue, than mere exactitude
of imitation, or exertions of technical skill;
and when more is attempted, its effect never
approaches to that of poetry; the artist being
not only confined to one point of time, but to
the mere exterior expressions of feature and
gesture; while the poet unlocks the mind, and
pours into his verses all its inward sentiments,
energies, and affections.

24. When the actor joins his talents to those
of the poet, the powers of painting, sculpture;
and poetry are all united and improved ; wherefore a fine drama well acted may justly be considered as one of the highest of all intellectual
gratifications. It is asserted, indeed, by a great
critic, that *familiar comedy only* is *more powerful in the theatre than* in *the page*; but that
imperial tragedy *is less so**; to which I can
by no means agree; for though it be true, as
this author observes, that *no voice or gesture
can add dignity or force to the soliloquy of
Cato*, they may add both to that of Lady Macbeth. The philosophical reflections of the stoic,
being free from all passion, admit of no enthusiastic expression in the actor, and are therefore
unfit for the stage : but the tumultuous effusions of aspiring hopes and atrocious desires,
which agitate the bosom of a daring and ambitious princess, on her first conceiving designs
of murder and usurpation, display the most
interesting variety of energetic passions ; and,
consequently, admit of a higher degree of embellishment from good acting than can be
employed in comedy of any kind.

25. As most of the crimes and enormities of
mankind arise from the violence of the passions,
moralists have endeavoured to win over pride

* Johnson's Preface to Shakspeare.

to the side of virtue, by representing all passion as weakness; and considering the energy of reason as the only real energy of the human mind: but, nevertheless, the powers of mental feeling are as much powers of the mind, as those of thinking; and the different degrees of energy, in both, equally mark the different degrees of perfection, or imperfection, in different individuals. Those philosophers, who would exalt the one by suppressing the other, attempt to form a model of human perfection from a design of their own; which may, indeed, excite our admiration, as a consummate work of art; but will never awaken our sympathies, as a vigorous effusion of nature. The Cato of Addison is the image of a perfect man drawn after one of these artificial models; but the Achilles of Homer is the image of a perfect man, such as came from the hands of the Creator, with every faculty of mind and body formed upon the same scale; so that every act that he does, and every sentence that he utters, is marked by the same bold and unrestrained energy of character. The one is like a yew in a garden, which has been pruned and shorn into a determinate and regular shape, that it may fit its place, and not overshadow or injure the more tender plants, that grow near it: but the other is like an oak in the forest, which spreads its branches widely and irregularly, in every direc-

tion, over the smaller trees that surround it;
and while it protects some, blights others.

26· No character can be interesting or impressive in poetry, that acts strictly according
to reason : for reason excites no sympathies,
nor awakens any affections ; and its effect is
always rather to chill than to inflame. It is
possible for the motives of passion in poetical
fiction to be too reasonable and too just ; so as
to give an appearance of sedate and considerate
moral sentiment to that, which can only fulfil
its purposes by appearing to be the spontaneous
effusion of glowing and enthusiastic feeling.
Had Agamemnon degraded Achilles from his
rank, or expelled him from his dominions,
instead of merely taking away his mistress,
his anger would have been more just, but
less interesting: as, in such a case, any man
would have felt anger; which would consequently have appeared only a common passion, arising from no peculiar nicety of sensibility, dignity of pride, or exaltation of honour.
The circumstances which excite the jealousy of
Othello have been thought by some, for whose
judgment I have the highest respect, to be too
weak : but, nevertheless, had the poet made
them much stronger, his infuriate jealousy
would have become reasonable suspicion·; and,
consequently, have lost all its interest, and all
its energy. It has often struck me that the

S

provocations given by Antonio to Shylock are
too great; and that the *calling him dog, and
spitting on his Jewish gabberdine,* weaken the
effect of his malignity, by making it appear
moral resentment. The authoress of the tragedy of de Montford has, therefore, in my
opinion, judged rightly in making the more·
dignified, but equally infuriate hatred of that
personage arise from slighter causes, magnified
into importance, and tinged with rancour by
the sour and gloomy malignity of the mind,
through which they are seen. By a strain of
poetry, admirably suited to the occasion, all
those petty offences of private society, which
are usually committed without design, and
borne without notice, are heightened into atrocious insults and deadly injuries, without any
intentional exaggeration, or wilful misrepre-
sentation, being in the smallest degree manifested *.

27. Such hatred, it may be justly said, is not
reasonable; but no more is any passion, that is
sufficiently energetic and enthusiastic to serve
the purposes of tragedy. All very violent passion verges towards madness; but provided it
does not, at the same time, verge towards folly,
it will not thereby be less effective in exciting
sympathy: for every display of perverted
energy, in the mind, may be, in the highest

* See Act ii. sc. ii.

degree, interesting and sublime; though its
weaknesses and defects can only be ridiculous
or contemptible. This extreme violence of.
passion, it is true, seldom appears in nature;
but if the passion itself appear, as the poet
has drawn it, he has a right to increase its
'degree : for, as the business, both of epic and
tragic poetry, is to display, and even to heighten
and embellish the energies of human nature,
both have equal liberty in heightening and embellishing those of the mind ; though the dramatic poet, for reasons before mentioned, be,
in other respects, more limited in the use of
this licence, than the epic.

28. Upon these principles, it is impossible
that tragedy should exhibit examples of pure
and strict morality, without becoming dull and
uninteresting; and, consequently, as useless as
insipid : for examples, which attract no attention, can convey no instruction. It has been
objected to the tragedy of the Fair Penitent,
by a critic who has entered into a specific examination of it, that the heroine *is very far
from being an amiable or unexceptionable
lady* *; upon which I can only observe, that,
if she had been either the one, or the other,
this critic would never have had an opportunity,

---

* See a review of this tragedy in a periodical paper
called the Lounger, published at Edinburgh, No. 25,

either of applauding, or censuring her: as the
play would scarcely have survived a first representation, and certainly not have lasted to a
second generation. Another critic, of the same
nation, hints that this want of moral example
in tragedy is owing to the want of talents in
our poets, and of taste in the public: *wisdom
and virtue*, he observes, *simple, uniform, and
unchanging, only superior artists can draw,
and superior spectators can enjoy* *. It seems
to me, on the contrary, that any-artists can
draw, but no spectators enjoy them; merely
because they *are* simple, uniform, and unchanging: for, what all spectators, of every degree,
both of rank and intellect, enjoy in representations of this kind, is the energy and variety of
just and appropriate expression of contending
passions, affections, and interests. Hence the
scenes of tragedy certainly do, and always must
present *passions and vices, round which the
poet throws the veil of magnanimity, which
he decorates with the pomp of verse and splendor of eloquence* † ; but that they thereby *familiarize the mind to their appearance, and take
from it that natural disgust which the crimes,
presented in their native form, would excite,*

* See some very able dissertations on the morality
of tragedy and comedy by Mr. Mackenzie, in the same
periodical paper, No. 27, 28, 49, and 50.
† Ibid. No. 27.

I cannot admit: for the pomp of verse and splendor of eloquence by no means tend to familiarize; but just the contrary: by giving supernatural force and energy to every image and expression, they tend to raise the mind above the contemplation of ordinary nature, instead of sinking it to a level with it. Besides, it is not for examples, to model their minds upon; or for lessons to direct their actions, that men frequent the theatre; but to hear a certain series of dialogues, arising out of a certain series of supposed events, recited with appropriate modulations of voice, countenance, and gesture. The events they know to be fictitious, and the persons concerned in them merely actors and actresses, who are to appear in other fictitious characters, and exhibit another series of events to-morrow night. It is impossible, therefore, for any person in his senses to consider, either the events, or the characters, as real examples, which he is to apply as rules for his own morals, or guides for his own prudence. Real events of great atrocity, happening frequently, certainly do harden the mind, by familiarizing it with enormities; of which we have lately had but too convincing proofs. Thirty years ago twenty persons being executed at once, for a state crime, would have thrown all Europe into consternation: but of late years we have been so satiated with such bloody events, that they scarcely excite any more emotion, than the news of a birth or a wedding. It is to the actual tyranny of Robespierre, however, that this change is owing, and not to the representations of that of King Richard, or Macbeth; * who had been continually uttering their atrocities, and committing their murders, upon the stage, for two centuries together; during the whole of which, manners, both public and private, had been rapidly and invariably growing milder.

29. When Horace, in the passage above cited, speaks of a dramatic poet *filling his breast with false terrors*, I conclude that he means terrors arising from false, or unreal causes: for terror is not a problem or a syllogism, that can, in itself, be true or false; but a passion, which is either felt or not; and which, if not felt, does not exist. Terror, therefore, if felt at all, must be real terror; and consequently the person, who feels it, must, at the time of feeling it, suppose the cause, which excites it, to be real and adequate; that is, real danger to himself, or some one else; otherwise, what he feels cannot be called terror, or any thing of the kind.

* γαιης εκ Γαλατων,
    ανθρωποις ολετειραι εριννυες εβλαστησαν.
                              Pison. Epigr.

· 30. This, however, is what no person ever does suppose at a theatrical representation ; and even if it were possible for any man in his senses to suffer, for a moment, the sort of delusion, which Don Quixote suffers at the puppet-show, it could only be at the first representation of the piece, and before he had read it : for afterwards, he must foresee all the incidents, which are to come ; and, therefore, can feel no fear or apprehension, lest they may take place ; or hope, that they may not. We all know, from the first drawing up of the curtain, that Othello is to kill his amiable and innocent wife, and afterwards to kill himself : but we know likewise that Othello is an actor, and Desdemona an actress ; and that neither are in danger of receiving any hurt : wherefore it is impossible that we should feel any apprehensions of such events being to happen, or pity, when they do happen. What we do feel, are the sentiments of heroic magnanimity, of warm and generous, but rash and impetuous affection, which the poet has put into the mouth of the one ; and those of innocent simplicity, mild resignation, and passive fortitude and fidelity, which he has attributed to the other. On the stage, we hear these sentiments uttered with all the appropriate accompaniments of action and gesture, and all the impressive graces of modulation of voice, and expression of countenance ;

whence they excite a degree of sympathy in us, so much beyond that which is felt from reading them in the closet.

31. It is by this kind of sympathy only, that pity can properly be said to melt the mind to love : for the pity, which we feel in contemplating the wants or miseries of a mendicant, or a maniac, how much soever it may affect us, does not, I believe, ever engender love of any kind, either towards its object, or any other. Even the tears of beauty only make it more lovely, when they seem to proceed from the pressure of real and serious distress ; and distress too, which is not only felt with the delicate sensibility of a tender mind, but endured with the mild and tranquil resignation of a firm one: for if the grief of the fair sufferer explode in rant and vociferation ; we may pity her, indeed, in a double sense ; but our pity will never melt the mind to love. If, too, her silent tears flow from any inadequate cause, such as being deprived of any frivolous gratification of vanity or dissipation, which does sometimes excite fair ladies' tears, they will certainly not enhance the effect of her own beauty, nor tend to conciliate the affections of beholders ; although pity may be felt for her weakness, as sincere as that which is felt for any other misery ; for

——————— to be weak is miserable
Doing or suffering ———————

32. It will, therefore, be found, I believe, that pity no further disposes the mind to love, than the distresses, which occasion it, display symptoms of such qualities, as we conceive to be amiable, estimable, or respectable; that is, of such energies of mind, whether active or passive, as appear suitable to the character, circumstances, and situation of the sufferer: for it is with these energies, that we sympathize; and it is our sympathy, and not our pity, that melts the mind to love.

33. The mild sensibility of passive courage naturally becomes the weaker sex: and, therefore, patience, gentleness, and meekness in suffering contribute to make women appear more lovely in the eyes of men: but the bold enterprise of active courage becomes the stronger; and is, therefore, that which wins the affections of women: Dido and Desdemona are, in this respect, images of the whole sex—" ferrum est quod amant— :" their minds are roused by admiration, and not melted by pity into love, but still it is equally a display of energy, that excites love in both; though of those different kinds of energy, which are suited by nature to the respective characters of each. The elegant moralist, who expresses his wonder at our fighting plays being such favourite entertainments of the tender sex, shows but little knowledge of that sex *.

* Lord Shaftesbury, Adv. to an Author, p. ii. f. iii.

34. Hence, in spite of all that the author of
the Inquiry into the Sublime and Beautiful has
said *, no real weaknesses, either of mind or
body, ever excite love ; but always either commiseration or contempt; which, considered in
the abstract, are nearly allied, and, on these
occasions, generally mixed.   In the human
race, indeed, nature has formed the female
weaker than the male; and consequently a
comparative degree of weakness is a general
characteristic of the sex ; and, of course, one
criterion of individual perfection : for, in such
cases, we can only judge of particular perfections by their conformity to general characteristics.   But that ever any individual woman
appeared more amiable or more beautiful for
appearing *peculiarly* weak, either in mind or
body, is so far from being true, that the almost
unanimous suffrage of the other sex will attest
the direct contrary ; and proclaim activity, as
well as health of body, to be one of the first
incentives to desire ; and vigour, as well as
sensibility of mind (which are both energies)
to be one of the first incentives to esteem and
mental affection. It is true, that the temporary
caprices of fashion do occasionally pervert
natural taste, in every thing ; and, I believe, a
certain degree of false delicacy and affected
timidity prevailed at the time when the treatise

* P. III. f. xvi.

in question was published : but the author happily lived to see it exploded, and left to cham-
bermaids and waiting women; whose invariable
characteristic it has been, from the time when
the Princess Nausicaa went from her father's
house, to wash her garments, to that when
Sophia Western went from hers to avoid her
lover.

35. This sort of selfish timidity, or extreme
solicitude for self-preservation, is always either
a real or affected weakness; and is, in either
case, equally odious and contemptible.. But
there is another quality of the mind, which is
frequently called timidity, though very improperly ; as it is so far from being incompatible
with personal courage, that it arises from that
principle, which is its best, and most secure
foundation.   This is that delicate and modest
reserve of behaviour, which proceeds from nice
sensibility, joined to a dignified, but not con-
fident pride ; and which, therefore, distinguishes
a mind, that dreads shame, but not danger ; and
trembles at moral, while it scorns physical evil.
Such a mind is surely not to be considered as
a weak one ; since, if it be, almost all human
virtue is weakness.

36. Neither is the yielding pliability of a
mild and gentle temper to be considered as a
mental weakness, though often called so : for,

to comply or yield with ease, dignity, and propriety, requires more real energy of mind, than can be displayed in any stubbornness and obstinacy of resistance: since that sort of stubbornness or obstinacy, which rests upon no principle of reason, honour, or integrity, is like the restiveness of a mule, nothing more than sullen stupidity. Hence fools are almost always ill-tempered; and generally sulky and obstinate; while persons of very enlarged minds, and very vigorous understandings are, as generally, good-tempered and compliant: for the high pride of conscious worth, and great talents, will not suffer its dignity to be discomposed by petty vexations; nor stoop to wrangle upon those paltry subjects of contention, which usually disturb the peace of families, and interrupt the harmony of private societies. Feeling how trivial such subjects of contention are, in the scale of their own contemplations; and knowing, at the same time, what serious consequences result from them, in the collision of little minds, they at once sacrifice their opinions to their peace; and so get that credit for amiable weakness, which they owe to exalted energy of mind. Thus it is that men, who lead armies, and govern empires, with the utmost vigour and ability, are in their own families often governed by their wives, their mistresses, or their children:—*That humoursome boy,* said Themistocles pointing to his infant son, *governs Greece; for he governs his mo-ther, his mother governs me, I govern Athens, and Athens governs Greece.*

37. Persons, on the contrary, of really weak characters, are always tenacious and opiniative in trifles: for, as their little vanity feels itself interested in maintaining any opinion, which they have once advanced, the more insignificant the object, and the more absurd the opinion, the more obstinately and violently will they contend; since the greater is the humiliation of confessing, and the shame of retracting error. Hence most of those opinions, in sup-port of which much blood has been shed, and great persecutions either inflicted or endured, have been, either extravagant paradoxes, in which neither party could discover any real meaning; or frivolous distinctions, in which both would have been equally puzzled to point out any real differences.

38. Whatever tends to exalt the soul to enthusiasm, tends to melt it at the same time: whence tears are the ultimate effect of all very sublime impressions on the mind;—as much of those of a joyous, as those of a melancholy cast:

————————— my plenteous joys
Wanton in fulness, seek to hide themselves
In drops of sorrow —————————

says the benevolent Duncan, on contemplating the prosperity of his kingdom, and the happiness and filial attachment of his subjects. Every generous, as well as every tender feeling of sympathy, when it reaches a certain pitch of rapture and enthusiasm, relieves its fulness in tears * ;—even those feelings, which are excited by the stern and unamiable passions of anger, hatred, envy, and jealousy. Of this we have very striking instances in the sudden bursts of anger in Lear, the gloomy effusions of hatred and envy in de Montford, and the impassioned expressions of jealousy in Othello ; all of which, in the glowing and enthusiastic parts, equally draw tears from the audience : not, indeed, from our sympathizing with any of those rough and turbulent passions; but because the pressure of such passions, upon great and elevated minds, exhibits an interesting struggle of contending affections; from which emanate the most striking flashes of glowing, pathetic, sublime, and vigorous sentiment; with all which we sympathize, in proportion to the truth, spirit, and energy, with which they are expressed. The most perfect instance of this kind is the tragedy of Macbeth; in which the character of an ungrateful traitor, murderer, usurper, and tyrant, is made, in the highest-degree, interesting, by

* ὗτω κοινον τι αρα χαρα και λυπη δακρυα εϛιν. Xenoph. Hellenic. vii. 1. f. 22.

A A 2

the sublime flashes of generosity, magnanimity, courage, and tenderness, which continually burst forth in the manly, but ineffective struggle of every exalted quality, that can dignify and adorn the human mind, first against the allurements of ambition, and afterwards against the pangs of remorse, and horrors of despair. Though his wife has been the cause of all his crimes and sufferings, neither the agony of his distress, nor the fury of his rage, ever draw from him an angry word or upbraiding expression towards her : but even when, at her instigation, he is about to add the murder of his friend, and late colleague, to that of his sovereign, kinsman, and benefactor, he is chiefly anxious that she should not share the guilt of his blood. " Be innocent of the knowledge, dearest chuck, till thou applaud the deed." How much more real grandeur and exaltation of character is displayed in one such simple expression from the heart, than in all the laboured pomp of rhetorical amplification!

39. In the tragedy of Venice Preserved, the unprincipled malignity, and sanguinary atrocity of the conspirators are studiously exposed ; and exaggerated to the utmost bounds of probability : while, in that of Julius Cæsar, their good qualities only are shown ; the stern patriotism of the one leader ; and the strict integrity, and amiable virtue of the other,

3

being drawn in brighter colours than the impartial testimony of history warrants. Yet,
though Shakspeare's poetry rises far above
Otway's, the gallant and profligate impetuosity
of Pierre; and the various conflicting passions
of his perfidious friend, are far more interesting
and impressive, than the republican firmness of
Cassius, or the philosophical benevolence of
Brutus; merely because they are more energetic:
for it is with the general energy, and not with
the particular passions, that we sympathize.
*Men fit to disturb the peace of all the world,
and rule it when 'tis wildest,* are the proper ·
materials for tragedy; since, how much soever
we may dread, or abhor them in reality, we are
always delighted with them in fiction.

40. The vindictive ferocity of Achilles has
been thought to need some apology, even by
the warmest admirers of the Iliad: but the
poet, who had looked into the inmost recesses
of the human mind, well knew that, had his
hero been less ferocious, he must have been
less energetic; and, consequently, less interesting and impressive. To rouse the feelings of
his audience—to exalt and melt them by turns,
was his object; and for that, he has shown as
much taste and knowledge in the selection of
his means, as genius and ability in the employment of them. Achilles weeps, with all the
ecstasy of woe, over his insulted honour, and

his: slaughtered friend; but meets his own impending death with careless and haughty indifference; and when struggling in the overwhelming torrents of the Scamander, only reproaches the Gods with not keeping their promise of an honourable and glorious termination to his life.

41. In all the fictions, either of poetry or imitative art, there can be nothing truly pathetic, unless it be, at the same time, in some degree, sublime: for, though, in scenes of real distress, pity may so far overcome scorn, that we may weep for sufferings, that are feebly or pusillanimously borne; yet, in fiction, scorn will always predominate, unless there be a display of vigour, as well as tenderness and sensibility of mind. Fiction is known to be fiction, even while it interests us most; and it is the dignified elevation of the sentiments of the actors or sufferers, that separates the interesting, or the pathetic, from the disgusting, or the ridiculous.

42. Scenes of extreme suffering, or hyperbolical atrocity, which, in real life, excite only the shudder of horror, are viewed only with disgust in fiction; whether it be in poetry, painting, or sculpture: for the mind is never deceived by such fictions; but always considers them as works of mere invention or imitation; and, as they are necessarily associated with

repulsive and horrible ideas, never gives them
that spontaneous attention, which alone can
induce it to sympathize with the energies, either
of active, or passive fortitude, displayed by the
sufferer. Such are the martyrdoms of Spagno-
let, the events in the play of Titus Andronicus,
and in the latter part of the novel of the Monk.
When really acted within the sphere of our
knowledge, the pruriency of curiosity will
seldom allow us to remain in ignorance even
of the details of such events, how much soever
we may wish them unknown, after the hideous
images have begun to haunt our memories:
but, when the poet or the artist presume to
obtrude such images upon us gratuitously, as
the means of exciting an extreme degree of
sympathy, they have no longer any incentives
to entice curiosity; and are consequently rejected with scorn, aversion, or disgust.

43. No merely selfish sorrow or affliction,
how justly and eloquently soever expressed,
can ever be pathetic in fiction; because it can
never be, in any degree, sublime; but must
always exhibit more of the weaknesses than the
energies of the mind. Hence tragedy, which,
as Aristotle has observed, in a passage before
cited, is conversant only in the higher ranks of
human nature; and which, to be interesting,
must always be, in some degree, sublime, never
dares to bring forward any scenes of distress,

of which self is the motive; while comedy (by which I mean comedy as opposed to tragedy, that is, ludicrous comedy) which, as the same great author observes, is conversant only with the lower ranks; and, consequently, seeks to please by the direct opposite of the sublime, never dares to bring forward any distress, which has any other motive than self: for distress, which has any other adequate motive, can never be ridiculous; and distress, which is founded in that motive solely, must necessarily be either ridiculous, contemptible, or disgusting, when exhibited in fiction.

44. On the other hand, it is equally true that no kind of mimic distress can be interesting, the motives for which are entirely unconnected with self; because such distress must necessarily be extravagant and unnatural; and therefore unfit for either tragedy or comedy. A philanthropist ranting upon the calamities of a remote country, which he never saw; or lamenting, in tragic pomp, the misfortunes of a foreign potentate, whom he never knew, would only exhibit the disgusting image of an idiot or a maniac, which would not be tolerated on any stage. All our social arise out of our selfish passions, and continue so far connected with them, that, in separation, the one verge towards mental insanity, and the other become utterly sordid and despicable.

Milton has been censured for making the devil too amiable and interesting a character; but Milton could not have done otherwise, without destroying all the interest of his poem: for to have exhibited so principal an actor in the events, which he relates, without passions or affections, would have been dull and insipid; and to have given him only selfish passions would have been rendering him a character more fit for one of the scriptural farces, or sacred drolls of the middle ages, than for a most serious, and even solemn epic composition. The passage, in which he appears most amiable, is perhaps the most striking and pathetic in the whole poem; and as it occurs in the beginning of it, confers no small degree of interest upon what follows:

———————— his face
Deep scars of thunder had entrench'd, and care
Sat on his faded cheek, but under brows
Of dauntless courage, and considerate pride,
Waiting revenge.   Cruel his eye, but cast
Signs of remorse and passion to behold
The fellows of his crime, the followers rather,
Far other once beheld in bliss, condemn'd
For ever now to have their lot in pain:
Millions of spirits, for his fault amerc'd
Of Heaven, and from eternal splendors flung,
For his revolt: yet faithful how they stood
Their glory withered: as when Heaven's fire
Hath scath'd the forest oaks or mountain pines,
With singed top, their stately growth, though bare,

Stands on the blasted heath.   He now prepar'd
To speak; whereat their doubled ranks they bend,
From wing to wing, and half enclose him round,
With all his peers: attention held them mute.
Thrice he essay'd, and thrice, in spite of scorn,
Tears such as angels weep burst forth.

Throughout the poem, the infernal excite
more interest than the celestial personages, because their passions and affections are more
violent and energetic.

45. We often feel a sort of sympathy with
our own past sufferings; which casts, over our
minds, a grateful tinge of melancholy, not unlike that produced by the fictitious distress of
tragedy or pathetic narrative.   Hence, *to delight, or gratify oneself by indulging sorrow**,
is an expression often employed by one of the
greatest masters of human nature; and one of
the few general maxims or sentences, that he
has left, is to the same effect †; nor is there
any person of common sensibility, who has not,
at some moments of his life, felt the propriety
of it.   We love to retrace images of affliction,
and scenes of distress; in which ourselves have
borne a part; and of which the recollection
fills the mind with sentiments, at once tender,
and pleasing: but it is only from past affliction,
that we feel this pleasure; and only from that
kind of past affliction, under the pressure of

* γοȣ τερψασθαι.
† —— μιτα γαρ τι και αλγισι τιρπιται ανηρ.—Od. O. 399.

which, we have felt and displayed sentiments honourable to ourselves; the remembrance of which exalts and expands, while it melts and softens the mind. The pain arising from wounds suffered in a battle, or grief for the loss of friends, who had fallen in it, might afterwards be remembered with sentiments of grateful, though melancholy reflection: but the sufferings of ignominious punishments, or the sorrows for the loss of accomplices condemned for disgraceful crimes, do not, probably, afford any pleasing materials for future recollections. The pleasures and pains of sympathy are therefore precisely the same, in their principle, when they relate to ourselves, as when they relate to others.

46. Every energetic exertion of great and commanding power; whether of body or mind; whether physical or moral; or whether it be, employed to preserve or destroy, will necessarily excite corresponding sympathies; and, of course, appear sublime: but, in all moral or political power, the sublimity is in the mental or personal energy exerted, and not in the power possessed: for a person of the meanest character and capacity; a Claudius, a Nero, or a Vitellius, may possess the most unlimited power; and yet be an object of contempt, even to those who are subject to it. A despot may command the actions of men, but cannot com-

mand their sentiments or opinions: wherefore, as Longinus observes, it is not the tyrant diffusing terror, whose character is sublime; but the man, whose exalted soul looks down upon empire, and scorns the transitory possessions, which it can bestow*. He displays real energy of mind; and, with that energy, we sympathize; in whatever manner, or to whatever end, it be exerted. The tyrant therefore may show it, as well as the philosopher; and, in that case, the character of the tyrant will be sublime; but not to those, who are under the actual impression of the terror, which he inspires: for it is as utterly impossible for a man at the same time, to sympathize with the effect and the cause, as it is for him to fill his cup, at the same time, from the mouth and the source of the river. Fear is the most humiliating and depressing of passions; and, when a person is under its influence, it is as unnatural for him to join in any sentiments of exultation with that which inspires it, as it would be for a man to share in the triumph or the feast of the lion, of which he was himself the victim and the prey.

47. All sublime feelings are, according to the principles of Longinus, which I have here endeavoured to illustrate and confirm, feelings

* S. vii.

of exultation and expansion of the mind, tend-
ing to rapture and enthusiasm; and whether
they be excited by sympathy with external objects, or arise from the internal operations of
the mind, they are still of the same nature. In
grasping at infinity, the mind exercises the
powers, before noticed, of multiplying without
end; and, in so doing, it expands and exalts
itself, by which means its feelings and sentiments become sublime.

The same effects result from contemplating
all vast and immense objects; such as very
spacious plains, lakes, or forests; extensive
ranges of extremely high mountains; mighty
rivers; unbounded seas; and, above all, the
endless expanse of unknown vacuity.

48. Upon a similar principle all works of
great labour, expence, and magnificence are
sublime; such as the wall of China; the colonnades of Palmyra; the pyramids of Egypt;
the aqueducts of Rome; and, in short, all
buildings of very great dimensions, or objects
of very great richness and splendor: for, in
contemplating them, the mind applies the ideas
of the greatness of exertion, necessary to produce such works, to the works themselves; and
therefore feels them to be grand and sublime,
as works of man; though, if compared with
the works of nature, their dimensions may be
small and contemptible. Great wealth, too, is

so nearly allied to great power, that the contemplation of its splendor equally exalts and expands the imagination. Phidias's colossal statue of Jupiter in ivory and gold might have been equally well executed in plaster gilt; but its effect upon the spectators would have been very different, as the priests and hierophants of Elis well knew. Every person, who has attended the celebration of high mass at any considerable ecclesiastical establishment, must have felt how much the splendor and magnificence of the Roman catholic worship tends to exalt the spirit of devotion, and to inspire the soul with rapture and enthusiasm. Not only the impressive melody of the vocal and instrumental music, and the imposing solemnity of the ceremonies, but the pomp and brilliancy of the sacerdotal garments, and the rich and costly decorations of the altar, raise the character of religion, and give it an air of dignity and majesty unknown to any of the reformed churches. Even in dramatic exhibitions, we find that splendid dress, rich scenery, and pompous ceremony are absolutely necessary to support the dignity of tragedy; and, indeed, such is their effect, that they often serve as an universal substitute, and compensate for the want of every other merit.

49. Darkness, vacuity, silence, and all other absolute privations of the same kind, may also

be sublime by partaking of infinity; which is equally a privation or negative existence: for infinity is that which is without bounds, as darkness is that which is without light, vacuity that which is without substance, and silence that which is without sound. In contemplating each, the mind expands itself in the same man ner; and, in expanding itself, will of course conceive grand and sublime ideas, if the imagination be in any degree susceptible of grandeur or sublimity.   .

50. All the great and terrible convulsions of nature; such as storms, tempests, hurricanes, earthquakes, volcanos, &c. excite sublime ideas, and impress sublime sentiments by the prodigious exertions of energy and power, which they seem to display: for, though these objects are, in their nature, terrible, and generally known to be so, it is not this attribute of terror that contributes, in the smallest degree, to render them sublime.

51. As far as feeling or sentiment is concerned, and it is of feeling or sentiment only that we are speaking, *that* alone is terrible, which impresses some degree of fear. I may *know* an object to be terrible; that is, I may know it to possess the *power* of hurting or destroying: but this is *knowledge*, and not *feeling* or *sentiment*; and the *object* of that knowledge is *power*, and not *terror*; so that, if any sym-

pathy results from it, it must be a sympathy
with power only. That alone is actually terrible to me, which actually impresses me with
fear : for, though I may *know* it to be dangerous, when I am beyond its reach, I cannot feel
that sentiment, which danger inspires, till I
either am, or imagine myself to be, within it;
and all agree that the effect of the sublime upon
the mind is a sentiment of feeling, and not a
result of science.

52. There is no image in poetry wrought up
with more true sublimity and grandeur than the
following of Virgil; but that it should be quoted
as an instance of terror being the cause of the
sublime is to me most unaccountable.

Ipse pater, media nimborum in nocte, corusca
Fulmina molitur dextra : quo maxima motu
Terra tremit, fugere feræ, et mortalia corda
Per gentes humilis stravit pavor ———— *

If sublimity is here in any degree the result
of terror, the poet must have very ill understood the effect of his own imagery : for he
expressly tells us that the effect of this dreadful
explosion of thunder and lightning, upon those
who felt it, was *humble fear*; and surely he
could not, by *humble fear*, mean any *sublime
sentiment*. The description, indeed, impresses
us with such sentiments, because we sympathize

* Georg. I. 328.

with the vast and energetic power displayed, and feel no terror whatsoever : but those who witnessed the reality and did feel terror, felt the effects of it, as the poet has stated them to be, humble and depressive, instead of elevating and expansive.

53. The principle features of this sublime image are taken from one, at least as sublime, and far more spirited, of Lucretius :

———— quoi non conrepunt membra pavore,
Fulminis horribili quum plaga, torrida tellus
Contremit, et magnum percurrunt murmura cælum?
Non populi gentesque tremunt ? regesque superbi
Conripiunt divom perculsi membra timore * ?

Here the effect described is the same ; abject fear and superstition, which are the direct reverse of the enthusiastic exultation of sublime sentiments.

54. It is true that both superstition and religious enthusiasm arise from excess of religious reverence : but, nevertheless, their principles, as well as their effects, in the human mind, are totally different, and even adverse to each other ; the one proceeding from excessive fear, and the other from excessive confidence. The superstitious man sees, in his God, a severe and relentless judge ; before whom he shrinks and trembles : the enthusiast sees a beneficent

* Lib. V. 1218.

B b

patron and protector ; by whose favour he is
preserved and exalted : the one imagines himself the object of perpetual anger, which it is
the business of his life to avert or propitiate :
the other conceives himself to be the object of
special love and regard ; the exhilarating idea
of which expands and invigorates every faculty
of his soul, and causes him to mistake its improved energies for supernatural inspirations.

55. A similar difference of feeling in different
minds manifests itself in the contemplation of
the ordinary appearances and events of nature.

Hunc solem, et stellas, et decedentia certis
Tempora momentis, sunt qui formidine nulla
Imbuti spectant ———— *

There are some men whom the actual sense
of danger does not impress with fear ; and who
can, therefore, enjoy the awful sublimity of a
storm at sea, even when the vessel, in which
they sail, is in immediate peril of being wrecked :
but to such persons the storm is not *terrible* ;
and the moment that it becomes so ; that is, the
moment when they feel the actual pressure of
fear, all sympathy with the cause that produces
it, and, consequently, all relish for the sublimity
of it, is at an end. Those, who are actually
frightened, if they give way to their feelings,
and are not restrained by shame, avoid the very

* Horat. Epist. I. vi. 3.

appearance of it; as we see timid women do on shore; who fly to a cellar, or a darkened room, to avoid the *sublime* effects of a thunder storm; because to them they are not sublime but terrible. To those only are they sublime, *qui formidine nulla imbuti spectant,* who behold them without any fear at all; and to whom, therefore, they are in no degree terrible.

56. Plague, pestilence, famine, discord, &c. are only sublime in the personifications of poetry; when the destructive energy of a general cause is presented collectively to the mind; which thus sympathizes with that energy; although its natural effects may be any thing but sublime: for, I believe, no one ever felt any sublimity in being diseased, starved, or beaten; or in feeling himself apprehensive of such calamities: nor do I conceive that he would present a very sublime image to any one else, when actually suffering them. Even in the inanimate objects of nature, if a general character of barrenness pervade the whole, even of the grandest scenery—if every plant seem starved and sickly, and every tree stunted and withered, the effects of meanness and poverty so far overbalance those of their opposites, that no sooner is the first impression of surprise passed, than we begin to find more matter of disgust than delight in the prospect. Weakness is always nearly allied to meanness in

vegetable, as well as animal productions ; so
that scenery of this kind, to be really sublime,
should be, not only wild and broken, but rich
and fertile ; such as that of Salvator Rosa, whose
ruined stems of gigantic trees proclaim at once
the vigour of the vegetation, that has produced
them, and of the tempests, that have shivered
and broken them. There is also a sort of comfort and satisfaction felt in beholding every
production around us strong and luxuriant ;
which, though it arise from sympathies of another class, is of no less importance in rendering the scenery pleasing.

57. The character of Achilles is, perhaps, the
most sublime and the most terrific, that ever
the boldness of poetical fiction dared to delineate : but, nevertheless, the terror and sublimity of it could never have been felt together.
To the Trojans he was only terrible : to us he
is only sublime ; as we only sympathize with
those prodigious energies of mind and body,
which made him terrible to them. The grandest display of his terrific appearance is, when
he approaches the walls of Troy ; and the most
spirited expression of his lofty and sublime
sentiments is, perhaps, in his address to the
prostrate Lycaon : yet neither the venerable
Priam, nor his suppliant son, express any
of that enthusiastic rapture, which sublimity
inspires ; but, on the contrary, both seem

impressed with all the dejection of the most humiliating fear.

58. My friend Mr. Price has quoted expressions in different languages, from the φοβερον and δεινον of Aristotle and Longinus, down to the *terrible high-bred cattle* of the Newmarket hawkers, to prove that *terrible* frequently signifies *sublime*; or at least *excellent* and *striking* *; and I could have supplied him with another, perhaps still more in point, from a Greek naturalist, who says that a rabbit's head is δεινως ασαρκος, *terribly lean*. He might also have heard, among the Newmarket hawkers, of *terrible jockeys*, as well as of *terrible horses*; and concluded, according to his system, and the natural consistency of language, that such jockeys must be *excellent*, or even *sublime* riders; but just the contrary : terrible here means *extremely bad—quite despicable* †. Among the same masters of language, he might also have heard of the weather being *devilish hot*, or *devilish cold*; and of some persons being *damned clever*, and others *damned stupid*; from which, I think, had his mind been quite free from the theories of the Sublime and Beautiful, he would have concluded, that all such expressions have nothing to do with

---

* Essay on the Picturesque, vol. i. p. 112, note; 2d ed.

† So Hippocrates says αδυναμιη δεινη, *terrible impotence,* *or weakness.* περι αρχ. ιητρικ. f. xix.

either ; but that men, in the laxity of colloquial speech, seize upon some impressive word, and use it as an augmentative, or superlative; or, perhaps, merely for the sake of emphasis, without any regard to its strict meaning or etymology. For this purpose words and objects of terror would naturally be adopted : for nothing is so impressive as fear; although the impression, which it makes, is invariably the opposite of sublime.

59. This notion of pain and terror being the cause of the sublime, appears, indeed, to me, to be, in every respect, so strange and unphilosophical, that were it not for the great name, under which it has been imposed on the world, I should feel shame in seriously controverting it. But, when I consider the deserved authority of that name, and the influence, which it has had, in spreading this notion, with the practical bad taste, that has resulted from it, I am rather apprehensive of not controverting it effectually. I admit, however, that this influence has principally appeared among artists, and other persons not much conversant with philosophical inquiries : for, except my friend before mentioned, I have never met with any man of learning, by whom the philosophy of the *Inquiry into the Sublime and Beautiful* was not as much despised and ridiculed, as the brilliancy and animation of its style were applauded, and admired.

60. It is, indeed, no easy matter to understand this philosophy, so far as relates to the sublime; which is first stated to proceed *from whatever is fitted in any sort to excite the ideas of pain and danger ; that is to say, whatever is in any sort terrible, or conversant about terrible objects, or operates in a manner analogous to terror **. But, nevertheless, as the author immediately adds, *when danger or pain press too nearly, they are incapable of giving any delight, and are simply terrible ; but at certain distances, and with certain modifications, they may be, and they are delightful, as we every day experience.*

61. It were to be wished that the author had informed us, what these particular delights are, which danger and pain every day afford us ; and at what specific distances, or under what particular modifications, they do afford them : for, in the common acceptation of these words, danger means the probability of evil, and pain the actual sensation of it ; and how the sense or feeling either of the probability of the evil, or of the evil itself, can exist any where but in

---

* P. I. f. vii.

When so clear and acute a writer, as Mr. Burke generally is, gives so indistinct and unphilosophical a definition, we may be assured that he had entangled himself in his own subtilties, and was more anxious to conceal his perplexity than explain his meaning.

the mind, no common understanding can conceive; and, indeed, the author himself does
not, in his subsequent arguments, consider
them as existing any where else; and, as he
speaks of *sensations* being *moderated in description,* and so rendered *sublime* *, we may
reasonably suppose that he here confounded
distance and *degree*; a stout instance of confusion even with every allowance that can be
made for the ardour of youth in an Hibernian
philosopher of five and twenty.

Certain degrees, however, would have answered his purpose no better : for be the degree
of danger ever so small; that is, be the evil
apprehended, or the probability of its happening ever so slight, the sentiment excited by it
must be equally fear : since, if it do not excite some degree of fear, the sense of danger,
as it is called, is mere *perception* or *knowledge,*
not either a *sentiment, sensation,* or *passion.*
Aristotle defines fear to be *mental pain or
trouble, arising from an idea of future evil,
either destructive or afflictive* †; and if this
definition be just, as it has hitherto been held
to be, the differences in its degrees cannot any-
wise change the mode of its existence, nor alter
the nature, though they may lessen the effect

* P. II. f. xxi.

† φοϐος, λυπη τις η ταραχη εκ φαντασιας μελλοντος κακου,
η φθαρτικου η λυπηρου. Rhetor. l. ii.

of its operation. Fear, therefore, which is humiliating and depressive in one degree, must be
proportionally so in another ; and consequently,
in every degree, the opposite of sublime.

62. As corporeal pain and physical evil are,
according to the system in question, the means
of the sublime, and self-preservation its principle * ; all the sentiments excited by it must,
of consequence, be merely corporeal, organic,
or nervous sensations ; as the author endeavours to prove them to be † ; and so far, his
system is consistent in itself, though not with
his general principles : for it leads directly to
materialism ; from which no man was ever
more averse.

63. The highest degree of these sublime sensations, he states to be *astonishment*; and the
subordinate degrees, *awe, reverence,* and *respect* ‡ ; all which, he considers as *modes of
terror, which exercise the finer parts of the
system, as common labour does the grosser :*
and thus, by a physical process, which he ex-
plains at length, but which no physiologist has
been able to understand, *become capable of
producing delight, not pleasure; but a sort of
delightful horror, a sort of tranquillity tinged
with terror; which, as it belongs to self-preservation, is one of the strongest of all the
passions* §.

* P. I. f. vi. and P. IV. f. vii.
† P. IV. f. v. ix. et seq.   ‡ Ibid.   § Ibid.

All this, however, obscure as, I confess, it is to me, seems perfectly clear to the more acute penetration of his disciple and commentator; who observes, in terms more direct and explicit than the author, perhaps, would have desired, *that the sublime, being founded on ideas of pain and terror, like them operates by stretching the fibres beyond their natural tone. The passion excited by beauty is love and complacency: it acts by relaxing the fibres somewhat below their natural tone; and this is accompanied by an inward sense of melting and languor.* *.

This *stretching* power of ideas of terror, no pathologist has, I believe, discovered or even surmised, though the *laxative* power of terror itself is so well known, as to have been celebrated even by poets; with more, indeed, of the accuracy of philosophy than the delicacy of poetry †. The *laxative* powers of beauty, the author has illustrated by the difference of our *feelings on a warm genial day in a spot full of the softest beauties of nature,* and, *when the fibres are braced by a keen air in a wild romantic situation* ‡: but I apprehend that this difference, so far as it depends upon the

---

* Essays on the Picturesque, Vol. i. p. 103.
† Aristoph. Ϭατραχ. 479. Ed. Brunk.   Gay's Fab.
True Story, &c.
‡ Essays on the Picturesque, Vol. i. p. 104.

relaxation or tension of the fibres, arises entirely from the difference of temperature in the atmosphere, and not at all from that of character in the scenery *:

64. As for the passions and sensations belonging to self-preservation they are certainly very strong; but how *tranquillity*, tinged with terror or any thing else, came to be one of them, surpasses all ordinary ingenuity to discover. Such passions, too, are always most strong in the weakest and meanest minds; those of the selfish, the cowardly, and the penurious: for, as avarice is a modification of vanity, so is penury of timidity. They are, therefore, the passions, which Longinus specially excluded

* I remember, many years ago, to have met with an account of an experiment to ascertain the pernicious effects of drinking tea; in which it was stated that a single ounce of that deleterious drug, having been steeped for only five minutes in a quart of boiling spring water, rendered it so corrosive, that it immediately took all the hairs off a raw pig's tail, that was put into it. What havock must it then make with the tender coats of the stomach! The chemist was too intent on proving his system to think of trying the effects of hot water without the infusion of tea: for all

—— Philosophers, who find
Some favorite system to their mind,
In every point to make it fit,
Will force all nature to submit.

SWIFT.

from all possibility of being sublime; and we accordingly find that, when poets or moralists would draw a sublime character, they represent him as free from them as is consistent with the infirmity of human nature, and oftentimes more so.   It is he whom,

> Si fractus illabatur orbis,
> Impavidum ferient ruinæ.

65. As for the author's graduated scale of the sublime from respect to astonishment, it cannot, perhaps, be better illustrated than by applying it to his own character.

He was certainly a very *respectable* man; and *reverenced* by all who knew him intimately. At one period of his life, too, when he became the disinterested patron of remote and injured nations, who had none to help them, his character was truly sublime; but unless upon those whom he so ably and eloquently arraigned, I do not believe that it impressed any *awe.*

66. If, during this period, he had suddenly appeared among the managers in Westminster-hall without his wig and coat; or had walked up St. James's street without his breeches, it would have occasioned great and universal *astonishment*; and if he had, at the same time, carried a loaded blunderbuss in his hands, the astonishment would have been mixed with no small portion of *terror*; but I do not believe

that the united effects of these two powerful passions would have produced any sentiment or sensation approaching to sublime, even in the breasts of those, who had the strongest sense of self-preservation, and the quickest sensibility of danger.

67. From this system the author has deduced many strange principles of taste ; against which, however, his feelings often seem to revolt : but those of his followers have been less scrupulous ; as abundantly appears from the works of many modern painters, poets, and romance writers ; which teem with all sorts of terrific and horrific monsters and hobgoblins ; but never stoop to the more humble but more difficult task of heightening and embellishing ordinary nature with the energies of poetical fiction, or the colouring of poetical diction.   This would be sinking into the tame drudgery of portrait painting and copying ; occupations wholly un-worthy of that exalted genius, which aims at realizing the visions of the sublime and beau-tiful.

68. An attempt was once made to introduce these charming delights of danger, pain, terror, and astonishment, into the art of landscape gardening ; and at least they would have given it some character : but, unfortunately, the author of the project had not the literary talents of the first discoverer of these exquisite

sources of the sublime; so that his noble designs were stifled in the birth, for want of being
sufficiently guarded against the malignant powers of ridicule *. We need not however despair
of yet seeing them put in practice; as far at
least as the heavy and half-frozen spirits of a
northern people are capable of comprehending
or enjoying them: for it is not long, since I
beheld a most edifying specimen of the happy
effects, which might be thus produced. Amidst
some very grand scenery of woods, rocks, and
mountains, was a spacious and picturesque
cave; which, as some improver of this school
naturally conceived, only wanted a little terror
to render it truly sublime. This, he easily supplied, by prevailing on the then proprietor to
place a monstrous figure of a giant or cyclops
over the entrance of it, with a huge stone sus-
pended in his hand, and ready to fall upon the
head of any person who should presume to
enter. Not, however, calculating correctly
the exact distance or degree of danger necessary to produce the desired effect, the stone
actually did fall; and, coming nearer to the
head of one of the spectators, than the laws of
the system allow, it has brought the scheme into
such disrepute among the ignorant mechanics

* See Treatise on Oriental Gardening, and Heroic
Epistle to its Author, Sir W. Chambers.

5

and barbarous country gentlemen of the neigh-
bourhood, that there is some danger of the
benefit of the example being lost to the public.

69. There is, nevertheless, another source of
the sublime applicable to the same art, which
is still untried ; though the same difficulty of
calculating the exact degree of proximity in
the danger may arise to obstruct it. The author
of the Inquiry into the Sublime and Beautiful
states that all noxious reptiles and wild beasts
of prey are sublime ; and all innocent and domesticated animals, mean and contemptible * :
wherefore a snake or a scorpion pent up in
the corner of a cave, or a wolf or a bear chained
at the mouth of it, may produce, perhaps, exactly the effect required ; though their being
pent up or chained is not compatible with
wildness. But, nevertheless, I know of no
other means of preventing the too near approximation of the danger; which, as the
author of the system allows, would dissipate
all the *delight*, and very probably produce a
degree of pain far beyond that, which he thinks
an ingredient of the sublime. I have lately
heard of a lion in plaster or wax being employed
for this purpose ; but though he is said to be
very correctly imitated, and to look very fierce,
I do not find that any person is at all afraid of

* P. II. f. ii. and v.

him, or that he adds at all to the sublimity of the scene.

70. Some tasteless persons, indeed, may deny altogether the justness of this distinction between noxious and innocent, or wild and tame animals ; and may even go so far into a contrary opinion, as to maintain that the game cock, who, in a naval engagement, stalked majestically about the deck, and crowed and clapped his wings after every broadside, presents a more sublime image to the mind, than any noxious reptile, that lurks concealed in its dark hiding place, ready to strike its envenomed sting into every unwary obtruder. Nay, it may be thought that this gallant and heroic bird is an object of more real dignity and elevation of character than the eagle or the falcon, that pounces upon its defenceless prey : though the latter may, indeed, afford a finer subject of description to the poet, both by displaying greater energy of body, and by leading the imagination into the wild haunts of forests and mountains, which would supply accompaniments of grand poetical, and picturesque scenery, instead of the humble accessories of the farm-yard, the dunghill, or the cock-pit.

71. It may also be thought that, independent of the effect of such accompaniments, the dog who fought against the murderers of his master, and, after being mortally wounded in his

defence, lay two days by his lifeless body, and
then expired in attempting to seize one of the
persons, who took it up, is an object of more
true sublimity, than a wolf worrying a sheep,
or a lion or tiger springing from the covert of a·
thicket upon their unsuspecting prey *.

72. No Dutch painter ever exhibited an
image less imposing, or less calculated to inspire awe and terror, or any other of the
above-mentioned author's symptoms or sources
of the sublime, (unless, indeed, it be a stink)
than the celebrated dog of Ulysses, lying upon a
dunghill, covered with vermin, and in the agonies
of death: yet when, in such circumstances, on
hearing the voice of his old master, who had
been absent twenty years, he pricks his ears,
wags his tail and expires, what heart is not at
once melted, elevated, and expanded with all
those glowing feelings, which Longinus has so
well described as the genuine effects of the
true sublime? That master, too—the patient,
crafty, and obdurate Ulysses; who encounters
every danger, and bears every calamity with a
constancy unshaken, a spirit undepressed, and
a temper unruffled; when he sees this faithful old servant perishing in want, misery, and
neglect—yet still remembering his long lost

* Lions and tigers, like all other animals of the cat
kind, are cowardly and treacherous; and never openly
face an enemy, but always attack by surprise.

C c

benefactor, and collecting the last effort of expiring nature to give a sign of joy and gratulation at his return—hides his face and wipes away the tear!—This is true sublimity of character, which is always mixed with tenderness; mere sanguinary ferocity being terrible and odious, but never sublime. αγαθοι πολυδακρυτοι ανδρες—*Men prone to tears are brave*, says the proverbial Greek hemistich: for courage, which does not arise from mere coarseness of organization, but from that sense of dignity and honour, which constitutes the generous pride of a high mind, is founded in sensibility.

73. It is true that, through all nature, the noxious and destructive powers are more vigorous and energetic in their operations than those of beneficence and preservation; whose efforts, being more gradual and progressive, are more tame and quiet. Consequently energy, which is the fundamental principle and indispensable requisite of all sublimity of character, is more frequently and more manifestly displayed in bad, than in good actions; and in the pernicious, than in the amiable qualities of the mind. But, nevertheless, the most amiable and beneficent qualities are not unsusceptible of it; and when it does invigorate their exertions, they rise far above any of their opposites. Weigh the emancipator of America and benefactor of mankind against any of the mighty conquerors

and usurpers, who have at different periods oppressed their respective countries, and trampled upon the rights of surrounding nations, and say which character is most truly sublime!

74. In animals, the energetic are more rarely found separate from the destructive qualities, than in the human race; wherefore wild beasts and birds of prey are more frequently and more generally employed as the materials of sublime imagery in poetry, than any of the domesticated kinds: but still their sublimity of character arises entirely from their being energetic, and not at all from their being destructive: for, where equal energy can be displayed in the exertion of beneficent qualities, it will be more sublime because more interesting; as the examples before cited are sufficient to prove. All kindred passions mutually vibrate to the movements of each other; and consequently that, which can melt and exalt at the same time, will be more efficient in both, than that, which can only melt, or only exalt, will ever be in either. Sublimity therefore of character and expression is always more affecting and impressive than any other kind.

75. It has already been observed that there are many things sublime in description, which are not so in reality; as there are objects beautiful in painting, which are not so in nature: for the poet seizes only the energetic qualities

C C 2

and expressions, which he heightens and embellishes, and suppresses the rest; as the painter
seizes only the beautiful effects of light and
shadow, to display the powers of his art upon,
while he sinks the rest in obscurity and indistinctness; as far as the limits of truth in imitation will allow: for, in this respect, poetry has
a great advantage over painting; since it is
confined by no laws of strict imitation; but
may bring forward those qualities only of an
object, which suit its purposes, and leave all
the rest entirely unnoticed. In expressing
mental energies, it is not under the necessity
of showing them through the medium of corporeal form; but darts them at once upon the
mind; and thus, without departing from the
truth of description, gives sublimity to 'objects,
whose bodily deformity, weakness, or minuteness may prevent them from appearing so in
reality.

76. No person, I believe, ever felt any
sublime emotions on viewing a swarm of bees
wrangling in the air; but Virgil's description
of it, though strictly true, is sublime in the
extreme:

Ergo ubi ver nactæ sudum, camposque patentes:
Erumpunt portis; concurritur; æthere in alto
Fit sonitus, magnum mixtæ glomerantur in orbem,
Præcipitesque cadunt. Non densior aëre grando
Nec de concussa tantum pluit ilice glandis.
Ipsi per medias acies, insignibus alis;

Ingentes animos angusto in pectore versant,
Usque adeo obnixi non cedere, dum gravis aut hos,
Aut hos, versa fuga victor dare terga coegit *.

77. Most of the similes in Homer, taken
from minute objects, are sublime upon the
same principle.   There are few persons, who
have not seen crowds of water-fowl fluttering
about a moor, without feeling any sublime
emotions from them : but, in the poet's numbers, no imagery was ever more grand, though
without one circumstance of exaggeration, or
one metaphor of embellishment :

Των δ', ωστ' ορνιθων πετεηνων εθνεα πολλα,
χηνων, η γερανων, η κυκνων δκλιχοδειρων,
Ασιω εν λειμωνι Καϋστρικ αμφι ρεεθρα,
ενθα και ενθα ποτωνται αγαλλομεναι πτερυγεσσι,
κλαγγηδον πρκκαθιζοντων, σμαραγει δε τε λειμων †.

78. It is true that persons of poetical minds,
or accustomed to enjoy descriptions of this
kind, learn to feel a relish for the circumstances
in nature, which give rise to them ; in the same
manner as persons conversant with painting
learn to relish things in nature, which are the
proper subjects of that art; but which otherwise they would not have noticed.   Both see
nature through the medium of art; though the
peculiarities of the respective arts direct their
attention to different qualities : for as painting

* Georgic iv. 77.   † Il. B. 459.

addresses itself principally to the senses and imagination, its objects are chiefly beauties; while poetry, addressing itself wholly to the imagination and the passions, seeks chiefly for energies.

79. All the expressions of painting and sculpture being fixed and stationary, and limited to exterior form, the influence of these arts upon the passions is, as before observed, very feeble, compared with that of poetry; whose images have all the motion and activity of animated nature. The lines of Horace therefore,

> Segnius irritant animos demissa per aures,
> Quam quæ sunt oculis subjecta fidelibus,

are not true, if applied to painting in opposition to poetry, as some eminent authors have applied them *: but Horace is not speaking of painting or sculpture; but of dramatic poetry; and of narration in dramatic poetry opposed to representation; in which sense his observation is perfectly just: for we undoubtedly sympathize more with the exterior expressions of passion, when we see them well represented, than when we hear them described; though, in the description, the images may be more grand, and the energies more vigorous and powerful; because the expansion of the imagination is not then limited and controlled by

* The Abbé du Bos, and Mr. Burke.

the evidence of the senses, as it is in the exhibition upon the stage.

80. Nothing can, therefore, be more remote from truth, than what the author of the Inquiry into the Sublime and Beautiful states of objects, or the qualities of objects, being rendered sublime, by being *moderated* in description * : for it is by being elevated and expanded in description that they are rendered sublime; and the peculiar business of poetry is so to elevate and expand them, that the imagination may conceive *distinct*, but not *determinate* ideas of them; and thus have an indefinite liberty of still exalting and expanding, without changing or confounding the images impressed upon it.

81. Further than this, all obscurity is imperfection; and, indeed, if obscurity means indistinctness, it is always imperfection. The more distinct a description; and the more clearly the qualities, properties, and energies, intended to be signified or expressed, are brought, as it were, before the eyes, the more effect it will have on the imagination and the passions: but then, it should be *distinct* without being *determinate*. In describing, for instance, a storm at sea, the rolling, the curling, the foaming, the dashing and roaring of the waves cannot be

* P. II. f. xxi.

C C 4

too clearly, too precisely, or too exactly expressed: but it should not be told how many
yards in a minute they advanced, how many
feet they rose, or with what precise weight or
momentum they descended. These are points,
which should always be left to the imagination;
and though the imagination will not fix any
precise bounds to its conceptions, it will always
expand them to the utmost verge of probability,
provided there be sufficient spirit in the style.
of the poetry to raise the mind to a tone of
enthusiasm.

82. Critics have been led into the notion that
imagery is rendered sublime by being indistinct
and obscure, by mistaking energies for images,
and looking for *pictures* where *powers* only
were meant to be expressed. Of this. kind is
Virgil's description of the materials employed.
by the Cyclops in forming the thunder-bolts of
Jupiter —

> Tres imbris torti radios, tres nubis aquosæ
> Addiderant; rutili tres ignis, et alitis Austri:
> Fulgores nunc terrificos, sonitumque metumque
> . Miscebant operi, flammisque sequacibus iras—

which all men feel to be extremely sublime; at
the same time that they are obliged to own that
no chimera of a madman ever presented a more
incoherent subject for a picture than *three rays
of twisted showers, three of watery clouds, three.
of red fire, and three of winged south winds*;

*with terrific lightnings, sound, fear, anger,
and pursuing flames mixed up in the work**.
But the poet never meant to produce a picture;
but merely to express, in the enthusiastic language of poetry, which gives corporeal form
and local existence to every thing, those energetic powers, which operate in this dreadful
engine of divine wrath. The materials of the
girdle of Venus are still more remote from any
thing like visible imagery:

ενϑ' ενι μεν φιλοτης, εν δ' ιμερος, εν δ'οαριστυς,
παρφασις ητ' εκλεψε νοον πυκα περ φρονεοντων.

But they are embodied energies or powers,
which are of the same nature as the personified
energies before treated of; and as such, there
is no obscurity or indistinctness whatever in
them; nor, indeed, are the expressions of Homer or Virgil, in any instance, either obscure
or indistinct, though those of Milton are in
many: clearness and distinctness are, on the
contrary, the peculiar characteristics of the
former,

Non tantum ut dici videantur, sed fieri res.

83. Obscurity and indistinctness are merely
degrees of privation in the images of thought,
as well as in those of vision; and if we allow
them to be efficient causes of the sublime, we

* See Sublime and Beautiful. P. V. f. v.

shall necessarily come to the same conclusion as the celebrated line of Dryden led to,

My wound's so great because it is small;

to which was replied,

Then 'twould be greater, were it none at all.

For if a certain degree of want of light and clearness produce a comparative degree of sublimity, it necessarily follows that a total want of them would produce the superlative degree of it; and to this conclusion the author of the Inquiry into the Sublime and Beautiful boldly and confidently advances: for he not only makes utter darkness to be an active and efficient cause of the sublime, by its physical operation on the organ of vision*; but he also makes utter nonsense to be an equally active and efficient cause, by the influence which habit has given to certain words and combinations of words upon the imagination and the passions; though the words themselves, at the time of exciting the sentiment, convey no ideas whatever to the mind; their operation being by a certain contagion of passion, which certain modes of speech mark in the writer, and communicate to the reader †.

84. I readily agree with this author in giving every possible degree of credit to enthusiastic

* P. IV. f. xv.　　　　† P. V.

and impassioned modes of speech. They are the great vehicles of sympathy—the sole means of conveying warm and animated sentiments from one mind to another: since that, which is not expressed with all the energetic glow of real ecstasy, will never excite any ecstatic feelings in the reader:

> ——— Si vis me flere, dolendum est
> Primum ipsi tibi : ———

and the same maxim may be extended to all expressions of serious or vehement passion. The sentiment must rise full from the source, and flow strong through the current, or its contagion will never communicate itself to those whom it approaches. This glowing energy of language, appropriated always to the sentiments which it is meant to express, is the very essence of poetry, and that which gives it all its power over the soul. Strip it of this, by transposing or changing the words, and its most glowing and animated effusions will become torpid and lifeless;—as unlike to what they were, as the skeleton of Helen to the beauty, that set the world in arms. But are ideas, therefore, of no importance ?—or can this contagion of passion be communicated by any other means, than through the ideas conveyed or excited by the expressions, which communicate it ? I say conveyed *or* excited ; because I am aware that a

single idea *conveyed* may excite trains of many
others, upon the principle of association : but
there must necessarily be some idea conveyed ;
for, in mind as in body, nothing can come
from nothing, and every effect will be proportioned to its cause ; so that, in proportion as
the idea conveyed is clear and energetic, and
expressed with force and propriety, will be its
power in exciting others. Mental feelings can
only arise from mental perceptions, and, consequently, every new mode or increased degree
of the one must be preceded by a new mode or
increased extension of the other. Nonsense
can no more be sublime, than darkness or vacuity can be ponderous or elastic ; and to controvert either position is, in some measure, to
participate in its extravagance ; nor should I
presume to do it, did I not every day see the
fatal effects of this seducing author's theories
on the taste of the public ; not only in England,
but on the continent, particularly in Germany,
where nonsense seems to have become the order
of the day. In England, it has been, in a great
measure, confined to harlequin farces, pantomime plays, and romances in prose : for, except
Fingal and Temora, I know of no entire poem
written upon the principles of the *Sublime and
Beautiful*; and had these been published as
the works of their real author, or as the productions of the eighteenth century, they would

3

have been consigned at once to the neglect and oblivion, into which they have sunk since the imposture has been detected, and from which another poem of the same kind, which the author did publish in his own name, never emerged *.' As the works of an ancient bard, discovered after the lapse of so many ages, in a remote corner of the world, amidst a rude and ignorant people, national vanity joined with antiquarian prejudice in extolling them; and, as they were found admirably to accord with these new principles of taste, every thing being, in the words of the comedy, *finely confused and alarmingly obscure*, the critics of the North exulted in having at length found, in an original work of one of their own countrymen, instances of the true sublime, which they had in vain sought for in the tamer productions of the Greek and Roman poets †; with whom, these

Versus inopes rerum, nugæque canoræ

* See a very able dissertation annexed to Mr. Laing's History of Scotland, in which is contained a full account and complete exposition of this most impudent imposture; in which some names of higher rank and respectability in literature than that of James Macpherson appear to have been concerned, so far at least as wilful misprision of fraud can implicate them.

† See Lord Kaims, Blair, Gerrard, &c. &c. particularly the first, who has opposed parallel passages from Fingal, and Pope's Homer, (for he went no higher) to each other, and invariably given the preference to the former.

were never in much repute*; notwithstanding
that the author of the Inquiry into the Sublime
and Beautiful found so admirable a specimen
of them in one of the most admired passages
of their most faultless poet.

85. Their fundamental maxim was, that
sound sense or intelligence was the only ｊust
principle of good writing of any kind;

Scribendi recte sapere est et principium et fons †.

and the more clearly and distinctly this was
expressed the better. Without it, all the
impassioned modes of speech, of which the
above-mentioned author speaks ‡, are nothing
but sonorous ｊargon,—the froth and tinsel of
rhetoric, which raise expectation only to dis-
appoint it‖. What is it, that makes the impassioned language of Achilles, Macbeth, and
Othello so interesting, but the strong sense and
energy of mind that beams through it? No
orator nor logician ever reasoned more strongly,

---

* εκ αν αληθες υψος ειη, μεχρι μονης της ακοης σωζομενον.
LONGIN. f. vii.

† " Est eloquentiæ, sicut reliquarum, fundamentum
sapientia." Cɪc. Orator. c. 70. vol. i. 610.

‡ Subl. and Beaut.

‖ " Quid est enim tam furiosum, quam verborum vel
optimorum atque ornatissimorum sonitus inanis, nulla
subjecta sententia nec scientia." Cɪc. de Orator. i. c. 12.

" Prima est eloquentiæ virtus perspicuitas.—

" Erit ergo obscurior etiam, quo quisque deterior."
QUINTIL. Instit. lib. ii. c. iii.

more clearly, or more correctly, than Achilles
does in his most eloquent and most impassioned
reply to the ambassadors of Agamemnon; and
it is this strength of reasoning, which makes us
sympathize so cordially with the expression of
passion; since it shows the vigour, as well as
the sensibility of his mind; and it is the union
of these two qualities, which constitutes true
sublimity of character.

86. The same principle of sound sense, correct intelligence, and clear expression manifests
itself in all the descriptive parts of the great
poets of antiquity; whether the subjects of
them be images, or energies; visible or intellectual properties: nor is it less manifested in
the description of the formation of the thunder-bolts above cited, than in that of the shield
of Achilles: for all the embodied powers or
energies, that are employed in it, are really
such as belong to thunder and lightning.   Had
the poet introduced others :—had he employed
frost for fire, drought for rain, silence for sound,
or mercy for wrath, it would really have been
sonorous nonsense, as the critic imagined; but,
in that case, I do not believe that any ordinary
reader would have discovered it to be sublime,
whatever a system-builder might have thought
of it.

87. I admit, however, that the impassioned
and enthusiastic language of poetry is absolutely

necessary to reconcile the mind to these bold
descriptions, composed of personified and embodied powers and energies: for, if such brilliant coruscations of fancy be shown through
the cold medium of reason instead of the glowing one of inspiration, the tone of colouring
becomes so inconsistent with the form, that we
can no longer recognize them. Not only a
poetical, therefore, but a metrical style, the
tone of which is highly exalted above that of
the common vehicle of common social intercourse, is absolutely necessary to convey them
with proper effect to the mind: wherefore we
never find them in any but the heroic or lyric
metres of the Greeks; the elegiac, or iambic,
not being sufficiently dignified and exalted to
bear them. Our blank verse, though used as
an heroic metre, and appropriated to the most
elevated subjects, is, like the Greek iambic,
too near to the tone of common colloquial
speech to accord well with such flights; nor
do I believe that it would be possible to trans-
late the above cited passage of Virgil into it,
without losing all its poetical spirit, and consequently making it appear nonsensical as well
as insipid.

88. The obscurity of the lyric style of Pindar
and the Greek tragedians does not arise from
any confusion or indistinctness in the imagery;
but from its conciseness and abruptness; and

from its being shown to the mind in sudden
flashes and coruscations, the connexion between
which is often scarcely perceptible. The sense,
as well as the metre of these compositions seems
to have been adapted to music ; the strong
contrasts, and quick transitions of which, it
seems to have been meant to accompany : but
in no good writer, is there any confusion or
indistinctness of imagery; though in Pindar
and Sophocles the transitions from one image
to another are often extremely rapid and unexpected ; as they are in Gray's admirable,
imitations of the Greek lyric style:

She wolf of France, with unrelenting fangs,
That tear'st the bowels of thy mangled mate,
From thee be born, who o'er thy country hangs,
The scourge of Heaven. What terrors round him wait !
Amazement in his van, with flight combin'd,
And Sorrow's faded form, and Solitude behind.

   Mighty victor, mighty lord,
     Low on his funeral couch he lies !
   No pitying heart, no eye, afford
     A tear to grace his obsequies.
   Is the sable warrior fled ?
Thy son is gone. He rests among the dead.
The swarm, that in thy noontide beam were born ?
Gone to salute the rising morn.
Fair laughs the morn, and soft the zephyr blows,
   While, proudly riding o'er the azure realm,
In gallant trim the gilded vessel goes ;
   Youth on the prow, and Pleasure at the helm ;
       D D

Regardless of the sweeping whirlwind's sway,
That, hush'd in grim repose, expects his evening prey.
Fill high the sparkling bowl,
The rich repast prepare,
'Reft of a crown, he still may share the feast:
Close by the regal chair
Fell Thirst and Famine scowl
A baleful smile upon their baffled guest, &c.

This is in Pindar's best manner; but surely here is no confusion, indistinctness, or obscurity of imagery; but only bold metaphors, strong contrasts, and abrupt transitions from triumph to dejection, from mourning to gaiety, and from festivity to famine; to which sudden and violent oppositions, the brilliancy of the effect in the whole is, in a great measure, owing.

89. The imagery of Milton, as before observed, is often confused and obscure; and so far it is faulty: but, nevertheless, I can find neither confusion nor obscurity in the passage, which has been so confidently quoted as an instance of both *.

He above the rest,
In shape and, gesture proudly eminent,
Stood like a tower: his form had yet not lost
All its original brightness, nor appear'd
Less than Archangel ruin'd, and th' excess
Of glory obscured: as when the sun new risen

* Sublime and Beautiful, P. II. f. iv.

Looks through the horizontal misty air
Shorn of his beams; or, from behind the moon,
In dim eclipse, disastrous twilight sheds
On half the nations; and, with fear of change,
Perplexes monarchs.

The firmness of the devil's station or posture
is here compared to that of a tower; and his
faded or diminished splendour to that of the
sun seen through a morning haze, or from
behind the moon during an eclipse; all which
is perfectly clear; the objects of comparison
being at once grand and illustrative; and the
description of them, as far as they are described,
distinct, correct, and circumstantial. The
properties of solidity and firmness only, in the
tower, being the objects of comparison, to have
described its form or magnitude would have
been silly and impertinent: but the diminution
of brightness is an occasional effect; and when
an occasional effect is made the object of
poetical comparison or description, it is always
necessary to state its causes and circumstances;
which the poet has here done with equal conciseness, precision, perspicuity, and energy;
and it is to this that its sublimity is, in a great
degree, owing.

90. The imagery in the description of the
allegorical personage of death by the same great
author must, however, be admitted to be indis-

tinct, confused, and obscure ; and, by being so, loses much of its sublimity :

—————————— *the other shape,*
If shape it might be call'd, that shape had none,

is a confused play of words in Milton's worst manner ; and

Fierce as ten furies, terrible as hell,

are comparisons that mean nothing; as we know still less of the fierceness of furies or terrors of hell, than we do of those of death ; and fierceness is a mental energy, and not a positive quality, that can be measured by a scale of number. Ten furies may have collectively more strength than one; because the mechanic strength of many individuals may be concentered into one act or exertion ; but this is not the case with fierceness.

91. The blind admiration, with which the mass of mankind read works of established reputation, precludes all discrimination, whether of judgment or feeling. Not to be delighted with what they have always heard, in general terms, is *fine*, might argue a want of capacity to comprehend, or a want of taste to relish its merits ; to avoid the imputation of which, they applaud without reserve ; and conclude that every peculiarity, which they meet with, is a peculiarity of excellence, whether they understand it or not. Upon this principle,

there is scarcely any anomaly of grammar in
Shakspeare, or of metre in Milton, that has
not found even professed critics to praise and
commend it as a beauty : for they do not reflect,
that if it be a beauty, it is of that sort which
any writer may easily display ; and which all
good writers are anxious to avoid.

92. Of the same kind, is the sublime, which
they have imagined to arise out of vastness of
dimensions and unlimited greatness of size. It
is of that description, which every grovelling
imagination may reach, without any other
effort, than that of multiplication.*. The Ghost
striding from hill to hill in Ossian ; or the giant
in Claudian, lifting a mountain on his shoulders, whilst a river runs down his back, are
images as vast and as incomprehensible as any
critic of this school can desire ; but for that
very reason they are not sublime : for the passions can sympathize with no images, that the
imagination does not comprehend distinctly.
They may sympathize, indeed, with mental
energies to any extent : for in them, neither the
evidence of sense, nor the deductions of analogy
can set any boundaries to physical probability ;

---

* —— " vitio male judicantium, qui majorem habere
yim credunt ea quæ non habent artem . . . . . .
evenit nonnunquam ut aliquid grande inveniat, qui semper
quærit quod nimium est."

QUINTILIAN, Inst. l. ii. c. xii.

D D 3

CHAP.
I.
Of the Su-
blime and
Pathetic.

whence he, *qui nihil molitur inepte*, does not say that the Aloidæ actually did pile mountains upon mountains; but only that they aimed at it, and might perhaps have done it, had they not been cut off by a premature death, before they arrived at their full growth :

Οσσαν επ᾽ Ουλυμπω μεμασαν θεμεν, αυταρ επ᾽ Οσση
Πηλιον εινοσιφυλλον, ιν᾽ ηρανος αμβατος ειη.
και νυ κεν εξετελεσσαν, ει ήβης μετρον ικοντο *.

* Odyss. λ. 314. The authenticity of these lines appears to have been questioned by some of the ancient
critics ; Eustath. p. 1687 : and Aristarchus and others
rejected all the latter part of this book, containing the
Visions of the Punishments of Hell, from v. 567 to 626
inclusive ; not on account of any faults or defects in the
poetry, which is most exquisite ; but on account of the
difficulty of reconciling it to the simple evocation of the
dead, related in the preceding part. See Schol. in Pindar. Ol. i. v. 91 ; and Schol. ined. in Odyss. v. 567, cited
in a note to v. 5 of the Orestes of Euripides, published in
London A. D. 1798.

This difficulty, it must be owned, is a serious one, and
if the whole passage be left out, the succeeding line con-
nects itself with the preceding one perfectly well. The
three lines too, relating to the deification of Hercules,
are manifestly spurious ; the deification of that hero,
being unknown to the writer or writers of the Iliad and
Odyssey, as was likewise that of Bacchus ; the lines relating to him in the Iliad being manifestly spurious. The
above-mentioned three lines appear, however, to have
been manifestly inserted into the text of the passage ; for
the placing Hercules among the souls of the defunct plainly

93. So apprehensive, indeed, was he, that this daring hyperbole might lead the imagination to grasp at any unlimited or incomprehensible image, that in this instance only, and that of the giant Tityos, he has descended to the particulars of number and quantity, and given their determinate measurements:

εννεωροι γαρ τοιγε και εννεαπηχεες ησαν.
ευρος, αταρ μηκος γε γενεσθην εννεοργυιοι.

proves that he was not then held to be a god; and the idea of his being a mere image or *ειδωλον*, different from the other shades, is contradicted by his subsequent address to Ulysses, in which he likewise speaks of himself as a mere man, whose life had been laborious and unfortunate. The very learned author, too, of the note to Euripides above cited, is mistaken when he says that the punishments of Tantalus, mentioned in this passage, appear to have been unknown to Pindar; for he has distinctly alluded to them; stating the suspension of the stone over his head to be *μετα τριων τεταρτον.πονον*—*a fourth punishment after the three suffered before*; which three are the *διψος, και λιμος, και στασις εν λιμνη* mentioned in the Odyssey. I am aware that de Pauw altered *τεταρτον* to *τεταρτος*; and refers it to Tantalus, as being the fourth person punished after Sisyphus, Tityos and Ixion; but though another German editor has inserted this strange depravation into his text, I can scarcely believe that the very learned Greek professor of Cambridge could swallow it. Still less can I believe that he would be satisfied with Heyne's interpretation, that *μετα τριων τεταρτον* means indefinitely *αλλον επ' αλλω.*

Virgil has perhaps hurt the effect by making them actually engage in the mighty attempt instead of merely designing or aiming at it—

Ter sunt conati imponere Pelio Ossam
Scilicet, atque Ossæ frondosum involvere Olympum :
Ter Pater extructos disjecit fulmine montes—

and Claudian has quite spoiled it by making his giants complete the attempt, in which he has been followed by Milton in his battle of the angels ; a part of the Paradise Lost, which has been more admired, than, I think, it deserves.

94. I do not mean, however, to deny that vastness may be a mean of exciting sublime sentiments ; but then it is upon the principle of indefinite extension before explained ; which cannot therefore extend to those images, which are merely exaggerated human forms, distinct and definite in their nature.; and incapable of acquiring grandeur of character from increase of dimensions. No reader ever discovered or imagined any thing sublime in Swift's Brobdignagians.

95. The influence of music upon the passions is much less than that of poetry ; but more than that of painting or sculpture : for, though inarticulate sounds convey no distinct images, or ideas, to the mind; certain modulations of tone naturally awaken correspondent sympathies ;

and certain combinations of it excite certain trains of ideas, by means of habitual associa- tion ; which, if of a kind to affect the passions, will affect them, when excited by these means, as well as when excited by any others. All the marvellous stories, however, told by the an- cients of the power of music over the soul, relate to the powers of music and poetry united ; and, as we hear of no persons among them, rendered eminent by mere musical com- position ; or who even professed the art of composing, we may conclude that the music was only of a secondary degree of importance ; and employed merely to give more effect to the sentiments, imagery, and expressions of the poet. The contrary is the case with almost all modern music ; the complicated melody of which overwhelms and buries the sense of the words ; so that poetry without music has now a much greater degree of influence upon the passions, than with it ; as must be evident to every person, who frequents the theatres ; where even a moderate tragedy, moderately acted, has manifestly a much greater effect on the feelings of the audience, than even the finest serious opera, performed by the first musicians of Europe, both vocal and instrumental. Even the dumb show of a pantomime dance seems, in our theatres, to excite more sympathy, and to attract more fixed attention than the highest

efforts of music can ; and perhaps it has really
more influence on the passions : for, when well
acted, it unites all the various expression of
countenance, attitude, and gesture, which can
be given by painting and sculpture ; and adds
to them the impressive embellishments of motion, animation, and succession. Music often
weakens the effect of such expression by too
great a display of technical skill ; than which,
nothing can be more adverse to the success of
whatever appeals to the passions.

96. Whether the story, which has afforded
Dryden so happy a subject for the display of
his great talents ;, or any other of the marvellous tales of the same kind, told by the Greeks,
have any foundation in truth ; or whether all
are not to be held in the same estimation as
that of Arion and the Dolphin, is a question,
which I shall not pretend to discuss : but,
nevertheless, I cannot but observe that, if any
such effects ever were produced, we might reasonably have expected to hear of them in the
Greek theatre ; where the most perfect combinations of music and poetry continually exerted their united powers upon collective multitudes, whose genuine feelings would necessarily
show themselves, free from all affectation or
restraint. No such miraculous effects are,
however, any where recorded ; nor does it
appear that the Greek tragedies, which were

all opera's, had, in representation, any degree of influence upon the passions, at all comparable to that, which we continually see produced by those of Shakspeare, Otway, and Rowe. It is probable, therefore, that the respective powers of music and poetry in exciting sympathy, whether considered jointly or separately, were always nearly the same as they are now; and that, though a pathetic air and expressive accompaniment might have heightened the effect of a lyric composition, yet a good rhapsodist would have made a greater impression upon the passions of his audience by reciting a book of the Iliad, than the first musicians of Greece could have done by singing a choral ode of Sophocles.

97. The verses of Homer, indeed, appear to have been originally accompanied by music; though of so rude and artless a kind, that we should now scarcely think it deserving of the name. The φορμιγξ or lyre, which consisted of four linen strings drawn over a wooden box, or the shell of a tortoise, could only have served to mark the pauses and cadences in the sort of chant, which was then called singing; and we accordingly find, that, though the fine voice of the bard is often celebrated, his skill or taste in touching his instrument is never once noticed; which we can only account for by supposing it to have been so imperfect as not to admit of either.

98· As for those fanciful theorists, who would persuade us that musick has such despotic and universal influence over the soul, that all its passions and affections vibrate as regularly to the strings of an instrument tuned in unison with them, as those strings do to the stroke of the bow or touch of the finger *, it will be sufficient to refer them to the story of Dr. Cornelius Scriblerus and his lyre †, which may serve as an explanatory comment to all the miraculous tales, upon which such theories have been founded. Without pretending to have such exalted notions of human nature, as either the Stoics of old, or the Philanthropists of modern times, have professed to entertain, we may at least presume that man, even in his most degraded state, is something better than the counterpart of a fiddle.

* Webb on Poetry and Music; and Kircher quoted by him.

† History of Martinus Scriblerus.

CHAPTER II.

OF THE RIDICULOUS.

1. DIAMETRICALLY opposite to the sublime and pathetic is the ridiculous : for laughter is an expression of joy and exultation; which arises not from sympathy but triumph ; and which seems therefore to have its principle in malignity. Those vices, which are not sufficiently baneful and destructive to excite detestation ; and those frailties and errors, which are not sufficiently serious and calamitous to excite pity, are generally such as excite laughter * : an involuntary convulsion communicated, in some unaccountable manner, from the mind to the features of the face, and the organs of respiration ; which seems to be peculiar to

---

* τε αισχρε ιστι το γελοιον μοριον· το γαρ γελοιον ιστιν αμαρ-τημα τι και αισχος ανωδυνον, και ε φθαρτικον.—ARIST. Poet. f. xi.

" Ea facillime luduntur, quæ neque odio magno, nec misericordia maxima digna sunt. Quamobrem materies omnis ridiculorum est in istis vitiis, quæ sunt in vita hominum neque clarorum neque calamitosorum, neque eorum qui ob facinus ad supplicium rapiendi videntur."—CIC. de Orat. lib. ii.

ὁ γελως παθος εν ηδονη. αι δ᾽ υπερβολαι καθαπερ επι το μειζον, εντω και επι τ᾽ ουλαττον.—LONGIN. f. xxxviii.

mankind ; or, at least, to be only participated in a degree by some tribes of monkeys.

2. Hence, as tragedy displays its powers in heightening and embellishing the general energies of human nature, so does comedy in exposing and exaggerating its particular weaknesses and defects. The one exhibits only the genuine feelings and sentiments of nature, expressed in the glowing language of enthusiasm ; while the other shows these feelings and sentiments weakened by the restraints, perverted by the habits, and modified by the rules of artificial society ; and expressed in the language appropriated to it by the artificial manners of particular ages and countries. The one delights in unity and simplicity of character, such as all character is when under the dominion of enthusiastic passion : but the other often produces its happiest effects by assembling and uniting those incongruities and inconsistencies, which, though neither incompatible nor unnatural, exhibit in their junction a perversion or degradation of the natural character of man : such as boasting and cowardice, ignorance and pedantry, dulness and conceit, rudeness and foppery ; with all the other heterogeneous combinations of impotent vanity, which generally affects excellence in that, which is most above its reach, because it is that, which it is most prone to admire.

11

3. The jealousy of Othello, and the ambition of Lady Macbeth, are those passions operating as the poet, from his general observation of human nature, conceived that they must operate upon great and atrocious minds : but the jealousy of Ford or Kitely, and the ambition of Malvolio, are the same passions operating as the poet had seen them operate on individuals of his own age and country. In the one, the general characteristics of human nature are merely heightened and embellished : but, in the other, they are modified and debased to suit the peculiarities, either natural or acquired, of particular individuals or classes of men.

4. The same difference is observable, in the character and expression of attitude and countenance, between the pictures of Raphael, and those of Rembrandt. Both drew from nature ; but the one drew the general energies and perfections of mankind, and the other their individual peculiarities and perversions : whence the compositions of the one are sublime, and those of the other ridiculous. Raphael raises us in our own estimation by showing us images of men, such as we think *might* exist ; and Rembrandt degrades us by showing us such as we know *do* exist : for the ridiculous, in whatsoever mode it be exhibited, will ever retain so much of its original principle, that the pleasure,

which it causes, will be in its nature a pleasure of malignity.

5. It has been observed by Locke that wit consists in facility of combination, and judgment in accuracy of discrimination * : but wit in this sense means, not merely pleasantry, but the power of imagination in general ; in which signification the word appears to have. been universally employed till lately. As limited to that particular species of wit, which excites mirth or pleasantry, it is equally comprehended in this definition : for whether the combinations of imagery be sublime or ludicrous ;—be intended to excite admiration or laughter, a facility in discovering resemblances will equally constitute the power of producing them ; since invention itself is nothing but a prompt, vigorous, and extensive power of combination.

6. Sublime imagery is not less sublime for being obvious ; but all ludicrous combinations must be new and uncommon, though just and natural : for it is in the sudden display of unforeseen resemblances between things of different or opposite character; such as the grave and the gay; the pompous and the familiar ; the exalted and the humble, &c. that what are called flashes of wit principally consist. In all, the principal feature or figure in the composi-

* Essay on Understanding, book ii. c. xi. f. 2.

tion is shown to the imagination, distorted or debased by being placed in an unfavourable light; or associated with degrading ideas; from the influence of which, the air of ridicule, which it acquires, arises.

7. Humour consists in similar coincidences of things generally dissimilar, displayed in manners instead of images and ideas: as when the auctioneer considers himself as a public character in the state, and imagines that his profession requires the talents of a consummate orator and rhetorician : or when a fishmonger, exalted to the rank of a major of militia, describes the moving of his regiment, from village to village, with all the pomp and pedantry of military diction, usually employed in describing the march of numerous armies from one kingdom to another.   In all cases, this kind of mock heroic is among the most powerful sources of the ludicrous : as, by joining the forms of the most momentous of human affairs to the most trivial of human actions, it at once amuses the imagination with novelty and contrast, and flatters that innate principle of selfish vanity or malignity, which makes us naturally delight in the degradation of whatsoever is exalted.

8. Of the same kind are the burlesque imitations or parodies of serious compositions; which being the most easy of all the tricks, by

which ridicule is produced, generally constitute
the wit and humour of those, who have no
other: for as the whole art of this species of
the ludicrous consists in employing, in a low
sense, or upon a low subject, those modes of
expression, which another person has employed
seriously, or upon an exalted one, it requires
neither invention, learning, nor ingenuity; but is
always in the power of any person, who will
condescend to employ it. The effect, too, is
always certain: for when the expressions, appropriated to grand or elevated subjects, are
transferred to those which are minute, humble,
or familiar, the contrast will necessarily be ridiculous in proportion as it is strong and abrupt.
The name of Boileau has preserved a parody,
of this kind, of a celebrated scene in the Cid
of Corneille; though it is a piece of wit, of
which Boileau's valet-de-chambre was just as
capable as his master. Ludicrous parodies of
some passages in the odes of Pindar are also
still extant, in a comedy of Aristophanes*;
and probably many more were made by the
lesser wits of that age: since no compositions
were ever more open to such kind of ridicule;
the change of a single word being, in many
instances, sufficient to direct all his dithyrambic
pomp of diction to some low or mean object;
and consequently to make it ludicrous, in pro-

* Fragm. Pindar. xiii. ed. Heyne.

portion to its inflation and magnificence. The ridiculous seems indeed to be always lying in wait on the extreme verge of the sublime and pathetic; and, as the chill of a single drop of cold water can condense into torpid dew an elastic mass of steam sufficient to give motion to the most powerful engine, so the damp of a single low word or incongruous circumstance is sufficient to sink into meanness and ridicule the most lofty imagery, or pathetic effusion, expressed otherwise in the most dignified and appropriate terms; and the higher the pitch, to which the strings of passion or enthusiasm are strained, the more sudden and complete will be their relaxation.

9. Upon the same principle, incongruities in dress, deportment, and dialect; such as dirt and finery, awkwardness and affectation, pomp and vulgarity, are ludicrous; and, above all, the heterogeneous confusion of accent and idiom, which a foreigner makes, when speaking a language, with which he is but imperfectly acquainted; a species of the ridiculous, which, howsoever low and contemptible it may appear to the polished courtier, or proud philosopher, has been a constant resource of comedy, from the time of Aristophanes, to the present day; Moliere being the only writer, distinguished for much vis comica, who has not condescended to employ it.

E E 2

10. The pleasure, which we receive from the imitations of a common mimic, who takes off, as it is called, the peculiarities of voice, gesture, manner, and expression of particular individuals, is of the same kind, and derived from the same principle: for, in the imitation, those peculiarities are always, in some degree, distorted and exaggerated; and, by being exhibited through organs and features, to which they do not naturally belong, they acquire a new character; which becomes ludicrous, in proportion as it becomes remote from the general style then in use in the polished ranks of society.   There is scarcely any person, whose manner a good mimic will not make appear ludicrous; or whose features a good caricaturist will not make appear ridiculous; without, in either case, losing the general resemblance: for there is scarcely any individual, who has not some peculiarity both in his manner and features; and by exaggerating this, and making it prominent, both the one and the other are enabled to give a vitiated and distorted; and, consequently, a ludicrous resemblance of him.

11. In all these cases, it is something of defect or deformity which pleases us; and consequently, how degrading soever it may be to own it, the passion flattered must be of the malignant kind.   Those persons, nevertheless,

who are most prone to laughter, and most ready to enjoy every kind of social pleasantry or ridicule, without reflecting at whose expence it is indulged, are commonly called *good-na-tured*; while those, on the contrary, who show no such disposition; but who chill with grave looks; or check with moral observations, the mirth, which a gay circle is deriving from a ludicrous display of the follies and foibles of a person, whom they, perhaps, all reverence and esteem, are as commonly styled *morose, sour, ill-natured fellows.* But in this case, we confound two qualities, which are extremely different, *good-nature,* and *good-humour. Good-nature* is that benevolent sensibility of mind, which disposes us to feel both the happiness and misery of others; and to endeavour to promote the one, and prevent or mitigate the other: but, as this is often quite impossible; and as spectacles of misery are more frequent and obtrusive than those of bliss; the good-natured man often finds his imagination so haunted with unpleasant images; and his memory so loaded with dismal recollections; that his whole mind becomes tinged with melancholy; which frequently shows itself in unseasonable gravity, and even austerity of countenance and deportment; and in a gloomy roughness of behaviour; which is easily mistaken for the sour morosity of the worst spe-

cies of malignant temper. *Good humour*, on
the contrary, is that prompt susceptibility of
every kind of social or festive gratification,
which a mind void of suffering or sorrow in
itself; and incapable, through want of thought
or sensibility, of feeling the sufferings or sorrows of others, ever enjoys. A certain degree
of vanity, or light pride, is absolutely necessary to feed and support it; and, though it is
never allied to dark envy or atrocious malignity,
it is never, I believe, entirely free from a certain share of sordid selfishness: for, as the
perpetual smile of gaiety can only flow from
the heart, which is perpetually at ease, it can
only flow from *that*, which carries the ingre-
dients of perpetual ease always within itself;
and these are affections, which never diverge
far from its own centre.

12. There is, nevertheless, a certain degree
of sympathy in joy, as well as in sorrow—in
laughter, as well as in tears—

> Ut ridentibus adrident, ita flentibus adflent
> Humani vultus.

But still, I think, the sympathy is weaker; and
the comparative degree of joy or exhilaration,
which we feel in beholding the gaiety and festivity of others, is much less than that of the
grief or pity, which we feel in beholding their
sufferings and sorrows. This, however, may

depend, in a great degree, on the respective constitutions of different individuals; for each will of course sympathize most with that pas- sion, to which he is most prone by nature or habit: but, nevertheless, in exciting laughter, sympathy seems, in all cases, to be less power- ful than contrast; for the dry joker or grave buffoon is always more successful, in creating mirth, than the gay giggling one. What the poet says of sympathetic sorrow—

———————— Si vis me flere dolendum est
Primum ipsi tibi" ————

is certainly not applicable to sympathetic mer- riment: for, in proportion as the wit laughs at his own joke, his audience are generally dis- posed to be serious *.

13˙ All the selfish passions, or those passions which peculiarly belong to self-preservation or self-gratification; such as fear, parsimony, avarice, vanity, gluttony, &c. are the most common and proper subjects of the ridiculous; and are consequently the leading characteristics in the most prominent personages of comic fiction: for, as they show vice without energy; and make human nature appear base without being atrocious, and vile without being destruc-

* " Quamquam gratiæ plurimum dictis severitas affert; fitque ridiculum id ipsum, quia qui dicit non ridet."— QUINCTIL. Inst. l. vi. c. iii.

tive, they excite the laugh of scorn instead of
the frown of indignation ; and receive, from
the insignificance of their effects, the ludicrous
character of folly, instead of the serious one
of wickedness.

14. Like all qualities, however, which are
vicious only in their excess, and meritorious
in their moderation, it is impossible to express
or represent them so, as that the characters
exhibited may not be liable to be misunderstood
or misapplied : for as the boundaries between
the vicious excess and the virtuous moderation
cannot be fixed by any geometrical admeasure-
ment, or mathematical calculation, every individual fixes them according to his particular
disposition, interest, or circumstances. That
degree of fear, which, to the soldier or the
seaman, may appear unmanly timidity, may,
to the merchant or mechanic, seem only necessary caution; and that degree of parsimony,
which the old and wary may think only laud-
able frugality, may, to the young and dissipated,
appear the meanest penury: whence every
rake or spendthrift, when he sees the comedy
of the Miser, will be apt to apply the character of Harpagon to the father or guardian, by
whose prudence he is restrained from ruining
himself and his family ; and conclude that it is
equally meritorious to rob or defraud him. But
would he not have made a similar application

of what he saw in real life, and drawn a similar conclusion, if he had never seen the play?
I think it is evident that he would: for comedy
is a fictitious imitation of the examples of real
life, and not an example, from which real life
is ever copied. No one ever goes to the theatre to learn how he is to act on a particular
emergency; or to hear the solution of any
general question of casuistical morality, that
may have arisen in his mind; but merely to
sympathize with the general energies, or laugh
at the particular weaknesses of human nature:
which, in the fictions of theatrical representation, he can do without the intermixture of
any of those painful or humiliating sentiments,
which would occur in contemplating them, as
they arise from similar events in real life.

15. As exhibiting the particular weaknesses
and follies of the human mind, the fictions of
comedy, and the characters which it employs,
must deviate from the common system, which
common prudence marks out for the conduct
of domestic life, equally with those of tragedy,
which displays its general energies. The usual
subject and principal action of all comedy is
love, and its termination marriage: but if this
union were to be, as it commonly is, or at least
ought to be in real life, the slow result of calm
and tried attachment—of deliberate and sober
preference, sanctified by virtue and directed by

prudence, how flat, tame, and insipid would be
the progress of it; and how impossible for any
powers of genius to make the representation of
such scenes interesting or amusing! To produce this effect, there must be difficulties and
embarrassments, obstacles and restrictions;
which are to be eluded by intrigue, controlled
by impudence, or surmounted by audacity.
The credulity of the simple is to be duped and
exposed by the artifice of the crafty; or the
circumspection of the wary baffled and frus-
trated by the enterprise of the bold; so that the
various peculiarities of manners, dispositions,
and affections may be displayed in a variety of
situations, and under the influence of a variety
of circumstances, to amuse the fancies, and
awaken the sympathies of the spectators.

16. These difficulties and embarrassments,
obstacles and restrictions, of course, arise from
guardians or parents; whose prudence or avarice, vanity or ambition, thwart the more disinterested inclinations of their wards and children. They are consequently the persons
whose credulity is to be duped, whose circumspection is to be eluded, and whose characters are to be exposed to the scorn and
ridicule of the spectators. Even where the plot
of the piece does not admit of such characters;
that scorn and ridicule are often pointed against
the simple and inoffensive—the weak and well-

meaning; who are cheated by the crafty, insulted by the insolent, and triumphed over by
all.

17. Comedy therefore, considered as holding
out examples for real life, is necessarily still
more immoral in its tendency than tragedy;
since the characters and incidents, which it
exhibits, are those which occur in the ordinary
ranks of civil society, and which it is therefore
in every one's power to imitate. The crimes
of King Richard, or Macbeth, are within the
reach of few; but the vices of Charles Surface,
and the indiscretions of Tom Jones, are within
the reach of every gentleman : nevertheless, I
do not believe that such vices, and such indiscretions, would have been less frequent, if those
popular instances of them had never been exhibited to the public: for the high spirits of
the gay and voluptuous think as little of the
examples held out in plays and romances, when
plunging into riot and intemperance, as the
aspiring minds of the ambitious do, when plan-
ning designs -of treason and usurpation. A
coxcomical highwayman may, indeed, affect
to imitate the character of Macheath ; but this
imitation commences after he becomes a highwayman, which he would equally have been,
had the Beggar's Opera never existed. Men
are driven to such courses by the urgent pressure of want, brought on, perhaps, by the

thoughtless indulgences of vice and extravagance: but no person, in his senses, was ever
led into enterprises of such dangerous importance by the romantic desire of imitating the
fictions of a drama. If the conduct of any persons is influenced by the examples exhibited in
such fictions, it is that of young ladies in the
affairs of love and marriage: but I believe that
such influence is much more rare, than severe
moralists are inclined to suppose; since there
were plenty of elopements, and stolen matches,
before comedies, or plays of any kind, were
known—" viderunt primos argentea secula
mœchos."—If, however, there are any romantic minds, which feel this influence, they may
draw an awful lesson concerning its consequences from the same source; namely, that
the same kind of marriage, which usually ends
a comedy, as usually begins a tragedy.

CHAPTER III.

OF NOVELTY.

1. IT has been observed, in a preceding part of this inquiry, that every natural sentiment or sensation, when long continued without variation or interruption, becomes an habitual mode of existence instead of a transitory affection; and, therefore, ceases to produce any marked degree either of pleasure or pain. Even if repeated very frequently, and always in the same mode and degree, it will become so far habitual as to be very insipid; though not quite neutral or imperceptible: for if the revival of it can so far awaken attention as to be perceived and noted, its impression must be either pleasing or the contrary; though, perhaps, in so slight a degree, as scarcely to relieve the mind from that painful listlessness, which arises from the sense of mere unemployed and unvaried existence.

2. Change and variety are, therefore, necessary to the enjoyment of all pleasure; whether sensual or intellectual: and so powerful is this principle, that all change, not so violent as to produce a degree of irritation in the organs

absolutely painful, is pleasing; and preferable to any uniform and unvaried gratification.

3. It might naturally be supposed, when standards of excellence were universally acknowledged and admired in every art; in poetry and elocution; in painting and sculpture; in personal dress, decoration, and demeanor; it might naturally be supposed, I say, that the style and manner at least of those standards would be universally followed; and that the wit and ingenuity of man would only be employed in adding the utmost refinements of execution to that, which admitted of no improvements from invention. But this is by no means the case:—on the contrary, *ita comparatum est humanum ingenium, ut optimarum rerum satietate defatigetur; unde fit, artes, necessitatis vi crescere, aut decrescere semper; et ad fastigium evectas, ibi non posse consistere.* Perfection in taste and style has no sooner been reached, than it has been abandoned, even by those, who not only professed the warmest, but felt the sincerest admiration for the models, which they forsook. The style of Virgil and Horace in poetry, and that of Cæsar and Cicero in prose, continued to be admired and applauded through all the succeeding ages of Roman eloquence, as the true standards of taste and eloquence in writing. Yet no one ever attempted to imitate them;

3

though there is no reason to suspect that their praises were not perfectly sincere: but all writers seek for applause; and applause is only to be gained by novelty. The style of Cicero and Virgil was new in the Latin language, when they wrote; but, in the age of Seneca and Lucan, it was no longer so; and though it still imposed by the stamp of authority, it could not even please without it; so that living writers, whose names depended on their works, and not their works upon their names, were obliged to seek for other means of exciting public attention, and acquiring public approbation. In the succeeding age the refinements of these writers became old and insipid; and those of Statius and Tacitus were successfully employed to gratify the restless pruriency of innovation. In all other ages and countries, where letters have been successfully cultivated, the progression has been nearly the same; and in none more distinctly than in our own: from Swift and Addison to Johnson, Burke and Gibbon, is a transition exactly similar to that from Cæsar and Cicero to Seneca and Tacitus.

4. In imitative art, the progress of corruption has been nearly the same. The taste for pure design in Italy arose and perished with Raphael; whose immediate scholars and successors deviated into extravagance and distortion, that they might appear original, and gain

the applause of their contemporaries by surpassing what was simply excellent; in which, if
they did not succeed, they at least succeeded
in producing something new; which equally
answered their purpose. In the following age,
novelties still more fascinating and various were
displayed by the masterly hands and luxuriant
imaginations of Lanfranc and Pietro da Cortona; whence the style of art became entirely
changed; and though Raphael was still looked
up to, as the most perfect master of design,
those, who most implicitly acknowledged the
authority of his name, had evidently lost all
relish for the merits, by which it was acquired.
They admired the vigour of his genius, and applauded the purity of his taste; but lamented
that he had not been acquainted with the principle of pyramidal grouping, the flowing line,
and all those systematic tricks of false refinement, to the want of which, he in a great degree
owed that reputation, which alone recommended
his works to their notice or approbation.

5. The words genius and taste are, like the
words beauty and virtue, mere terms of general
approbation, which men apply to whatever they
approve, without annexing any specific ideas to
them. They are, therefore, as often employed
to signify extravagant novelty as genuine merit;
and it is only time that arrests the abuse. Purity, simplicity, grace, and elegance, are, as well

as beauty, qualities, that are always equally admired, because the words, by which they are expressed, are terms of approbation. But, nevertheless, these terms are entirely under the influence of fashion; and are applied to every novelty of style or manner, to which accident or caprice gives a momentary currency. Pietro da Cortona and Bernini would, without doubt, have maintained their pretensions to them as firmly, and, probably, as sincerely as Raphael, Annibal Caracci, or Nicolas Poussin; and their admirers would have supported their claims with equal obstinacy: for no person ever adopted or admired a style, which he felt or thought to be inelegant, ungraceful, or impure; but the meaning, which the words elegance, grace, and purity bear, differs, not only in different individuals, but in the same individuals, accordingly as they are differently applied. We often hear the same persons talk of the grace and elegance of a Greek statue, and of a French dancer; and, perhaps, with equal sincerity: for, either they feel neither, and are guided, in the one instance, by the authority of criticism; and, in the other, by that of fashion; or, perhaps, they feel both; but, in the latter instance, misapply the terms, or mistake the causes of their feelings: for, as novelty and difficulty, displayed in extraordinary feats of bodily strength and agility, are really and universally

F F

pleasing, it is no wonder that they should, in the laxity of colloquial language, be called by those terms, which are generally and indiscriminately employed to signify pleasing modifications of form and action.

6. There is no extravagance or absurdity of dress, or personal decoration or disguise, to which the same terms have not been applied with equal sincerity, so long as it has borne the gloss of novelty, or stamp of fashion; and, perhaps, painters, sculptors, and writers may be no further answerable for the corruptions of taste in art and eloquence, than taylors and milliners are for those in dress; since, in all professions—

Those, who live to please, must please to live.

The restless desire of novelty, so general among all mankind, may, perhaps, be the principle of both; to the extravagancies and caprices of which, those, who make it their business to supply the gratifications, must, of course, conform: for whether an artist or an author work for money or for fame, he is equally dependent upon public opinion; since mere posthumous fame is but a cold and distant reward; and is, moreover, one of which no person can be certain *.

---

* " Semper oratorum eloquentiæ moderatrix fuit auditorum prudentia. Omnes enim, qui probari volunt, volun-

3

7. The corruptions of art and the extravagancies of dress have, as far as I have been
able to observe, universally accompanied each
other : but poetry and elocution have never
manifested any symptoms of sympathy with
either. From the middle of the seventeenth
to the middle of the eighteenth century, the
fashions in dress were carried to the utmost
extreme of absurdity; and imitative art sunk
to its lowest state of degradation ; at the same
time that taste in literary composition, both in
England and France, attained a degree of
purity and perfection only surpassed by that of
the finest ages of Greece and Rome. The case
is that imitative art, being employed in exhibiting exterior and visible forms only, necessarily
catches its style of imitation, in some degree
at least, from those, with which it is most
familiar ; while writing, being employed in expressing mind only, is entirely independent,
even in its imitations, of all external appearances.

8. Perhaps one great cause of the permanency
of style, and continued identity of taste, in ancient art, was the permanency and unvaried
simplicity of dress. From the age of Pericles
to that of Hadrian, during a period of between

tatem eorum, qui audiunt, intuentur, ad eamque, et ad
eorum arbitrium et nutum totos se fingunt, et accom-
modant." Cic. Orat. ad Brutum, c. 24.

F F 2

five and six hundred years, under the successive domination of the Athenians, the
Lacedæmonians, the Macedonians, and the
Romans, there was less variation in the style
and taste of imitative art, through all the different states, that composed those empires,
excepting only Egypt, than there is, not only
between those of any two schools, but between
those of any two successive ages of the same
school, in modern Europe. During all that
period also, a simplicity of dress, bordering
upon negligence, and even approaching to nu-
dity, universally prevailed ; and any deviation
from it was deemed a symptom of barbarism
and corruption of manners unbecoming a man
of rank and education *. Even the women,
during that period, never attempted to ex-
change their native charms for the adscititious
ornaments of dress : for, though the limbs and
body were more or less concealed, as general
custom or individual modesty occasionally required, they never were so disguised, but that
the general forms of a human creature were

---

* Thucyd. lib. i. 6.
   " Sed tibi nec ferro placeat torquere capillos:
     Nec tua mordaci pumice crura teras.
   Ista jube faciant quorum Cybeleïa mater .
     Concinitur Phrygiis exululata modis.
   Forma viros neglecta decet———"
                    Ovid. de Arte Amandi, l. i. v. 505.
   See also the Portraits upon Coins, &c.

suffered to appear; which is not the case with
a lady in stays and a hoop. About the age of
Hadrian, the Roman women of fashion began
to dress their hair in fantastic forms, wholly
unlike those of nature; and when once disguise was thus mistaken for embellishment,
there was no longer any principle to check
the extravagancies of caprice. Consequently
novelty and splendor were soon mistaken for
grace and elegance ; and as the contagion immediately communicated itself to the other sex,
all simplicity of taste in dress and manners;
and, with it, all purity of style in art were
banished; and the licentious and operose
barbarism of the Byzantine court gradually
succeeded.

9. But though the passion for novelty has
been the principal means of corrupting taste,
it has also been a principal mean of polishing
and perfecting it* ; for, imitation being in itself
pleasing, men are always delighted with the
best specimens, which they have seen of it, be
they ever so bad ; and it is merely the desire
of something new, and not any preconceived
ideas of something better, that urges them on
to seek for improvement. As long as this rest-

* ἅπαντα μεν τοι, τα οὑτως ασεμνα, δια μιαν εμφυιται τοις
λογοις αιτιαν, δια το περι τας νοησεις καινοσπυδον . . . . .
αφ᾽ ὡν γαρ ἡμιν τ᾽ αγαθα, σχεδον απ᾽ αυτων τυτων και τα κακα
γιγνισθαι φιλει.—LONGIN. f. v.

F F 3

less desire of novelty can restrain itself, in imitative art, to the imitation of real genuine nature, it will only tend to real improvement, and limit its gratifications to varieties of perfection, and degrees of refinement : but, when it calls upon invention to usurp the place of imitation ; or substitute to genuine, or merely embellished nature, nature sophisticated and corrupted by artificial habits, it immediately produces vice and extravagance of manner. Of the first, Michael Angelo was a memorable instance ; and of the second, Bernini ; both of whom were men of extraordinary genius and talents ; but stimulated into manner and extravagance of opposite kinds by an insatiate desire of novelty and originality ; which was, nevertheless, more, perhaps, the general vice of the times, in which they respectively lived, than their own peculiarly : for we may observe that it operates, in modes and degrees nearly similar, in the contemporary Italian poets Ariosto and Marino ; who were likewise men of uncommon talents ; and who, in their respective faults and merits of this kind, nearly resemble the sculptors, with whom they respectively flourished. Ariosto, like Michael Angelo, is bold and spirited, but extravagant ; while Marino, like Bernini, is redundant, smooth, and ingenious ; but frivolous and affected. The merits and faults of the two first are certainly of a higher class; and the judgment of the public has, therefore, justly given them a higher rank and station in literature and art. Ariosto's extravagance is, indeed, of a very different kind from Michael Angelo's, whose genius more resembled Milton's; but still it is equally extravagance,

10. There is, however, another cause, besides the mere love of novelty, for that profusion of ornament, and unremitted affectation of elegance and splendor, which distinguish the decline or corruption of taste in every species of literary composition. When a language has been cultivated with success, and enriched with popular works in prose and verse, the brilliant and prominent passages of the most popular and admired of them become fixed in every person's memory; and are thus made the scale, by which they measure, and the criterion, by which they judge the general style of succeeding compositions; which are consequently condemned as flat, trite, or unpolished, if they do not uniformly stand this unfair test. If, on the contrary, they do, they necessarily display ornament, where the subject requires plainness and simplicity; and thus acquire that tawdry character, which, though generally abused, can alone secure attention; and authors can bear abuse, at all times, with much more patience than neglect.

11: It is observed by a great critic that men judge of the merits of a living writer by his worst performances; and of those of a dead one, by his best * : and this they do, not so much from any principle of malignity or envy, as because they remember only the most brilliant passages of the one; and consequently apply them, even mechanically and unintentionally, as the standards, by which they try the least brilliant of the others. Hence, an unvaried degree of brilliance and ornament being required, those, whose business it is to gratify public taste, strive to dress every part of their compositions alike; whether the subject admit of such dress and decoration or not : and as they thus get into a habit of adorning their style by rule and system, instead of by taste and feeling, they adorn all parts of it ill; and are always either frivolous or extravagant : for, when just feeling and a discriminating tact cease to be the legitimate criteria of excellence, the caprices of novelty are freed from all restraint; and the fashion of the day becomes the only test of merit †,

---

* Dr. Johnson, Pref. to Shakspeare.

† Quæ non laudantur modo a plerisque, sed (quod pejus est) propter hoc ipsum, quod sunt prava laudantur: nam sermo rectus, et secundum naturam enunciatus, nihil habere ex ingenio videtur.

QUINTILIANI, Instit, l. ii, c, v,

12. As writers and readers multiply in a language, every plain and easy mode of expression, which it affords, becomes trite and common by frequent repetition ; and certain degrees of vicious refinement and affectation become absolutely necessary to exalt the style above the familiar vulgarity of common colloquial speech ; and as this common colloquial speech is constantly extending its usurpations, and vulgarising refinement ; refinement can only maintain its character and keep out of its reach, by constantly retreating from it, and becoming more refined ; and consequently more affected and constrained : this will be found to be the progress of all highly polished languages.

13. In no art has the passion for novelty had more influence, than in that of landscape gardening, or embellishing and improving grounds ; of which it appears hitherto to have been almost the sole principle. Whenever this art has been practised in countries only partially and imperfectly cultivated ; as in the ancient Persian and Roman empires ; and in the modern kingdoms and states of Europe till lately ; it always appeared to delight in a profuse display of labour and expense ; and in deviating as much as possible from ordinary nature. Rivers, springs, groves, lawns, and forests were to be seen every where ; and the country was covered with fine trees, which exhibited every variety of natural

form : but canals, fountains, quincunxes, and parterres were only to be seen where art and industry had formed them ; and trees cut into the shapes of pyramids and colonnades, men and animals, were new and unusual objects ; and such as were only to be found in highly dressed gardens. Novelty, contrast, and sur-prise are naturally so pleasing, that every per-son was delighted with objects of this kind; and as the word *beauty* is always applied indis-criminately to every visible object that is, in any way, pleasing, no one hesitated in calling them *beautiful.* A great writer has, indeed, gone still further, and so completely sacrificed both his feelings and his philosophy to the fashion of the day, that, in investigating the subject, he discovers that surprise, arising from novelty and contrast, is the genuine principle of beauty ; and that consequently the Boromean island, in which all these tricks of art are con-trasted with wild uncultivated mountains sur-rounding an extensive lake, is the most beautiful spot on the globe *. Another great writer after-wards discovered that surprise or astonishment was the genuine principle, not of the beautiful, but of the sublime ; which, according to him, is as diametrically opposite to beauty, as pain is to pleasure †. When Montesquieu and

---

* Montesquieu, Fragm. sur le Gout.
† Inquiry into the Sublime and Beautiful.

Burke thus differ upon a subject of common sense and feeling, which each had made the particular object of his investigation, who shall hope to escape error in any theoretical inquiry? *

14. By taking a comparative view of the style of ornamental gardening in the remotest parts of Asia, we shall find a further illustration of the influence of the same principle of novelty in a directly contrary mode of practice. In the vast and populous empire of China, every spot capable of producing food for either man or beast is cultivated to the utmost extent of art and industry; and there the gardens of luxury and grounds devoted to amusement are affectedly diversified with artificial rocks, irregular lakes and ponds, and other imitations of the wild varieties of uncultivated nature : for there, such objects are rare and novel; and consequently the possessing them displays wealth, taste, and magnificence.

15. With the general extension of cultivation and enclosing in England, this style, or at least an imperfect imitation of it, was introduced among us ; and, as novelty recommended it to fashion, it soon obtained the sanction of general usage ; which it has now possessed so long

---

* ουδεν εν ανθρωποισι διακριδον εστι νοημα

αλλ' ὁ συ θαυμαζεις, τους' ετεροισι γελως.

LUCIAN. Epigr. V.

that it will probably soon lose it by the influence of the same restless power which first
introduced it. At least it has no other principle to rest upon; and this is, in its nature, a
changeable one. It may serve, indeed, to distinguish the great man's place from the adjoining country; and a large space of ground,
enclosed by a belt, and dotted with clumps,
may show his wealth and magnificence; and
the sacrifices which he makes to his taste: but
these sacrifices afford no gratification but to
vanity; since by the very act of sacrificing it;
that is, of throwing it open, all the charms of
intricacy and variety are demolished, and no
other substituted in their place.

16. These charms of intricacy and variety,
which ought peculiarly to be cherished and
cultivated in this art *, owe all their effect to
the natural love of novelty, of which we are
here treating; for, though contrast and surprise
cannot constitute beauty, they can render it
more impressive; and, though a number of
objects seen together are still the same, as
when seen separately, yet their effect upon the
eye and the imagination is extremely different.
By being skilfully divided and arranged in
separate compositions, and shown successively

---

* Let not each beauty every where be spy'd,
Where half the skill is decently to hide.

Pope, Epist. on Taste.

in scenes artfully contrasted with each other,
each acquires separately the charm of novelty, and contributes to bestow it on the next; and as all is never shown at once, the spectator never knows when he has seen all; but still imagines that there are other beauties unrevealed, which fancy decorates with its own colours. The proprietor or contriver, indeed, who knows all, can suffer no such pleasing delusions : but, nevertheless, the changes produced by every variation of season, or even of weather, in confined scenery are so great; and the alterations made in a composition by the growth or amputation of the branch of a tree, so important, that the novelty of it is inexhaustible and everlasting ; especially if the proprietor improve, not by a preconcerted plan, but by the more safe and certain method of gradual experiment and observation. It is often impossible to know what ought to be done, till we know the effect of what has been done ; and if this depend upon the growth of trees, it cannot be ascertained by any calculation, but must wait the discovery of time ; and, by thus waiting, we both diversify and prolong the amusement ; and have the pleasure of contemplating, every year, new varieties of still improving scenery. The planter, too, is apt to think that, if his plantations grow, his work is done : but if he plant for timber, either useful

or ornamental, his plantations must be thinned gradually; and, if they be meant for orna- ment, the cutting down requires infinitely more skill and attention than the planting. The one is only the dead colouring of the picture, or rough hewing of the statue, in which any error may be amended; but the other is the finish- ing of it, in which a single false stroke may be fatal.

17. As every new impression, either upon the organs of sense, or upon the mind, that is not absolutely painful, is pleasing, curiosity is one of the most universal passions; and one, of which the gratifications afford, perhaps, the most pure and unmixed, if not the most exqui- site pleasures. Not only every acquisition of knowledge, but every new idea or new image, from what source soever it may be derived, affords real delight * : whence we are all pleased at hearing narrations of miraculous and extra- ordinary events, and feel a natural inclination to believe them true. So strong, indeed, is this inclination, that I have often observed persons employ, imperceptibly, no small degree of arti- fice to deceive themselves into a belief of mi- racles, in the truth of which they were no ways interested : whence I have been led to suspect that many persons, who have passed in the world

* το δε θαυμαστον ηδυ· σημειον δε· παντες γαρ προστιθεντες απαγγελλουσιν, ως χαριζομενοι.—ARISTOT. Poet. f. xliii.

for impostors, have been, in fact, the dupes of their own unintentional frauds. The natural desire of belief becomes, by indulgence, a predominant passion; and such persons practise deceit, first on themselves, and then upon others.

18. What adds still to the pleasure of hearing and believing miraculous events, is the grateful emotion caused by surprise; an emotion, which men seem to have equal pleasure in receiving and communicating; the eagerness for relating wonders being fully as keen as that of listening to them; so that it almost always happens that a wonderful tale grows more wonderful, in proportion to the number of mouths, through which it has passed. The vanity of displaying more knowledge, or affording more entertainment, induces every retailer to add something; till at last credulity is overstrained, and the miracle literally dies of repletion.

19. This eagerness of curiosity is not at all damped or impeded by the object of it being known to be offensive and disagreeable; children listening greedily to stories of ghosts, at the same time, that they tremble at every word; and persons of all ages and descriptions anxiously looking out for, and reading all narratives of atrocious murders, and horrible executions; though, perhaps, they previously know that the events, with which they are to be made ac-

quainted, are such as they shall afterwards wish in vain to blot from their memories. It is more than twenty years ago that I read, in a collection of French trials, the detailed accounts of the dreadful sufferings of Urban Grandier and Francis Damiens, and I have ever since anxiously wished that I had not read them; since, at certain moments, I find the horrid images haunt my imagination, in such a manner, that I feel it impossible to expel them, or keep my mind from fluttering round them. Start what new trains of ideas I will, they all lead to the same horrible and disgusting centre; from which no efforts can withhold or disentangle them : and yet were such direful scenes to be again acted in Europe (which God forbid!) I am not certain that the natural pruriency and restlessness of curiosity would suffer me to remain in ignorance of them.

20. Though no events, but such as are supposed, at least, to have really happened, can make this very strong and indelible impression upon the mind, yet known and avowed fiction, by merely holding forth new combinations of circumstances and images, can always excite a sufficient degree of curiosity, among the mass of mankind, to procure numerous and indefatigable readers; as is abundantly proved by the swarms of novels, with which the English

and French presses constantly teem. Most of these compositions have no other merit, than that of relating, in intelligible language, events of familiar life, not quite incredible, nor quite common; and yet the worst of them are constantly read with all the avidity of eager curiosity.

21. Perhaps the feeding and pampering this kind of curiosity, to a degree of morbid restlessness, is the principal, if not the only, moral evil resulting from such reading; and this, it must be owned, is a considerable one : for the habit, which young persons get, of reading merely for events, without any attention to language, thought, or sentiment, so completely unnerves all the powers of application, that their minds become incapable of learning, or retaining any thing. Whatever they read, they read without studying; and merely for the purpose of becoming acquainted with the contents of the book, which they never attempt to analyze, or digest; or turn into nutriment for their own minds; without which, reading is, at best, but a mere innocent and idle amusement. By the vicious indulgence of a prurient appetite, the mind, like the body, may be reduced to a state of atrophy.; in which, knowledge, like food, may pass through it, without adding either to its strength, its bulk, or its beauty.

G G

22. Besides this atrophy, arising from the habit of reading without attention, there is likewise a sort of sickly sensibility of mind, nourished, if not engendered, by compositions of this kind; which is equally adverse to the acquisition of all useful knowledge and sound morality; and which is the more dangerous and seductive, as it assumes the name and character of a most amiable virtue; and of one, which constitutes the principal charm of the softer sex. That fluttering and fidgetty curiosity;—that trembling irritability of habit, which cannot stoop to the tameness of reality, or the insipidity of common life; but is always interesting itself in the more animated and brilliant events of fiction, is often mistaken for real tenderness and sensibility of temper; and attributed to what, in the cant language of the times, is called a *good heart*; whereas it properly belongs to a deranged head. It is nearly of kin to a certain species of charity, (very common in the present age) which interests itself for the calamities of all mankind, except those, which it has the power to relieve. It has been said of another species of charity, that it begins at home; and sometimes ends, where it began: but this is so much in the contrary extreme, that home is the only part of the universe, which entirely escapes its attention.

It is continually stretching itself out to the
east, and to the west, and to the north, and to
the south; but always towards objects, which
it knows to be beyond its reach. Moral and
physical impossibilities sink before it; and
even excite instead of impeding its indefatigable exertions; for mere good intentions are
neither wearied by labour, exhausted by expense, nor baffled by obstructions; and kind
wishes and benevolent professions easily extend
themselves to the whole human race; while
the rancour and malignity of practice is only
felt by the comparatively few individuals, who
are within its reach. Conscience, therefore,
seldom hesitates in accepting this compromise;
which, either faith invests with the armour of
grace, or philosophy decks with the trappings
of virtue; both equally well adapted to exalt
the mind above the influence of natural affection; and teach it to look down, with contempt, upon the plain, simple, unassuming character of common practical benevolence *.

23. Even those writers of novels, whose
intention is to expose and ridicule this sickly
habit of mind, do, in fact, feed and promote it,
as much as any others: for their satire is only
pointed against the affectation of it; whereas
the reality, in these cases, is much worse than

* See the admirably drawn characters of Thwackum
and Square in Fielding's History of a Foundling.

the counterfeit. The capricious wife, or humor-some daughter, who only acts a fit of hysterics, or extreme nervous dejection, cannot long escape detection; and when the imposture is exposed, it is cured: but she, who has brought her nervous system into such a state of subser-viency to her temper, as to be really disordered and ill, whenever she is thwarted or opposed, appeals to the best feelings of man; and by thus putting her own vicious infirmities under the protection of others' virtues, secures their indulgence; and, of course, their increase. Like those, who by frequently telling a falsehood, become at length dupes to their own imposture, such persons become slaves to their own weak-ness, by habitually making others slaves to it: for, as this kind of weakness both feeds, and is fed by vanity, it, at first, affords them a spe-cious claim to every selfish and unreasonable indulgence; and, ultimately, excuses, in their own estimation, not only every omission, but almost every violation of the practical duties of their station in society. Like the theories of the philosophical politician, or the calculations of the abstract mathematician, the benevolence of persons afflicted with this eccentric sort of sensibility, is too refined for the ordinary occurrences of life, which are either too insipid to attract their observation, or too coarse to merit their attention.

3

24. When this nervous effervescence of feeling, or froth of sentiment, is still further sublimated by a dogmatical spirit of devotion, its selfishness becomes still more arrogant, by adding the more exalted pretensions of superior sanctity to those of superior sensibility. Of late this spirit has been much pampered by some of the sentimental narratives in question; the fair authoresses of which, in their zeal for revelation, boldly bring forward their love-sick heroes and heroines into the fields of religious controversy; and, as the same hands wield the weapons on both sides, they find as little difficulty in silencing all the cavils, and overturning all the objections of the fictitious disciples of Hume, Gibbon, and the French academy, as a colonel of the guards does in routing a regiment of fictitious French soldiers, in a review on Blackheath. When victory seems so easily obtained, it is no wonder that many are ready to enter the lists; especially, as the shortest and pleasantest way of becoming a saint is by converting a sinner. According to the Italian proverb, *those, who know nothing, doubt nothing*; whence it has frequently happened to me of late to hear questions of sacred criticism and philosophy decided, upon the authority of a dialogue in a novel, from which Grotius and Le Clerc, Mosheim and Michaelis shrank in despair, or passed by in timid perplexity.

25. In other respects, what has been before said of the moral influence of tragedy and comedy, may with equal propriety be applied to that of novels: for there is the same relation between a comedy and a novel, as between a tragedy and an epic poem. The end of morality is to restrain and subdue all the irregularities of passion and affection; and to subject the conduct of life to the dominion of abstract reason, and the uniformity of established rule: but the business of poetry, whether tragic or comic, whether epic or dramatic, is to display, and even exaggerate those irregularities; and to exhibit the events of life diversified by all the wild varieties of ungoverned affections, or chequered by all the fantastic modes of anomalous and vitiated habits. It is, therefore, utterly impossible for the latter to afford models for the former; and, the instant that it attempts it, it necessarily becomes tame and vapid; and, in short, ceases to be poetry:

——— caderent omnes a crinibus hydri :
Surda nihil gemeret grave buccina,

26. Men, however, do not search either epic or dramatic fictions for examples to guide them, either in the moral or prudential conduct of their affairs; and, if there be any that do, they will be more likely to become mad, than wicked; as they will exactly follow the steps of the

Knight of la Mancha, who sought for practical
examples in the species of poetical fiction then
most in fashion. Narrative fictions are, indeed,

generally more extravagant than dramatic, for
reasons before mentioned ; and consequently a
general, who should attempt to imitate Achilles,
might be guilty of more wild absurdities, than
a lover, who should attempt to imitate Lotha-
rio : but nevertheless, I believe, there is as
little danger in the example of the one, as of
the other : at least those heads that can be
turned, and those hearts that can be tainted by
such examples, would not have remained long
unturned, and untainted, if they had never been
acquainted with them. Alexander is said to
have dragged a man at his chariot wheels in
imitation of Achilles : but Alexander would
have been furious, cruel, and implacable, if he
had never read the Iliad, nor heard of the siege
of Troy : the torturing of Philotas, and assas-
sination of Parmenio, were certainly not in imitation of the hero of Homer.

27. It is natural for the professors of every
art and science to imagine, that the particular
objects of their respective pursuits are as important to the whole human race, as they are
to themselves individually ; whence there have
been, not only poets, but painters, to whom
the productions of their own art have appeared,
in the high character of bodies of universal

ethics, which were to correct national manners, and to improve and promote the practice
of every social virtue, by exhibiting examples
for the imitation, and recording events for the
instruction of mankind; as if men ever applied
to such sources of information for directions
how to act in the moral or prudential concerns
of life; or ever looked at pictures for any
thing but amusement. The most excellent of
all ethic painters is unquestionably our coun-
tryman Hogarth; but though his humorous
and expressive characters and compositions
have been viewed with delight by almost all
ranks and conditions of persons for more than
half a century, we may safely affirm that there
has not been one rake, prostitute, or idle ap-
prentice the less for them. Real examples may,
indeed, have some effect : but fiction is always
treated as fiction; and considered as mere
matter of amusement. Every glutton can be
diverted with the story of Helluo*; and yet
persevere in his course of sensuality without
intermission : but if another glutton of his

* Pope's Moral Essays, Ep. i. 238; who seems to have
taken it from la Fontaine. Had he been acquainted with
the original of Macho, a comic poet, who has told the
story, with much humour, of Philoxenus, a writer of dithyrambics in the court of the elder Dionysius, he would
probably have made more of it. The fragment is preserved by Athenæus, and edited, with other fragments of
the same poet, by Grotius, Excerpt. p. 851.

own age die of apoplexy or suffocation, it generally produces a short fit of abstinence; though never any permanent reformation: for the terror, even of real examples, constantly subsides, as the remembrance of them is gradually obliterated.

28. The only moral good, that appears to result from either poetry, music, painting, or sculpture, arises from their influence in civilizing and softening mankind, by substituting intellectual, to sensual pleasures; and turning the mind from violent and sanguinary, to mild and peaceful pursuits. The lovers of these arts seldom or never disturb the tranquillity either of kingdoms or families; and, if their lives be not very useful, they are always harmless, and often ornamental to society. The human mind cannot subsist without occupation, even during its intervals of relaxation from useful or serious employment; and if it have no intellectual amusements to soothe its lassitude and inquietude, during those intervals, it will fly for relief to ruinous dissipation or gross sensuality. It is true, that excessive attention to any of these arts often withdraws the mind from the study or cultivation of others more important and beneficial: but it oftener withdraws it from indulgences, which are more criminal and destructive, both to the individual and society. The frequenting of theatres, and

reading of romances and novels, often occupy
time, which *might·* be more profitably employed in the active pursuits of life; but
which probably *would* be more profusely
wasted in the more. frivolous amusements of
the coffee-house or assembly-room, or in the
more ruinous indulgences of the tavern or the
·brothel,

29. The erroneous estimates, which young
persons of quick sensibility and vivid imagination form of life and manners; and the false
hopes, which they consequently entertain·of
conjugal happiness, are undoubtedly confirmed
and strengthened by the exaggerated pictures
of human perfections, which they find in compositions of this kind : but, nevertheless, such
persons will always be drawing such visionary
pictures ; and will equally find imaginary pro-
totypes for them in real life, whether they read
such compositions, or not; and the restlessness
and discontent arising from such a-disposition
is equally adverse to regular morals and social
happiness. Finding nothing in the persons,
with whom they are united, corresponding with
the-extravagant ideas, which their heated imaginations had formed ; but still persuaded that
these ideas are taken from reality and not from
fancy, they become dissatisfied with all that
they had so eagerly desired, and appropriate
all the general vices and infirmities of human

nature to the particular object, whose vices' or
infirmities are most exposed to their constant
observation. Hence they are always easily
disgusted ; and it often happens that the very
qualities, which contributed to win their esteem,
and inflame their passion, while viewed at a
distance, become the means of turning their
esteem to scorn, and their love to hatred, when
constantly and unseasonably obtruded upon
them.

30. There is no virtue more amiable in the
softer sex, than that mild and quiescent spirit
of devotion ; which, without entangling itself
in the dogmas of religion, is melted by its cha-
rities, and exhilarated by its hopes : but, nevertheless, it frequently happens that women, who
have been educated in all the strictness of its
pure morality, do so blend and confound the
ideas of sin and sensuality, that they estimate
the virtue of modesty only as it tends to check
appetite and control desire : whence they neglect all the means of inspiring respect in their
husbands, but such as can only be employed at
the expense of that passion, which it should be
their constant study to cherish, perpetuate, and
exalt. Thus their freedom and reserve are
equally unseasonable ; the one being ever employed to excite personal disgust, and the other
to damp personal affection.

31. It has been observed by moralists that the sorrows and inquietudes, which embitter private life, are caused more by little acts of vexation, insult, and oppression often repeated, than by any of those great vices and atrocious crimes, against which nature revolts; and which, therefore, occur but seldom. With equal truth, it may be observed, that those reciprocal disgusts, which grow up between persons thus nearly and dearly connected, and gradually poison their happiness and embitter their existence, do not proceed so much from any marked violations of decency and decorum, as from little neglects and inattentions, so often repeated that they become constitutional habits, operating the more steadily and securely, because slowly and unobserved. Such is the perverse constitution of human nature, that, while every personal charm loses, every disgusting quality acquires influence by a repetition of its exertion; and as no charms are so perfect as to be entirely exempt from such qualities, the empire of mere personal beauty is always of short duration:

———— medio de fonte leporum
Surgit amari aliquid, quod in ipsis floribus angat.

So long as imagination is guided and stimulated by desire, it embellishes every image, that sense supplies: but, as soon as desire is sated, imagination changes sides, and all its powers of embellishment are at once inverted.

32. It is not merely in our sexual connections, but in every object of our desires or pursuits, that imagination acts this double part. Prior to attainment or possession, it employs every artifice to augment its charms and enhance its value; but immediately afterwards becomes equally busy and active in exposing its defects and heightening its faults; which, of course, acquire influence as their opposites lose it. Thus it happens that in moral as well as physical—in intellectual as well as sensual gratifications, the circles of pleasure are expanded only in a simple ratio, and to a limited degree; while those of pain spread in a compound rate of progression; and are only limited in their degree by the limits of our existence. At the same time, therefore, that, by enlarging the sphere of our connections, and the range of our enjoyments, we extend and multiply our pleasures and gratifications, we also extend and multiply, and that too in a compound proportion, our pains, disgusts, and disappointments. We satiate desire, indeed, and satisfy curiosity; but without reflecting that by so doing we extinguish both; and, with them, extinguish the lights that principally serve to cheer our way through life, and render inte-

resting the objects that break and diversify its tedious uniformity.

38. Of all our desires, perhaps, the desire of knowledge is that, of which the gratifications are the most pure and unmixed, as well as the most permanent; and which being, at the same time, the most difficult to cloy or satiate, affords the most certain and ample means of durable and solid happiness. But, nevertheless, when the acquisition of new ideas ceases to be new, it generally ceases to charm; and the possession itself brings, perhaps, more of humiliation than triumph—more of dissatisfaction than comfort or content—

> 'Tis but to know how little can be known
> To pity others' faults, and feel our own.

It has been the triumphant boast of fanatics of all sects and all times that the meanest among them have been able to look down with scorn upon the pride of human science; and to decide, without study or investigation, those abstruse questions concerning final causes, from which its wisest professors turned away in doubt, or shrank in despair: for as the ignorance of such persons never allows them to doubt, their mental continue to be as limited as their corporeal views, which see nothing between themselves and heaven; of which they soon conceive themselves to be the chosen ministers and special organs. The science of

the philosopher on the contrary, by giving him
a more extensive and comprehensive view of
things, makes him sensible of his own insignificance in the scale of being; and, whilst it
enlarges his understanding, narrows his pretensions and humbles his pride: for whatever
may be said of the pride of science, it is always
meek and humble compared with the pride of
ignorance *.

84. But not only the presumption of pride,
but the ardour of affection is diluted, and reduced to a lower tone, as the boundaries of
knowledge are expanded: for as the connections of the mind are multiplied and extended,
its relish for each individual object becomes
less keen. The flattering visions of hope, too,
fade before a more steady but less brilliant
light; and though the materials for forming
pleasant schemes and specious projects be increased, the time for employing them is cur-
tailed, and the foundations upon which the
edifices were to stand, shaken and dissolved
by the very power that was to raise them.
Thus even the solitary amusement, commonly
called *building castles in the air*, ceases; and
mental employment, the last and best source
of happiness, loses, by continued exertion, all
its power to entertain or delight. Our facul-

* ουκ εστ ανοιας ουδεν, ως εμοι δοκει, τολμηροτερον.

MENANDR.

ties have no new modes of exercise, nor the objects, which employ them, any new modes of presenting themselves; and those, that are old, are become stale by repetition, and can no longer excite interest, or awaken attention. Thus, as we grow old, every thing, that surrounds us, seems to grow old with us, and the mind is gradually prepared for the approaching dissolution of its habitation.

35. Nevertheless, life seems to be more valued in its last stages than in its first: at least we always find it guarded with more care, and preserved with more caution, by those who are labouring under all the hopeless infirmities of age and decrepitude, than by those who are rioting in the full enjoyment of youth, health, and vigour. But for this there are several reasons to be assigned: in the first place, that, which appears to be love of life, is often nothing more than fear of death; which, like all other objects of terror, becomes more terrible, as it approaches nearer, and as the mind, upon which it acts, grows weaker: in the next place, we are, by a sort of natural and instinctive impulse, always disposed to be sparing of any thing, of which we have but little left; more especially in cases, where, by the necessary laws of progression, that little is, every instant, becoming less: and lastly, though the affections and attachments of the young are more ardent

and violent, those of the old are more steady and permanent, as well as more widely diffused. In youth, while the powers of enjoyment are fresh and vigorous, and every object around us wears the unsullied bloom of novelty, we are led from one to another in a succession so rapid that we have not time to attach ourselves to any in particular. But as this bloom of novelty fades by use, the mind becomes less restless, and our desultory pleasures and amusements gradually subside into regular pursuits and fixed habits, which produce regular and fixed, though seldom very ardent attachments, to every object, with which they connect us; and the number of these objects will of course be increased, as life is lengthened, and the causes and opportunities of habitual attachment varied and extended. Thus the hooks and links, which hold the affections of age, are more numerous and complicated, than those which hold the passions of youth; and though each individually be less strong, their united force, joined to that of the other causes above mentioned, renders them more effective. Love may be extinct, and friendship buried in the grave with deceased contemporaries: but, nevertheless, both will be replaced by habitual attachment to inanimate objects :—to the trees, that we have planted or protected :—to the houses, that we have built or inhabited :—to

H H

the lands, that we have purchased or improved:
—to the books, that we have studied or admired :—to the curiosities, that we have collected or valued :—and even to the money, that
we have amassed. Long and constant association will render them all more or less dear to us ;
and rather than leave them for ever, we would
be content to bear for ever the accumulated
miseries of weakness, decrepitude, and pain.

36. Upon the same principle, the love of
property, as well as the love of life, increases
in proportion as the powers of enjoying it, and
the probable period of possessing it, are diminished : for, though the importance, which it
confers, and the power exercised in bequeathing it, may be weighty considerations, this
habitual attachment seems to be universally the
ruling motive. Hence the characteristic foible
of old age is not so much avarice as parsimony :
—to be careful in saving and accumulating,
rather than eager and ambitious in acquiring.
The bold speculations of usury or commerce,
which stake the chances of enormous gain
against those of enormous loss, seldom either
enrich or ruin the old ; whose love of what they
possess is generally more powerful than the desire of possessing more. In bequeathing, too,
they most commonly show more tenderness and
concern for the property itself, than either for
their own good fame, or for the comfort and

well-being of those upon whom they bestow it: whence the last anxious wish of the expiring miser is, almost invariably, that his possessions may be kept, together undiminished and unimpaired. For this reason it has been found expedient, in almost all countries, where property has been secure and the disposal of it free, to enact laws similar to our statute of Mortmain: for as old men feel but little attachment to persons and much to things, they will naturally be disposed to leave what they possess to a permanent corporation, where it must necessarily remain entire, rather than expose it to be embezzled or dispersed by individual caprice or extravagance. Personal vanity, indeed, and the desire of recording and perpetuating a name, may often greatly promote this disposition: but, nevertheless, its root seems to be in an habitual attachment to the possession itself, and a consequent anxiety for its integral preservation: whence it has often appeared most prevalent, where there has been no symptom of such vanity.

37. Though this habitual attachment to objects of property or possession may with propriety be ranked among our selfish attachments; as it arises, in a great degree, from selfish affections; it is, nevertheless, much less purely or sordidly selfish than many of those gratifications of vanity or sensuality, which pass, in

the general estimation of mankind, for social, liberal, and generous pleasures. The dissipated rake, and voracious glutton, who spend their property in the unlimited indulgence of their passions and appetites, are surely more thoroughly selfish than any of those, who, through parsimony or frugality, do not spend it at all. The pursuits of the former begin and end with themselves, and have no object but their own personal indulgence; whereas those of the latter must necessarily extend to a greater distance, and embrace the good of some objects beyond their own existence : but still as the gratifications of the former are generally in company, and those of the latter in solitude, the one are reckoned liberal and social, and the other sordid and selfish; as if persons could not seek their own peculiar indulgence when with others, or employ themselves for the good of others' when alone. Even that facility in giving, which so often distinguishes the gay and dissipated, may be purely selfish: for as there is a degree of humiliation in receiving favours of this kind, there is a proportionate gratification of pride and insolence in conferring them; and when they are conferred indiscriminately, without prudence or circumspection as to the means or the objects, we may safely conclude that this gratification is the real motive and spring of action; though, perhaps, it may lie concealed even from the person, whom it actuates. In the payment of a just debt or discharge of a legal demand, there can be no gratification of this kind; wherefore, he, who cannot make his justice keep pace with his generosity, but squanders in profuse donations what is due to expecting creditors, may be assured that his real motive is such gratification, and that his generosity is as sordidly selfish as the avarice of the usurer who supplies the means of it *.

38. As every natural or social affection is weakened, and every habitual attachment strengthened by time, it frequently happens, in the last stages of life, that the objects of the one are only valued as the links, which are to extend our connections with the other : whence arises that anxious desire of extending this connection as far as possible, which so often induces old persons to entail their property to the latest period possible, and to transfer all power over it from known and approved children to grandchildren or great,

---

* " Qui aliis nocent, ut in alios liberales sint, in eadem sunt injustitia, ut si in suam rem aliena convertant. . . nihil est enim liberale, quod non idem justum."

Cic. Off. l. i. f. xiv.

——— ὐκ ἐϛὶ κακως κεχϛημένον ανδϛα τοις ιδιοις, ἐιναι πιϛον ἐν αλλοτϛιοις.

Lucian, Epigr. xxx.

grandchildren, whose future dispositions cannot even be guessed at: but still by these means, the beloved possession is rendered secure for another generation; and that consideration is sufficient to supersede every feeble claim of expiring affection. In the ower orders of society, where there are no such objects of habitual attachment, but where

> The modest wants of every day
> The toil of every day supplies—

the parental affections generally die away, as in the brute creation, with the necessities for their exertion, and the habits of continued intercourse, which those necessities produced.

39. To be secluded from every object of attachment or pursuit, whether animate or inanimate; and reduced to dead silent solitude, in which the mind is left to the unvaried and uninterrupted sense of its own mere existence, without any hope of change but in the termination of it, is perhaps the most extreme state of suffering, that human nature can long endure. Such is perpetual solitary imprisonment, the most cruel, because the most permanent and lingering mode of torture, of any, which the malignant ingenuity of man hath invented to torment man; and which has this peculiarity of injustice over most others, that

3

while it guards the sufferer merely to make him suffer, it holds out no example of terror to deter others from committing his crime. His sufferings being unseen, no one observes or thinks of them : for liberty, occupation, and society are, like health, reputation, and fortune, blessings, of which no one ever knows or considers the value, till he feels the loss *.

40. Even without confinement, were we doomed to spend our lives with one set of unchanging objects, which could afford no new varieties, either of sensations, images, or ideas ; nor produce any new modifications or dispositions in those previously felt or acquired, all around us would soon have the tiresome sameness of the walls of a cell. If to this were added prescience of every event that was to happen to us through life ; so as to extinguish hope and expectation, and every feeling of suspense or pleasure of novelty, it would scarcely be possible for any gratifications, that remained, to render existence endurable. Thus, if we suppose the world and its inhabitants to be fixed in one unchangeable state for ever, deprived of all variation of seasons, and of every kind of progressive or successive growth, decay, or reproduction, how

---

* φιλει πως το ανθρωπειον ουχ ουτω τι ευπαθεν της ευδαιμονιας αισθανεσθαι, ως και δυστυχησαι ποθειν αυτην.

Ρ   DION, Hist. lvi. f. 45.

perfect soever we may suppose that fixed state to be, we should soon become so tired of it, were it realized, that we should eagerly covet any change, and agree with the poet that even death itself is to be reckoned among the gifts or benefactions of nature *. Man, as he now is, is formed for the world, as it now is, in which

He never is, but always to be blest—

that is, his real happiness consists in the *means* and not in the *end* :—in *acquisition*, and not in *possession*. The source and principle of it is, therefore, *novelty :* the attaiment of new ideas ; the formation of new trains of thought; the renewal and extension of affections and attachments ; the new circumstances and situations, in which all the objects of those affections and attachments appear by periodical or progressive change ; the new lights, in which we ourselves view them, as we advance from infancy to maturity, and from maturity to decay ; the consequent new exertions and variations of pursuit adapted to every period of life ; and, above all, the unlimited power of fancy in multiplying and varying the objects, the results, nd the gratifications of our pursuits beyond ₂ bounds of reality, or the probable duraof existence. A state of abstract perfection

* Juvenal, Sat. x.

would, according to our present weak and inadequate notions of things, be a state of perfect misery; as it would necessarily preclude
almost every mental exercise and intellectual
gratification, from which our happiness here
arises. If every thing were known, there would
be nothing to be learned; if every good were
possessed, there would be none to be acquired;
and if none were wanting, or there were no
evil, there would be none to be done; and
consequently all would be dead inaction, or
action without motive or effect. So absurd
and presumptuous is it in us to attempt to
form any ideas of the beatitude of superior
beings, whose faculties and modes of intelligence have, perhaps, nothing in common with
our own.

THE END.

Luke Hansard, printer,
Great Turnstile, Lincoln's-Inn Fields.

'ained

18B/492/P

CPSIA information can be obtained
at www.ICGtesting.com
Printed in the USA
BVHW06s0005270418
514512BV00018B/492/P

9 780282 237295